Rick Steves'
SCANDINAVIA

John Muir Publications
Santa Fe, New Mexico

Other JMP travel guidebooks by Rick Steves
Asia Through the Back Door (with Bob Effertz)
Europe Through the Back Door
Europe 101: History and Art for the Traveler (with Gene Openshaw)
Mona Winks: Self-Guided Tours of Europe's Top Museums
  (with Gene Openshaw)
Rick Steves' Best of Europe
Rick Steves' Germany, Austria & Switzerland
Rick Steves' Great Britain & Ireland
Rick Steves' France, Belgium & the Netherlands (with Steve Smith)
Rick Steves' Italy
Rick Steves' Russia & the Baltics (with Ian Watson)
Rick Steves' Spain & Portugal
Rick Steves' Phrase Books: German, French, Italian,
  Spanish/Portuguese, and French/Italian/German

Thanks to Brian Carr Smith and Jane Klausen for research help and to
my wife, Anne, for making home my favorite travel destination.
Thanks also to Thor, Hanne, Geir, Hege, and Kari-Anne, our Norwegian family. In loving memory of Berit Kristiansen, whose house was
my house for 20 years of Norwegian travel.

John Muir Publications, P.O. Box 613, Santa Fe, NM 87504
Copyright © 1998, 1997, 1996, 1995 by Rick Steves and Steve Smith
Cover copyright © 1998 by John Muir Publications. All rights reserved.

Printed in the United States of America
Second printing April 1998

Previously published as *2 to 22 Days in Norway, Sweden, and Denmark*
copyright © 1988, 1989, 1991, 1992, 1994

For the latest on Rick's lectures, guidebooks, tours, and public
television series, contact Europe Through the Back Door, Box 2009,
Edmonds, WA 98020, tel. 425/771-8303, fax 425/771-0833, Web site:
www.ricksteves.com, or e-mail: rick@ricksteves.com.

ISSN 1084-7206
ISBN 1-56261-390-1

Europe Through the Back Door Editor Risa Laib
John Muir Publications Editors Krista Lyons-Gould, Nancy Gillan
Production Mladen Baudrand
Design Linda Braun
Cover Design Janine Lehmann
Typesetting Kathleen Sparkes, White Hart Design
Maps David C. Hoerlein
Printer Banta Company
Cover Photo Stave church, Oslo, Norway; Leo de Wys Inc./Fridmar
  Damm

Distributed to the book trade by
Publishers Group West
Berkeley, California

CONTENTS

The Best Destinations in Scandinavia

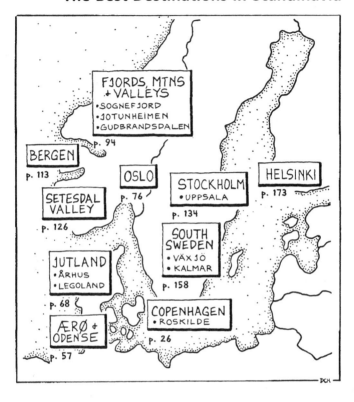

FJORDS, MTNS
+ VALLEYS
• SOGNEFJORD
• JOTUNHEIMEN
• GUDBRANDSDALEN
p. 94

BERGEN
p. 113

OSLO
p. 76

STOCKHOLM
• UPPSALA
p. 134

HELSINKI
p. 173

SETESDAL
VALLEY
p. 126

SOUTH
SWEDEN
• VÄXJÖ
• KALMAR
p. 158

JUTLAND
• ÅRHUS
• LEGOLAND
p. 68

COPENHAGEN
• ROSKILDE
p. 26

ÆRØ +
ODENSE
p. 57

INTRODUCTION

This book breaks Scandinavia into its top big-city, small-town, and rural destinations. It gives you all the information and opinions necessary to wring the maximum value out of your limited time and money in each of these destinations. If you plan a month or less in Scandinavia and have a normal appetite for information, this lean and mean little book is all you need.

Experiencing the culture, people, and natural wonders of Scandinavia economically and hassle-free has been my goal for over 20 years of traveling, tour guiding, and travel writing. With this book, I pass on to you the lessons I've learned.

Rick Steves' Scandinavia is your smiling Swede, your Nordic navigator, a tour guide in your pocket. This book is balanced to include a comfortable mix of exciting capital cities and cozy small towns. It covers the predictable biggies and mixes in a healthy dose of Back Door intimacy. Along with seeing Tivoli Gardens, Hans Christian Andersen's house, and *The Little Mermaid*, you'll take a bike tour of a sleepy remote Danish isle, dock at a time-passed fjord village, and wander among eerie, prehistoric monoliths in Sweden. To save time, maximize diversity, and avoid tourist burnout, I've been very selective. We won't cruise both the Geirangerfjord and Sognefjord, just the better of the two—Sognefjord.

The best is, of course, only my opinion. But after more than two busy decades of travel writing, lecturing, and tour guiding, I've developed a sixth sense of what tickles the traveler's fancy.

This Information Is Accurate and Up-to-Date

With this book, you can travel foot-loose and fancy-free, knowing you've goot good, solid information to guide you through the best of Scandinavia. Since this book is selective, covering only the places I think make the top month or so, I'm able to update it personally—by visiting my recommended hotels, restaurants, and sights. (Some publishers save money by updating their guidebooks only by letter.)

Please travel with the most current edition of this book. If you're packing an old book, you'll learn the seriousness of your mistake . . . in Scandinavia. Your trip costs about $10 per waking hour. Your time is valuable. This guidebook will save you lots of time.

Planning Your Trip

This book is organized by destinations. Each of these destinations is a mini-vacation on its own, filled with exciting sights and homey, affordable places to stay. In each chapter, you'll find:

Planning Your Time, a suggested schedule with thoughts on how best to use your limited time.

Orientation, including tourist information, city transportation, and an easy-to-read map designed to make the text clear and your arrival smooth.

Sights with ratings: ▲▲▲—Don't miss; ▲▲—Try hard to see; ▲—Worthwhile if you can make it; no rating—Worth knowing about.

Sleeping and **Eating**, with addresses and phone numbers of my favorite budget hotels and restaurants.

Transportation Connections to nearby destinations by train and route tips for drivers.

The **Appendix** is a traveler's tool kit, with telephone tips, a climate chart, and public transportation routes.

Browse through this book, choose your favorite destinations, and link them up. Then have a great trip! You'll travel like a temporary local, getting the absolute most out of every mile, minute, and kroner. You won't waste time on mediocre sights because, unlike other guidebooks, I cover only the best. Since your major financial pitfall is lousy expensive hotels, I've worked hard to assemble the best accommodations values for each stop. And as you travel the route I know and love, I'm happy you'll be meeting some of my favorite Scandinavian people.

Trip Costs

Five components make up the cost of your trip: airfare, surface transportation, room and board, sightseeing, and shopping/entertainment/miscellaneous.

Airfare: Don't try to sort through the mess. Get and use a good travel agent. A basic round-trip U.S.A.-to-Copenhagen flight should cost $800 to $1,000, depending on where you fly from and when. Always consider saving time and money in Europe by flying "open jaws" (for instance, flying into Copenhagen and out of Bergen).

Surface Transportation: For a three-week whirlwind trip of all my recommended destinations, allow $500 per person for public transportation (first class, 21-day Scanrail pass and extra boat rides; only $400 if you go second class), or $600 per person (based on two people sharing car and gas) for a three-week car rental, ~olls, gas, and insurance. Car rental is usually cheapest if arranged from the U.S.A.

Room and Board: You can eat and sleep well in Scandinavia for $60 a day for room and board. A $60-a-day budget allows $10 for lunch, $15 for dinner, and $35 for lodging (based on two people splitting the cost of a $70 double room that includes breakfast). That's basic and alcohol-free, but doable. Students and tightwads do it on $40 ($15–20 a bed, $20 for meals and snacks). But budget sleeping and eating requires the skills and information covered in this book (and in greater detail in my book *Europe Through the Back Door*).

Sightseeing: In big cities, figure $5 to $8 per major sight, $2 for minor ones, and $25 for splurge experiences (e.g., tours or folk concerts). The major cities have cards giving you a 24-hour free run of the public transit system and entrance to all the sights for about $20. An overall average of $15 per day works for most people. Don't skimp here. After all, this category directly powers most of the experiences all the other expenses are designed to make possible.

Shopping/Entertainment/Miscellaneous: In Scandinavia, this category can brutalize your budget. While Scandinavia is expensive, transportation passes, groceries, alternative accommodations, admissions, and enjoying nature are affordable (about what you'd pay in England or Italy). When things are expensive, remind yourself you're not getting less for your travel dollar. Up here, there simply aren't any lousy or cheap alternatives to classy, cozy, sleek Scandinavia. Electronic eyes flush youth-hostel toilets and breakfasts are all-you-can-eat.

If you take full advantage of this book, you'll save a shipload of money and days of headaches. Read it carefully from start to finish. Many of the general skills and tricks used in Copenhagen work in Oslo and Stockholm as well.

Exchange Rates
I've priced things in local currencies throughout the book. While each of the Scandinavian countries' kroner (crowns) have different values, they are close.

> 7 Danish kroner = $1
> 7.4 Norwegian kroner = $1
> 7.9 Swedish kroner = $1

Kroner are decimalized: 100 øre = 1 krone. Kroner are not accepted abroad (except at foreign exchange services and banks).

Standard abbreviations are: Danish krone, DKK; Swedish krone, SEK; and Norwegian krone, NOK. I'll keep it simple. For all three countries, I'll use the krone abbreviation, "kr," and "7 kr = $1" as the exchange rate. To translate local Scandinavian prices into U.S. dollars, divide by seven (80 kr = about $11).

Finland's markka (FIM or mk) is worth about 20 cents (5 mk = $1). To convert to U.S. dollars, divide Finnish prices by five (40 mk = about $8).

Prices, Times, and Discounts

I've done all I can to insure that the hours, prices, telephone numbers, and addresses in this book are accurate and up-to-date, but I know you'll understand that this, like any other guidebook, starts to yellow even before it's printed.

In Scandinavia—and in this book—you'll be using the 24-hour clock. After 12:00 noon, keep going—13:00, 14:00, etc. For anything over 12, subtract 12 and add p.m. (14:00 is 2:00 p.m.)

This book lists peak-season hours for sightseeing attractions (July and August). Off-season, roughly October through April, expect shorter hours and fewer activities. Confirm your sightseeing plans locally, especially when traveling between October and May.

I have not listed special age discounts in this book. But in keeping with its social orientation, Scandinavia is Europe's most generous corner when it comes to youth, student, senior, and family discounts. If you are any of the above, always mention it. Students should travel with the ISIC card (International Student Identity Card, normally available at university foreign study offices in North America). Spouses often pay half-price when doing things as a couple. Children usually pay half-price or less (for example, in hostels).

When to Go

Summer is by far the best time to go. Scandinavia bustles and glistens under the July and August sun. Scandinavian schools get out around June 20, most local industries take July off, and the British and central Europeans tend to visit Scandinavia in August. You'll notice crowds during these times, but it's never as crowded as southern Europe. While you could do the trip without hotel reservations, I compare prices and reserve my favorite places by calling a day or two in advance as I go.

"Shoulder season" travel (in late May, early June, and September), with minimal crowds, decent weather, and sights and tourist fun spots still open, lacks the vitality of summer (although the big cities tend to be very crowded in early June). Things quiet down when the local kids go back to school (around August 20).

Winter has no tourist crowds for good reason. It's a bad time to explore Scandinavia. Many sights and accommodations are closed or open on a limited schedule. Business travelers drive hotel prices way up. Winter weather can be cold and dreary, and nighttime will draw the shades on your sightseeing well before dinner.

Sightseeing Priorities

Depending on the length of your trip, here are my recommended priorities:

3 days:	Copenhagen, Stockholm, Oslo, connected by night trains
5 days, add:	More time in capitals
7 days, add:	"Norway in a Nutshell" fjord trip, Bergen
10 days, add:	14-hour cruise to Helsinki, and slow down
14 days, add:	Ærø, Odense, Roskilde, Frederiksborg
17 days, add:	Jutland, Kalmar
21 days, add:	Lillehammer, Jotunheimen, Växjö, Setesdal
24 days, add:	Riga, Latvia, and Tallinn, Estonia
30 days, add:	Side trip to St. Petersburg, and slow down

Red Tape

Traveling throughout this region requires only a passport— no shots and no visas. Border crossings between Norway, Sweden, Denmark, and Finland are a wave-through. When you change countries, however, you do change money, postage stamps, and more. Local sales taxes on souvenirs and gifts purchased are refunded when you leave Scandinavia. When purchasing expensive items, ask the local merchant for tax-refund instructions.

Banking

Bring traveler's checks in dollars along with some plastic (ATM, credit, or debit cards). Banking in Scandinavia is straightforward. You'll have almost no loss because of the buy

Whirlwind Three-Week Tour

and sell rates (they're within about 2 percent of each other). Exchange rates are nearly standard. The banks make their money off a stiff 20-to-40-kr-per-check fee. Bring traveler's checks in large denominations. If you have only small-denomination checks, shop around.

In Norway, some banks charge 1 or 2 percent rather than per check. In many cases, small cash exchanges are cheaper outside of banks, at places that offer worse rates but smaller (or no) fees such as exchange desks on international boats and the handy FOREX windows at the Copenhagen and Stockholm train stations. American Express offices in each capital change AmExCo checks (and sometimes other brands as well) for no extra fee. Even with their worse-than-banks' exchange rates, AmExCo can save you money if you're changing less than $1,000. Post offices (with longer hours, nearly the same rates, and smaller fees) can be a good place to change money.

Scandinavia's Best Three-Week Trip

Days	Plan	Sleep in
1	Arrive in Copenhagen	Copenhagen
2	Copenhagen	Copenhagen
3	Copenhagen	Copenhagen
4	North Zealand, into Sweden	Växjö
5	Växjö, Kalmar, Glass Country	Kalmar
6	Kalmar to Stockholm	Stockholm
7	Stockholm	Stockholm
8	Stockholm	boat
9	Helsinki	boat
10	Uppsala to Oslo	Oslo
11	Oslo	Oslo
12	Oslo	Oslo
13	Lillehammer, Gudbrandsdalen	Jotunheimen: Sogndal
14	Jotunheimen Country	Sogndal: Aurland
15	Sognefjord, Norway in Nutshell	Bergen
16	Bergen	Bergen
17	Long drive south, Setesdal	boat
18	Jutland, Århus, Legoland	Århus/Billund
19	Jutland to Ærø	Ærøskøbing
20	Ærø	Ærøskøbing
21	Odense, Roskilde	Copenhagen

While this three-week itinerary is designed to be done by car, it can be done by train and bus. Scandinavia in 21 days by train is most efficient with a little reworking: I'd go overnight whenever possible on any train ride six or more hours long. Streamline by doing North Zealand, Odense, and Ærø as a three-day side trip from Copenhagen, skipping the Växjö–Stockholm train (there is no Copenhagen–Kalmar overnight train). The Bergen/Setesdal/Århus/Copenhagen leg is possible on public transit, but Setesdal (between Bergen and Kristiansand) is not worth the trouble if you don't have the freedom a car gives you.

If you really want to see Legos and the Bogman, do Jutland from Copenhagen. A flight home from Bergen is wonderfully efficient. Otherwise, it's about 20 hours by train from Bergen to Copenhagen via Oslo. British Midland has $139 flights from Bergen to London (800/788-0555 in U.S.A.).

ATM machines are everywhere, and offer a good exchange rate. To get a cash advance from a bank machine you'll need a four-digit PIN (numbers only, no letters) with your bank card. Before you go, verify with your bank that your card will work, then use it whenever possible.

Visa and MasterCard are more commonly accepted than American Express. Just like at home, credit or debit cards work easily at larger hotels, restaurants, and shops, but smaller businesses prefer payment in hard kroner.

You should use a money belt. Thieves target tourists. A money belt (call 425/771-8303 for our free newsletter/catalog) provides peace of mind. You can carry lots of cash safely in a money belt.

Don't be petty about changing money. The greatest avoidable money-changing expense is having to waste time every few days returning to a bank. Change a week's worth of money, get big bills, stuff them in your money belt, and travel!

Travel Smart

Upon arrival in a new town, lay the groundwork for a smooth departure. Reread this book as you travel and visit local tourist information offices. Buy a phone card and use it for reservations, reconfirmations, and double-checking hours. Enjoy the friendliness of the local people. Ask questions. Most locals are eager to point you in their idea of the right direction. Wear your money belt, learn the local currency, and develop a simple formula to quickly estimate rough prices in dollars. Keep a notepad in your pocket for organizing your thoughts, and practice the virtue of simplicity. Those who expect to travel smart, do.

Plan ahead for banking, laundry, post office visits, and picnics. Mix intense and relaxed periods. Every trip (and every traveler) needs at least a few slack days. Pace yourself. Assume you will return.

Tourist Information

Any town with much tourism has a well-organized, English-speaking tourist information office (which I'll abbreviate as "TI" in this book). The TI should be your first stop in a new city. Prepare. Have a list of questions and a proposed plan to double-check. If you're arriving late, telephone ahead (and try to get a map for your next destination from a TI in the town you're leaving). Important: Each big city publishes a "This

Week In ..." guide (to Copenhagen, Stockholm, Helsinki, Oslo, and Bergen). These are free, found all over town, and packed with all the tedious details about each city (24-hour pharmacy, embassies, tram fares, restaurants, sights with hours/admissions/phone numbers), plus a great calendar of events and a map of the town center.

While the TIs offer room-finding services, this is a good deal only if you're in search of summer and weekend deals on business hotels. The TIs can help you with small pensions and private homes, but you'll save both yourself and your host money by going direct with the listings in this book.

The **Scandinavian National Tourist Office** in the U.S.A. is a wealth of information (P.O. Box 4649, Grand Central Station, New York, NY 10163-4649, tel. 212/885-9700, fax 212/885-9710, Web site: www.goscandinavia.com, e-mail: info@goscandinavia.com). Before your trip, get their free general information booklet about the Scandinavian countries and request any specific information you may want (city maps, calendars of events, and lists of festivals).

Roger Greenwald's Scandinavia Links has the best collection of online resources I've seen: www.chass.utoronto.ca/~roger/scand.html.

Recommended Guidebooks

Especially if you'll be traveling beyond my recommended destinations, you may want some supplemental information. When you consider the improvements they'll make in your $3,000 vacation, $30 for extra maps and books is money well spent. Especially for several people traveling by car, the weight and expense are negligible. One simple budget tip can easily save the price of an extra guidebook.

Lonely Planet's *Scandinavian & Baltic Europe* is thorough, well-researched, and packed with good maps and hotel recommendations for low- to moderate-budget travelers. The hip Rough Guide's *Scandinavia* is thick. *Let's Go: Europe* has skimpy chapters on Scandinavia. Due to the relatively small market, there just aren't many guidebooks out on Scandinavia. Of all my European destination guidebooks, this one fills the biggest void.

Rick Steves' Books and Videos

Rick Steves' *Europe Through the Back Door* (Santa Fe, N.M.: John Muir Publications) gives you budget travel skills on minimizing jet lag, packing light, planning your itinerary, traveling by car or train, finding budget beds without reservations, changing money, avoiding rip-offs, outsmarting thieves, hurdling the language barrier, staying healthy, taking great photographs, using your bidet, and much more. The book also includes chapters on 37 of my favorite "Back Doors," three of which are in Scandinavia.

Rick Steves' Country Guides are a series of eight guidebooks covering Europe, Russia/Baltics, Britain/Ireland, France/Belgium/Netherlands, Germany/Austria/Switzerland, Italy, and Spain/Portugal, just as this one covers Scandinavia.

Europe 101: History and Art for the Traveler (co-written with Gene Openshaw; Santa Fe, N.M.: John Muir Publications) gives you the interesting story of Europe's people, history, and art. Written for smart people who were asleep during their history and art classes before they knew they were going to Europe, *101* helps resurrect the rubble. (Like most European histories, it has little to say about Scandinavia, but it will broaden your knowledge of Europe and give depth to your sightseeing.)

Mona Winks: Self-Guided Tours of Europe's Top Museums (co-written with Gene Openshaw; Santa Fe, N.M.: John Muir Publications) gives you one- to three-hour self-guided tours through Europe's 20 most exhausting and important museums (but nothing on Scandinavia).

While I've designed a series of four phrase books, there is virtually no language barrier in Scandinavia, so I wouldn't bother with a phrase book for traveling here.

My television series, *Travels in Europe with Rick Steves*, is now in its fourth season with 13 new shows airing throughout the U.S.A. this year. Three of these shows feature Scandinavia (Copenhagen/Ærø, Stockholm/Helsinki, and Oslo/Fjords/Bergen). All 52 *Travels in Europe* shows, which cover Europe from top to bottom, are aired over and over on most public television stations and most of these appear on the Travel Channel. They are also available as home videos (two or three shows per tape). Our new Scandinavia home video, with all three shows, is a particularly good value. (For specifics on these tapes along with my two-hour video slideshow lecture on Scandinavia, call 425/771-8303 for our free newsletter/catalog).

Maps

The maps in this book, drawn by Dave Hoerlein, are concise and simple. Dave, who is well-traveled in Scandinavia, has designed the maps to help you locate recommended places and the tourist offices, where you'll find more in-depth maps of the necessary cities or regions (cheap or free).

Train travelers can do fine with a simple rail map (such as the one that comes with your train pass) and with city maps picked up from the TI as you travel. But drivers shouldn't skimp on maps—get one good overall road map for Scandinavia (either the Michelin "Scandinavia" or the Kummerly and Frey "Southern Scandinavia" 1:1,000,000 edition). The only detailed map worth considering is the "Southern Norway-North" (Sør Norge-nord, 1:325,000) by Cappelens Kart ($12 in Scandinavian bookstores). Study the key carefully to get the most sightseeing value out of your map. Excellent city and regional maps are available from local TIs, and are usually free.

Transportation

Getting to Scandinavia

Copenhagen is the most direct and least expensive Scandinavian capital to fly into from the U.S.A. It is also Europe's gateway to Scandinavia from points south. There are often cheaper flights from the U.S.A. into Frankfurt and Amsterdam than into Copenhagen, but it's a long, rather dull, one-day drive (with a two-hour, $60-per-car-and-passenger ferry crossing at Puttgarten, Germany). By train, the trip is effortless—overnight from Amsterdam, Paris, or Frankfurt. The $120 trip is free with your Eurailpass (not with the Scanrail pass).

In Scandinavia: By Car or Train?

While a car gives you the ultimate in mobility and freedom, enables you to search for hotels more easily, and carries your bags for you, the train zips you effortlessly from city to city, usually dropping you in the center and near the tourist office. Cars are great in the countryside but an expensive headache in places like Oslo, Copenhagen, and Bergen. Three or four people travel cheaper by car. With a few exceptions, trains cover my recommended destinations wonderfully. On the web, check the European Railway Server at http://mercurio. iet.unipi.it.

Cost of Public Transportation

SCANRAIL PASS *

	1st cl	1st cl under 26	1st cl over 54	2nd cl	2nd cl under 26	2nd cl over 54
Any 5 out of 15 days	$228	$171	$203	$182	$137	$162
Any 10 days out of 1 month	364	273	324	292	219	324
1 month of consec. days	532	399	473	426	320	379

Trolls 4-11 half price. Most of these passes are available in Scandinavia at higher prices.

SCANRAIL & DRIVE PASS

Any 5 rail days and 3 car days in a 15 day period.

	2 adults 1st	2 adults 2nd	1 adult 1st	1 adult 2nd	extra car days (maximum 5)
A-Economy car	$300	$265	$385	$345	$58
B-Compact car	330	285	445	395	78
C-Intermediate car	350	305	475	435	88

Prices are approximate. No additional rail days available.

NORWAY RAILPASS

	1st cl	2nd cl
3 days in a month	$175	$135
7 consecutive days	250	195
14 consecutive days	335	255

Few Norwegian trains offer 1st class, so go with a 2nd class pass. Prices are about 20% less between October and April. Kids 5-16 half price, under 4 free.

SWEDEN RAILPASS

	1st cl	2nd cl
3 days within a 7 day period	$170	$130

Two kids under age 15 can ride along for free.

FINNRAIL PASS

	1st class	2nd class
3 days in a month	$169	$109

Children 6-17 half price, under 6 free.

Scandinavia:
Point-to-point 1-way 2nd class rail fares in $US. Add up fares for your itinerary to see whether a railpass will save you money.

* 1998 prices. 1999 prices may change.

Trains

The Scanrail pass is one of the great Nordic bargains. There are two types (each with several variations): one sold in the U.S.A. (the best value for most travelers) and one in Scandinavia. The one sold in Scandinavia is purchased easily on the spot at any major train station. Both give you free run of many boats (such as Stockholm to Finland) and all trains in the region (though you'll need reservations for long rides and express trains and there's a supplement for Norway's Myrdal–Flåm ride). Both passes go easy on the upgrade to first class. Even though Scandinavian second class is like southern European first class, for $7 a day extra, you might consider first class.

A Eurailpass, which costs much more than a comparable Scanrail pass, is a good value only for those coming to Scandinavia from central Europe (a three-week first-class Eurailpass costs about $678).

Scanrail 'n' Drive passes offer a flexible and economical way to mix rail and car rental (handy if you plan to explore Sweden's Glass Country or the Norwegian mountains and fjords).

Consider the efficiency of night travel. The *couchette* supplement (a bed in a compartment with two triple bunks) costs $20 beyond your first- or second-class ticket or pass. A "sleeper," giving you the privacy of a double or triple compartment, costs about $40 per bed.

Car Rental

Car rental is usually cheapest when arranged (well in advance) in the U.S.A. through your travel agent, rather than in Scandinavia. You'll want a weekly rate with unlimited mileage. If you're traveling for more than three weeks, ask about leasing a car. Each major rental agency has an office in the Copenhagen airport. Comparison-shop through your agent and Rafco, a small Danish company near the Copenhagen airport that rents nearly new Seat (Volkswagen) cars at almost troublemaking prices. The manager, Ken, promises my readers a 10 percent discount over his "Money Saver" rates: about $40/day (includes Collision Damage Waiver insurance) to rent an economy Seat Ibiza for a minimum of 21 days. Similar deals exist on larger cars and minibuses. Rafco has small motor homes (ideal for families on a budget) for about $750/week peak season, less otherwise (with gear, four to six beds, kitchen, WC, and a 10 percent discount for travelers with this book). For a brochure, contact Rafco, Englandsvej 380, DK-2770 Kastrup, Denmark, tel. 45/32 51 15 00, fax 45/32 51 10 89 (www.rafco.dk, e-mail: rafco@dk-online.dk).

Driving

Except for the dangers posed by the scenic distractions and moose crossings, Scandinavia is a great place to drive. Your American license is accepted. Gas is expensive, over $4 per gallon (gas in Denmark is cheaper than in its northern neighbors); but roads are good (though nerve-wrackingly skinny in western Norway); traffic is generally sparse; drivers are sober and civil; signs and road maps are excellent; local road etiquette is similar to that of the U.S.A.; and seat belts are required. Use your headlights day and night; it's required in most of Scandinavia. Bikes whiz by close and quiet, so be on guard.

There are plenty of good facilities, gas stations, and scenic rest stops. Snow is a serious problem off-season in the mountains. Parking is a headache only in major cities, where expensive garages are safe and plentiful. Denmark uses a parking windshield-clock disk (free at TIs, post offices, and newsstands; set it when you arrive and be back before your posted time limit is up). Even in the Nordic countries, thieves break into cars. Park carefully, use the trunk, and show no valuables. Never drink and drive. Even one drink can get a driver into serious trouble.

As you navigate, you'll find town signs followed by the letters N, S, Ø, V, or C. These stand for north, south, east, west, and center, respectively, and understanding them will save you lots of wrong exits. Due to recent changes, many maps have the wrong road numbers. It's safest to navigate by town names.

Telephones and Mail

Smart travelers use the telephone every day: for making hotel reservations, calling tourist information offices, and phoning home. The key to dialing long distance is understanding area codes and having a phone card.

Scandinavia's phone cards aren't credit cards, just handy cards you insert in the phone instead of coins. Each country sells a card (usually in denominations of about $5 and $10) good for use only in that country. You can buy phone cards at post offices, newsstands, and tobacco shops.

Dialing Direct: Norway and Denmark do not use area codes. Just dial local numbers direct from anywhere in the country. Sweden and Finland do have area codes. When making calls within Sweden or Finland, include the entire area code (which starts with a zero).

Calling internationally, you'll need to:

1. Dial the international access code of the country you're calling from.

2. Then dial the country code of the country you're calling.

3. If the country uses area codes, dial the area code next, *omitting the initial zero*. If the country does not use area codes, skip this step.

4. Then dial the local number.

To call one of my favorite B&Bs in Copenhagen from anywhere in Denmark, just dial its local number directly (32 95 96 22). To call the Copenhagen B&B from the U.S.A., dial 011 (the U.S.A.'s international access code), 45 (Denmark's country code), then 32 95 96 22.

To call Stockholm's hostel-in-a-ship from anywhere in Sweden, dial 08 (Stockholm's area code), then the local number: 679-5015. To call the Stockholm hostel from the U.S.A., dial 011 (our international access code), 46 (Sweden's country code), 8 (Stockholm's area code without the zero), then 679-5015. To call my office from Sweden, dial 009 (Sweden's international access code), 1 (the U.S.A.'s country code), then 425/771-8303. For a listing of international access codes and country codes, see the Appendix.

Hotel-room phones are a terrible rip-off for calls to the U.S.A. Never call home from your hotel room unless your hotel allows toll-free access to your USA Direct Service (many don't).

USA Direct Services: Calling the U.S.A. from any kind of phone is easy if you have an AT&T, MCI, or Sprint calling card. Each card company has a toll-free number in each European country that puts you in touch with an English-speaking operator. The operator will take your card number and the number you want to call, put you through, and bill your home phone number for the call (at the cheaper U.S.A. rate of about $1 a minute plus $3 for the first minute and a $2.50 service charge). You'll save money on calls of three minutes or more. Hanging up when you hear an answering machine is a $5.50 mistake. First use a coin or a Scandinavian phone card to call home for five seconds—long enough to say "call me," or to make sure an answering machine is off so you can call back, using your USA Direct number, to connect with a person. European time is six/nine hours ahead of the east/west coast of the U.S.A. For a list of AT&T, MCI, and Sprint calling-card operators, see the Appendix. Avoid using USA Direct for calls between European countries; it's much cheaper to call direct using coins or a Scandinavian phone card.

Mail: If you must have mail stops, consider a few pre-reserved hotels along your route or use American Express Mail Services. Most American Express offices will hold mail for one month. (They mail out a free listing of addresses.) This service is free to anyone using an AmExCo card or traveler's checks (and available for a small fee to others). Allow ten days for U.S.A.-to-Scandinavia mail delivery. Federal Express makes two-day deliveries, for a price. Phoning is so easy that I've dispensed with mail stops altogether.

Sleeping

Accommodations expenses will make or break your budget. Vagabonds sleep happily everywhere for $15 per night. An overall average of $60 per night per double is possible using this book's listings. Unless noted, the accommodations I've listed will hold a room with a phone call until 18:00 with no deposit, and the proprietors speak English. I like small, central, clean, traditional, friendly places that aren't listed in other guidebooks. Most places listed meet five of these six virtues.

In the interest of smart use of your time, I favor hotels and restaurants handy to your sightseeing activities and public transportation. Rather than list hotels scattered throughout a city, I choose a convenient, colorful neighborhood and recommend its best accommodations values, from $10 bunk beds to $140 doubles.

Tourist information offices' room-finding services, if you have no place in mind, can be worth the 30-kr fee. Be very clear about what you want. (Say "cheap," and mention that you have sheets or a sleeping bag, and whether you will take a twin or double, if you require a shower, and so on.) They know the hotel quirks and private-room scene better than anybody. Official price listings are often misleading, since they omit cheaper oddball rooms and special clearance deals.

To sleep cheap, bring your own sheet or sleeping bag and offer to provide it in low-priced establishments. This can save $10 per person per night, especially in rural areas. Families can get a price break; normally a child can sleep very cheaply in mom and dad's room. To get the most sleep for your dollar, pull the dark shades (and even consider bringing your own night shades) to keep out the very early morning sun.

Sleep Code

To save space while giving more specific information for people with special concerns, I've described my recommended hotels with a standard code. When there is a range of prices in one category, the price will fluctuate with the season, size of room, or length of stay. Prices listed are for the room, not per person.

S = Single room or price for one person using a double.

D = Double or twin room. Double beds are very often two twins pushed together.

T = Three-person room (often a double bed with a single bed moved in).

Q = Four-adult room (extra child's bed is usually less).

b = Private bathroom with toilet and shower or tub. (Rooms without a "b" have access to a shower and toilet down the hall.)

s = Private shower only. (The toilet is down the hall.)

CC = Accepts credit cards (**V** = **V**isa, **M** = **M**asterCard, **A** = **A**merican Express). If CC isn't mentioned, assume you'll need to pay cash.

If a hotel is listed in this book as "D-360 kr, Db-450 kr, CC:V," the hotel charges 360 kr (about $50) for a double room without a private bathroom, 450 kr (about $65) for a double with bathroom, and accepts Visa or hard kroner in payment.

Hotels

Hotels are expensive ($80–150 doubles) with some exceptions. Business-class hotels dump prices to attract tourists with "summer" and "weekend" rates (Friday, Saturday, and sometimes Sunday). The much-advertised hotel discount cards or clubs offer nothing more than these rates, which are available to everyone anyway. To sleep in a fancy hotel, it's cheapest to arrive without a reservation and let the local tourist office book you a room. Hotels are expensive, but when a classy, modern $200 place has a $100 summer special that includes two $10 buffet breakfasts, the dumpy $60 hotel room without breakfast becomes less exciting.

There are actually several tiers of rates, including tourist office, weekend, summer, summer weekend, and walk-in. "Walk-ins" at the end of a quiet day can often get a room even below the summer rate. Many modern hotels have "combi" rooms (singles with a sofa that makes into a perfectly good double), which are cheaper than a full double. Also, many places have low-grade older rooms, considered unacceptable for the general public and often used by workers on weekdays outside of summer. If you're on a budget, ask for cheaper rooms with no windows or no water. And if a hotel is not full, any day can become a summer day.

Hostels

Scandinavian hostels, Europe's finest, are open to travelers of all ages. They offer classy facilities, members' kitchens, cheap hot meals (often breakfast buffets), plenty of doubles (for a few extra kroner), and great people experiences. Receptionists speak English and will hold a room if you promise to arrive by 18:00. Many close in the off-season. Buy a membership card before you leave home. Those without cards are admitted for a $5-per-night guest membership fee. Bring bedsheets from home or plan on renting them for about $5 per stay. You'll find lots of Volvos in hostel parking lots, as Scandinavians know hostels provide the best (and usually only) $15 beds in town. Hosteling is ideal for the two-bunk family (four-bed rooms, kitchens, washing machines, discount family memberships). Pick up each country's free hostel directory at any hostel or TI.

Making Reservations

During most of the year (except, for instance, in the capitals during conventions—early June is packed in Oslo and Stockholm), you can do this entire trip easily without reservations or by making reservations a day in advance as you travel. Still, given the high stakes, erratic accommodations values, and the quality of the gems I've found for this book, I'd highly recommend calling ahead for rooms a day or two in advance as you travel. If tourist crowds are down, you might make a habit of calling between 9:00 and 10:00 on the day you plan to arrive, when the hotel knows who'll be checking out and just which rooms will be available. If you know your itinerary in advance, consider making telephone reservations before leaving home. I've taken great pains to list telephone numbers with long-distance instructions (see Telephone and Mail, above, and the Appendix). Use the telephone and the convenient telephone cards.

Most hotels listed are accustomed to English-only speakers. A hotel receptionist will trust you and hold a room until 18:00 without a deposit, though some will ask for a credit-card number. Honor (or cancel by phone) your reservations. Long distance is cheap and easy from public phone booths. Don't let these people down—I promised you'd call and cancel if for some reason you won't show up. Don't needlessly confirm rooms through the tourist office, because they'll take a commission.

If you know which dates you need and want a particular place, reserve a room before you leave home. To reserve from home, call, fax, or write the hotel. Phone and fax costs are reasonable, and simple English is fine. To fax, use the form in the Appendix. If you're writing, add the zip code and confirm the need and method for a deposit. In Europe, dates appear as day/month/year, so a two-night stay in August would be "2 nights, 16/8/99 to 18/8/99"—European hotel jargon uses your day of departure. You'll often receive a letter back from the hotel requesting one night's deposit. A credit card will usually be accepted as a deposit, though you may need to send a signed traveler's check or a bank draft in the local currency. If you provide your credit-card number as the deposit, you can pay with your card or with cash when you arrive; if you don't show up, you'll be billed for one night. Reconfirm your reservations a day in advance for safety.

Private Rooms
Throughout Scandinavia, people rent out rooms in their homes to travelers for around $40 per double. Prices are so cheap because it's a "taxation optional" form of income in Europe's most highly taxed corner. While some put out a "Værelse," "Rom," "Rum," or "Hus Rum" sign, most operate solely through the local TI (which occasionally keeps these B&Bs a secret until all hotel rooms are taken). You'll get your own key to a lived-in, clean, and comfortable (but usually simple) private room with free access to the family shower and WC. Booking direct saves both you and your host the cut the TI takes. (The TIs are very protective of their lists. If you enjoy a big-city private home that would like to be listed in this book, I'd love to hear from you.) Many private rooms come with no sinks in the room and showers a series of steep stairs away.

Camping
Scandinavian campgrounds are practical, comfortable, and cheap ($5 per person with camping card, available on the spot). The

national tourist office has a fine brochure/map listing all their campgrounds. This is the middle-class Scandinavian family way to travel: safe, great social fun, and no reservation problems.

Huts

Most campgrounds provide huts *(hytter)* for wanna-be campers with no gear. Huts normally sleep four to six in bunk beds, come with blankets and a kitchenette, and charge one fee (around $40), plus extra if you need sheets. Since locals typically move in for a week or two, many campground huts are booked for summer long in advance. If you're driving late with no place to stay, find a campground and grab a hut.

Eating

The smartest budget travelers do as most Scandinavians do—avoid restaurants. Prepared food is heavily taxed, and the local cuisine isn't worth trip bankruptcy. Especially outside Denmark, alcohol will floor your budget. Of course, you'll want to take an occasional splurge into each culture's high cuisine, but the "high" refers mostly to the price tag. Why not think of eating on the road as eating at home without your kitchen? Get creative with cold food and picnics. I eat well on a budget in Scandinavia using the following tips.

Breakfast

Hotel breakfasts are a huge and filling buffet, about an $8 to $10 option. This includes cereal or porridge, *let* (low fat) or *sød* (whole) milk, various kinds of drinkable yogurt (pour the yogurt in the bowl and sprinkle the cereal over it), bread, crackers, cheese (the brown stuff is goat's cheese—your trip will go better when you develop a taste for it), cold cuts, jam, fruit, juice, and coffee or tea. Coffee addicts can buy a thermos and get it filled in most hotels and hostels for $3 or $4.

I bring a baggie to breakfast and leave with a light lunch—sandwich and apple or a can of yogurt. Yes, I know, this is almost stealing, but here's how I rationalize it: Throughout my trip, I'm paying lots of taxes to support a social system that my host (but not me) will enjoy; I could have eaten what I take at that all-you-can-eat sitting, but choose to finish breakfast elsewhere . . . later. And the Vikings did much worse things. After a big breakfast, a light baggie lunch fits nicely into a busy sightseeing day.

If you skip your hotel's breakfast, you can visit a bakery to get a sandwich and cup of coffee. Bakeries have wonderful inexpensive pastries. The only cheap breakfast is one you make yourself. Many simple accommodations provide kitchenettes, or at least hot pads and coffee pots.

Lunch
Scandinavians aren't big on lunch, often just grabbing a sandwich (*smørrebrød*) and a cup of coffee at their work desk. Follow suit with a quick picnic or a light meal at a sandwich shop or snack bar.

Picnics
Scandinavia has colorful markets and economical supermarkets. Picnic-friendly mini-markets at gas and train stations are open late. Some shopping tips: Wasa cracker bread (Sport is my favorite; Ideal *flatbrød* is ideal for munchies), packaged meat and cheese, goat cheese (*geitost*; *ekte* means pure and stronger), yogurt (drink it out of the carton), freshly cooked fish in markets, fresh fruit and vegetables, lingonberries, mustard and sandwich spreads (shrimp, caviar) in a squeeze tube, boxes of juice, milk, *pytt i panna* (Swedish hash), and rye bread. Grocery stores sell a cheap, light breakfast: a handy yogurt with cereal and a spoon. If you're lazy, most places offer cheap ready-made sandwiches. If you're bored, some groceries and most delis have hot chicken, salads by the portion, fresh and cheap liver pâté, and other ways to picnic without sandwiches.

Dinner
The large meal of the Nordic day is an early dinner. Alternate between cheap, forgettable, but filling cafeteria or fast-food dinners ($12), and atmospheric, carefully chosen restaurants popular with locals ($20). Look for the *dagens rett*, an affordable one-plate daily special. One main course and two salads or soups fill up two travelers without emptying their pocketbooks. The cheap eateries close early. In Scandinavia, a normal, practical, fill-the-tank dinner is usually eaten around 18:00. Anyone eating out later is "dining," will linger longer, and can expect to pay much more. A $15 Scandinavian meal is not that much more than a $10 American meal, since tax and tip are included in the menu price.

In most Scandinavian restaurants, you can ask for more potatoes or vegetables, so a restaurant entrée is basically an all-you-can-eat deal. First servings are often small, so take advantage of this. Fast-food joints, pizzerias, Chinese food, and salad bars are inexpensive. Booze will break you. A small beer costs $5 in Oslo. Drink water (served free with an understanding smile at most restaurants). Waitresses and waiters are well paid, and tips are normally included, although it's polite to round up the bill.

Most Scandinavian nations have one inedible dish that is cherished with a perverse but patriotic sentimentality. These dishes which often originated with a famine, now remind the young of their ancestors' suffering. Norway's penitential food, lutefisk (dried cod marinated for days in potash and water), is used for Christmas and jokes.

The Language Barrier

In Scandinavia, English is all you need. Especially among the young, English is the foreign language of choice.

A few words you'll see a lot: *gamla* (old), *lille* (small), *stor* (big), *takk* (thanks), *slot* (palace), *fart* (trip), *centrum* (center), *gate* (street), *øl* (beer), *forbudt* (not allowed), and *udsalg* or *salg* (sale).

Each country has its own language. Except for Finnish, they are similar to English but with a few letters we don't have (Æ, Ø, Å). These letters barely affect pronunciation, but do affect alphabetizing. If you can't find, say, Århus in a map index, look after "Z."

One Region, Different Countries

Scandinavia is western Europe's least populated, most literate, most prosperous, most demographically homogenous, least churchgoing, most highly taxed, and most socialistic corner.

While Finland and Iceland are odd ducks, Denmark, Norway, and Sweden are similar. They have closely related languages (so close that they can laugh at each other's TV comedies). While the state religion is Lutheran, only a small percentage actually attend church other than at Easter or Christmas.

Each country is a constitutional monarchy with a royal family who knows how to stay out of the tabloids and work with the parliaments. Scandinavia is the home of cradle-to-grave security, and consequently, the most highly taxed corner of Europe. Blessed with a pristine nature, the Scandinavians are environmentalists (except for the Norwegian appetite for whaling). The region is also a leader in progressive lifestyles. More than half the couples in Denmark are "married" only because they've lived together for so long and have children.

Denmark, packing 5 million fun-loving Danes into a flat land the size of Switzerland, is the most densely populated. Sweden, the size of California, has 8.5 million, and 4.2 million Norwegians stretch out in skinny Norway. Oslo is as far from the north tip of Norway as it is from Rome.

Stranger in a Strange Land

We travel all the way to Scandinavia to enjoy differences—to become temporary locals. One of the beauties of travel is the opportunity to see that there are logical, civil, and even better alternatives to "truths" we always considered God-given and self-evident. While the materialistic culture of the United States is sneaking into these countries, simplicity has yet to become subversive. Scandinavians are into "sustainable affluence." They have experimented aggressively in the area of social welfare—with mixed results. Travel in Scandinavia can rattle a Republican. Fit in, don't look for things American on the other side of the Atlantic, and you're sure to enjoy a full dose of Scandinavian hospitality.

Send Me a Postcard, Drop Me a Line

If you enjoy a successful trip with the help of this book and would like to share your discoveries, please fill out the survey at the end of this book and send it to me at Europe Through the Back Door, Box 2009, Edmonds, WA 98020. I personally read and value all feedback. Thanks in advance—it helps a lot.

For our latest travel information, tap into our web site: www.ricksteves.com. My e-mail address is rick@ricksteves.com. Anyone can request a free issue of our newsletter.

Judging from the happy postcards I receive, it's safe to assume you're on your way to a great Scandinavian vacation. Thanks, and happy travels!

BACK DOOR TRAVEL PHILOSOPHY
As Taught in Rick Steves' *Europe Through the Back Door*

Travel is intensified living—maximum thrills per minute and one of the last great sources of legal adventure. Travel is freedom. It's recess, and we need it.

Experiencing the real Europe requires catching it by surprise, going casual . . . "Through the Back Door."

Affording travel is a matter of priorities. (Make do with the old car.) You can travel—simply, safely, and comfortably—anywhere in Europe for $60 a day plus transportation costs. In many ways, spending more money only builds a thicker wall between you and what you came to see. Europe is a cultural carnival, and time after time, you'll find that its best acts are free and the best seats are the cheap ones.

A tight budget forces you to travel close to the ground, meeting and communicating with the people, not relying on service with a purchased smile. Never sacrifice sleep, nutrition, safety, or cleanliness in the name of budget. Simply enjoy the local-style alternatives to expensive hotels and restaurants.

Extroverts have more fun. If your trip is low on magic moments, kick yourself and make things happen. If you don't enjoy a place, maybe you don't know enough about it. Seek the truth. Recognize tourist traps. Give a culture the benefit of your open mind. See things as different but not better or worse. Any culture has much to share.

Of course, travel, like the world, is a series of hills and valleys. Be fanatically positive and militantly optimistic. If something's not to your liking, change your liking. Travel is addicting. It can make you a happier American, as well as a citizen of the world. Our Earth is home to nearly 6 billion equally important people. It's humbling to travel and find that people don't envy Americans. They like us but, with all due respect, they wouldn't trade passports.

Globetrotting destroys ethnocentricity. It helps you understand and appreciate different cultures. Travel changes people. It broadens perspectives and teaches new ways to measure quality of life. Many travelers toss aside their hometown blinders. Their prized souvenirs are the strands of different cultures they decide to knit into their own character. The world is a cultural yarn shop. And Back Door travelers are weaving the ultimate tapestry. Come on, join in!

DENMARK

COPENHAGEN

Copenhagen (København) is Scandinavia's largest city. With over a million people, it's home to more than a quarter of all Danes. A busy day cruising the canals, wandering through the palace, taking a historic walking tour, and strolling the Strøget (Europe's greatest pedestrian shopping mall) will get you oriented, and you'll feel right at home. Copenhagen is Scandinavia's cheapest and most fun-loving capital, so live it up.

Planning Your Time

A first visit deserves two days.

Day 1: If staying in Christianshavn, start the day browsing through the neighborhood, called Copenhagen's "Little Amsterdam." Catch the 10:30 city walking tour. After a Riz-Raz lunch, visit the Use It information center and catch the relaxing canal boat tour out to *The Little Mermaid*. Spend the rest of the afternoon tracing Denmark's cultural roots in the National Museum and/or touring the Ny Carlsberg Glyptotek art gallery; spend the evening strolling or biking Strøget (follow "Heart and Soul" walk described below) or Christianshavn.

Day 2: At 10:00 explore the subterranean Christiansborg Castle ruins under today's palace. At 11:00 take the 50-minute guided tour of Denmark's royal Christiansborg Palace. The afternoon is free, with many options, including a smørrebrød lunch, tour of the Rosenborg Castle/crown jewels, brewery tour, or Nazi Resistance museum (free tour

often at 14:00). Evening at Tivoli Gardens before catching a
night train out.

With a third day, side trip out to Roskilde and Frederiksborg. Remember the efficiency of sleeping in-and-out by train.
If flying in, most flights from the States arrive in the morning.
After that, head for Stockholm and Oslo. Kamikaze sightseers
see Copenhagen as a Scandinavian bottleneck. They sleep in-
and-out heading north and in-and-out heading south, with two
days and no nights in the city. Considering the joy of Oslo and
Stockholm, this isn't that crazy if you have limited time. You
can check your bag at the station and take a 10-kr shower in
the Interail Center.

You can set yourself up in my best rooms for your entire
Scandinavian tour with a quick trip to a pay phone. This is
probably a wise thing to do.

Orientation

Nearly all of your sightseeing is in Copenhagen's compact old
town. By doing things by bike or on foot you'll stumble into
some surprisingly cozy corners, charming bits of Copenhagen
that many miss. Study the map. The medieval walls are now
roads that define the center: Vestervoldgade (literally, "western
wall street"), Nørrevoldgade, and Østervoldgade. The fourth
side is the harbor and the island of Slotsholmen where København ("merchants' harbor") was born in 1167. The next of the
city's islands is Amager, where you'll find the local "Little
Amsterdam" district of Christianshavn. What was Copenhagen's moat is now a string of pleasant lakes and parks,
including Tivoli Gardens. To the north is the old "new town,"
where the Amalienborg Palace is surrounded by streets on a
grid plan, and *The Little Mermaid* poses relentlessly, waiting for
her sailor to return and the tourists to leave.

The core of the town, as far as most visitors are concerned, is the axis formed by the train station, Tivoli Gardens,
the Rådhus (city hall) square, and the Strøget pedestrian street.
It's a great walking town, bubbling with street life and colorful
pedestrian zones. But be sure to get off the Strøget.

The character in Copenhagen's history who matters most
is Christian IV, who ruled from 1588 to 1648. He was Denmark's Renaissance king, the royal Danish party animal
whose personal energy kindled a Golden Age when Copenhagen prospered and many of the city's grandest buildings

Copenhagen

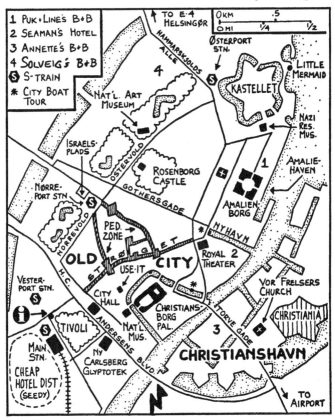

1 PUK + LINE'S B+B
2 SEAMAN'S HOTEL
3 ANNETTE'S B+B
4 SOLVEIG'S B+B
Ⓢ S-TRAIN
✱ CITY BOAT TOUR

TO E·4 HELSINGØR

0 KM   ·5
0 MI   ¼   ½

ØSTERPORT STN.

LITTLE MERMAID

KASTELLET

HAMMARSKJOLDS ALLE

NAT'L. ART MUSEUM

NAZI RES. MUS.

ISRAELS-PLADS

ROSENBORG CASTLE

OSTERVOLD

AMALIE-HAVEN

NØRRE-PORT STN.

GOTHERSGADE

AMALIEN-BORG

PED. ZONE

NØRREVOLD

OLD   CITY

STRØGET

NYHAVN

ROYAL THEATER 2

VOR FRELSERS CHURCH

VESTER-PORT STN.

H.C.

USE·IT

CITY HALL

CHRISTIANS BORG PAL.

TORVE GADE

CHRISTIANIA

TIVOLI

ANDERSENS BLVD.

NAT'L MUS.

3

MAIN STN.

CHEAP HOTEL DIST. (SEEDY)

NY CARLSBERG GLYPTOTEK

CHRISTIANSHAVN

TO AIRPORT

were built. Locals love to tell great stories of everyone's favorite king.

Tourist Information

The tourist office is now run by a for-profit consortium called "Wonderful Copenhagen." This colors the advice and information it provides. Still, it's worth a quick stop for the topnotch freebies it provides, such as a city map and *Copenhagen This Week* (a free, handy, and misnamed monthly guide to the city, worth reading for its good maps, museum hours with telephone numbers, sightseeing tour ideas, shopping suggestions, and calendar of events, including free English tours and concerts). The TI is across from the train station, near the corner of Vesterbrogade and Bernstorffsgade, next to the Tivoli entrance (daily May through mid-September 9:00–21:00; mid-September to April weekdays 9:00–17:00, Saturday 9:00–14:00, closed Sunday; tel. 33 11 13 25). Corporate dictates prohibit the TI from freely offering other brochures (such as walking-tour schedules and brochures on any sights of special interest), but ask and you shall receive. Thinking ahead, get information and ferry schedules for your entire trip in Denmark (Frederiksborg Castle, Louisiana Museum, Kronborg Castle, Roskilde, Odense, Ærø, Århus, and Legoland). The TI's room-finding service charges you and the hotel a fee and cannot give hard opinions. Do not use it. Get on the phone and call direct—everyone speaks English.

Use It is a better information service. This "branch" of Huset, a hip, city government–sponsored, student-run cluster of cafés, theaters, and galleries, caters to Copenhagen's young but welcomes travelers of any age. It's a friendly, driven-to-help, energetic, no-nonsense source of budget travel information, with a free budget room-finding service, ride-finding board, free luggage lockers, pen-pals-wanted scrapbook, free condoms, and Copenhagen's best free city maps. Their free *Playtime* publication is full of Back Door–style travel articles on Copenhagen and the Danish culture, special budget tips, and events. They have brochures on just about everything, including self-guided tours for bikers, walkers, and those riding scenic bus #6. They have a list of private rooms (250-kr doubles without breakfast). Use It is a ten-minute walk from the station: head down Strøget, then turn right on Rådhus-træde for 3 blocks to #13 (daily June–September 9:00–19:00; off-season open weekdays 10:00–16:00 and closed weekends; tel. 33 15 65 18, fax 33 15 75 18). After hours, their computer touch screen lists the cheapest rooms available in town.

The **Copenhagen Card** covers the public transportation system and admissions to nearly all the sights in greater Copenhagen, which stretches from Helsingør to Roskilde. It includes virtually all the city sights, Tivoli, and the bus from the airport. Available at any tourist office (including the airport's) and the central station: 24 hours, 140 kr; 48 hours, 230 kr; 72 hours, 295 kr. It's hard to break even, unless you're planning to side trip on the included (and otherwise expensive) rail service. It comes with a handy book explaining the 60 included sights, such as: Christiansborg Palace (normally 35 kr), Castle Ruins (20 kr), National Museum (30 kr), Ny Carlsberg Glyptotek (15 kr), Rosenborg Castle (40 kr), Tivoli (39 kr), Frederiksborg Castle (40 kr), and Roskilde Viking Ships (40 kr), plus round-trip train rides to Roskilde (70 kr) and Frederiksborg Castle (70 kr).

Arrival in Copenhagen

By Train: The main train station, Hovedbanegården (HOETH-ban-gorn; learn that word—you'll need to recognize it) is a temple of travel and a hive of travel-related activity. You'll find lockers (25 kr/day), a *garderobe* (35 kr/day per rucksack), a post office, a grocery store (daily 8:00–24:00), 24-hour thievery, and bike rentals. The Interail Center, a service the station offers to mostly young travelers (but anyone with a Eurailpass, Scanrail, student BIGE or Transalpino ticket, or Interail pass is welcome) is a pleasant lounge with 10-kr showers, free (if risky) luggage storage, city maps, snacks, information, and other young travelers (June through mid–September 6:30–22:00). If you just need the map and *Playtime*, a visit here is quicker than going to the TI.

Most travelers arrive in Copenhagen after an overnight train ride. The station has two long-hours money exchange desks. Den Danske Bank is fair—charging the standard 40-kr minimum or 20-kr-per-check fee for traveler's checks (daily 7:00–20:00). FOREX, which has a worse rate but charges only 10 kr per traveler's check with no minimum, is better for small exchanges (daily 8:00–21:00). On a $100 exchange, I saved 22 kr at FOREX. (The American Express office—a 20-minute walk away, off Strøget—may be even better; see Helpful Hints, below). While you're in the station, reserve your overnight train seat or couchette out (at Rejse-bureau). International rides and all IC trains require reservations (usually 20 kr). Bus #8 (in front of the station on the station side of Bernstorffsgade) goes to Christianshavn B&Bs. Note the time the bus departs, then stop by the TI (across the street on the left) and pick up a free Copenhagen city map that shows bus routes.

By Plane: Copenhagen's International Airport is a traveler's dream, with a tourist office, bank (standard rates), post office, telephone center, shopping mall, grocery store, and bakery. You can use American cash at the airport and get

change back in kroner. (Phone service for all airline offices is
split between two switchboards: SAS services—tel. 31 54 17
01 and Copenhagen Air Service—tel. 32 47 47 47. SAS ticket
hotline—tel. 32 32 68 00.) If you need to kill a night at the
airport, try the fetal rest cabins, the *hvilekabiner* (Sb-270 kr,
Db-405 kr, rented by the eight-hour period; reception open
6:00–22:00; easy telephone reservations, CC:VMA, tel. 32 31
32 31, fax 32 31 31 09).

Getting Downtown from the Airport: Taxis are fast and
easy, accept credit cards, and, at about 150 kr to the town center, are a good deal for foursomes. The SAS **shuttle bus** zips
between the central train station and airport in 20 minutes for
35 kr. **City bus** #250s gets you downtown (City Hall Square,
TI) in 30 minutes for 17 kr (12/hour, across the street and to
the right as you exit the airport). If you're going from the airport to Christianshavn, ride #9 just past Christianshavn Torv
to the last stop before Knippels Bridge.

Helpful Hints

Ferries: Book any ferries you plan to use in Scandinavia now.
Any travel agent can book the boat rides you plan to take later
on your trip, such as the Denmark–Norway ferry (ask for special discounts on this crossing) or the Stockholm–Helsinki–
Stockholm cruise (the Silja Line office is directly across from
the station at Nyhavn 43A, open Monday–Friday 9:00–17:00,
tel. 33 14 40 80). Drivers heading to Sweden by ferry should
call for a reservation (two competing Helsingør lines: 33 15 15
15 and 49 26 01 55, and the often cheaper Dragør line: 32 53
15 85). Reservations are free and easy and assure that you
won't be stuck in a long line.

Jazz Festival: The Copenhagen Jazz Festival—ten days
starting the first Friday in July (July 3–12 in 1998)—puts the
town in a rollicking slide-trombone mood. The Danes are
Europe's jazz enthusiasts and, more than most music festivals,
this one fills the town with happiness. The TI prints up an
extensive listing of each year's festival events (as well as a listing of other festivals).

Telephones: Use the telephone liberally. Everyone speaks
English, and *This Week* and this book list phone numbers for
everything you'll be doing. All telephone numbers in Denmark
are eight digits, and there are no area codes. Calls anywhere in
Denmark are cheap; calls to Norway and Sweden cost 6 kr per

minute from a booth (half of that from a private home). Coin-
op booths are often broken. Get a phone card (from newsstands, starting at 20 kr).

Traveler's Checks: The American Express Company
does not charge any fee on their checks and only 15 kr per
transaction on any other checks and cash (Strøget at Amager-
torv 18, Monday–Friday 9:00–17:00, summer Saturdays
9:00–14:00, tel. 33 12 23 01).

Getting Around Copenhagen

By Bus and Subway: Take advantage of the fine bus (tel. 36 45
45 45) and subway system called S-tog (Eurail valid on S-tog, tel.
33 14 17 01). A joint fare system covers greater Copenhagen.
You pay 11 kr as you board for an hour's travel within two zones,
or buy a blue two-zone *klippekort* from the driver (75 kr for ten
one-hour "rides"). A 24-hour pass costs 70 kr. Don't worry much
about "zones." Assume you'll be within the middle two zones.
Board at the front, tell the driver where you're going, and he'll
sell you the appropriate ticket. Drivers are patient, have change,
and speak English. City maps list bus and subway routes. Locals
are friendly and helpful. Copenhagen is a bit torn up as it puts
together a slick new subway system to celebrate the year 2000.

By Bus Tour: The city tour bus scene is in flux, but there
are always tours leaving from the City Hall Square (under the
statue of the two Lur Blowers, in front of Palace Hotel, one hour
blitz overview—with a short stop only at the *Mermaid*, two
departures per hour, 100 kr, also longer tours, tel. 31 54 06 06).
There is a new "hop-on-hop-off" tour bus making a general cir-
cuit of the town's top sights (daily 9:00–18:00, 100 kr, tel. 36 77
77 66). Budget do-it-yourselfers simply ride city bus #6: from the
Carlsberg Brewery, it stops at Tivoli, town hall, national
museum, palace, Nyhavn, Amalienborg castle, the Kastellet, and
the *Mermaid* (11 kr for one stop-and-go hour). The entire tour is
clearly described in a free Use It brochure.

By Taxi: Taxis are plentiful and easy to call or flag down
(22-kr drop charge, then 9 kr per km). For a short ride, four people can travel cheaper by taxi than by bus (e.g., 50 kr from train
station to Christianshavn B&Bs). Taxis accept all major credit
cards. Calling 31 35 35 35 will get you a taxi within minutes.

Free Bikes! Copenhagen's radical "city bike" program is
great for sightseers. Two thousand clunky but practical little
bikes are scattered around the old town center (basically the

terrain covered in the Copenhagen map in this chapter). Simply locate one of the 150 racks, unlock a bike by popping a 20-kr coin into the handlebar, and pedal away. When you're done, park the bike at any other rack, pop in the lock and you get your deposit coin back (if you can't find a rack, leave the bike on the street anywhere and a bum will take it back and pocket your coin). These simple bikes come with "theft-proof" parts (unusable on regular bikes) and—they claim—computer tracer chips embedded in them so bike patrols can retrieve strays. These are constructed with prison labor and funded by advertisements painted on the wheels and by a progressive electorate. Try this once and you'll find Copenhagen suddenly a lot smaller and easier.

For a serious bike tour, rent a more comfortable bike. Use It has a great biking guide brochure and information about city bike tours (50 kr including bike, two hours, grunge approach). You can rent bikes at Central Station's Cykelcenter (50 kr/day, weekdays 8:00–18:00, Saturday 9:00–13:00, summer Sundays 10:00–13:00, closed Sunday off-season, tel. 33 33 86 13) and Dan Wheel (35 kr/day, 60 kr/2 days, weekdays 9:00–18:00, Saturday and Sunday 9:00–14:00, 2 blocks from the station at 3 Colbjørnsensgade, on the corner of Vesterbrogade, tel. 31 21 22 27).

Do-It-Yourself Orientation Walk: "Strøget and Copenhagen's Heart and Soul"

Start from Rådhuspladsen (City Hall Square), the bustling heart of Copenhagen, dominated by the city hall spire. This used to be the fortified west end of town. The king cleverly quelled a French Revolution–type thirst for democracy by giving his people Europe's first great public amusement park. Tivoli was built just outside the city walls in 1843. When the train lines came, the station was placed just beyond Tivoli. The golden girls high up on the building on the square opposite the Strøget's entrance tell the weather: on a bike (fair) or with an umbrella. These two have been called the only women in Copenhagen you can trust. Here in the traffic hub of this huge city you'll notice . . . not many cars. Denmark's 200 percent tax on car purchases makes the bus or bike a sweeter option.

Old Hans Christian Andersen sits to the right of the city hall, almost begging to be in another photo (as he did in real life). On a pedestal left of the city hall, note the Lur-Blowers sculpture. The *lur* is a horn that was used 3,500 years ago.

Central Copenhagen

The ancient originals (which still play) are displayed in the National Museum.

The American trio of Burger King, 7-Eleven, and McDonald's marks the start of the otherwise charming Strøget (stroy-et). Copenhagen's 25-year-old experimental, tremendously successful, and most-copied pedestrian shopping mall is a string of lively (and individually named) streets and lovely squares that bunny-hop through the old town from the city hall to Nyhavn, a 15-minute stroll (or "strøget") away.

As you wander down this street, remember that the commercial focus of a historic street like Strøget drives up the land value, which generally tears down the old buildings. While Strøget has become quite hamburgerized, charm lurks in adjacent areas and many historic bits and pieces of old Copenhagen are just off this commercial cancan.

After 1 block you can side trip 2 blocks left up Larsbjørnsstræde into Copenhagen's colorful university district. Formerly the old brothel area, today this is Soho-chic.

Back on Strøget, the first segment, Frederiksberggade, ends at Gammel Torv and Nytorv (Old Square and New Square). This was the old town center. The Oriental-looking kiosk was one of the city's first community telephone centers before phones were privately owned. The squirting woman and boy on the very old fountain was so offensive to people from the Victorian age that the pedestal was added, raising it—they hoped—out of view. The brick church at the start of Amager Torv is the oldest building you'll see here.

Side trip 2 blocks north of Amager Torv to the leafy and caffeine-stained Gråbrødretorv (Grey Brothers' Square). At the next big intersection, Kobmagergade—an equally lively but less-touristy pedestrian street—is worth exploring.

The final stretch of Strøget leads past the American Express office, Pistolstræde (a cute street of shops in restored 18th-century buildings leading off Strøget to the right from Ostergade), McDonald's (good view from top floor), and major department stores (Illum and Magasin, see below) to a big square called Kongens Nytorv, where you'll find the Royal Theater.

Nyhavn, a recently gentrified sailors' quarter, is just opposite Kongens Nytorv. This formerly sleazy harbor is an interesting mix of tattoo parlors, taverns, and trendy (mostly expensive) cafés lining a canal filled with glamorous old sailboats of all sizes. Any historic sloop is welcome to moor here in Copenhagen's ever-changing boat museum. Hans Christian Andersen lived and wrote his first stories here.

Continuing north, along the harborside (from end of Nyhavn canal, turn left), you'll pass a huge ship that sails to Oslo every evening. Follow the water to the modern fountain of Amaliehave Park. The Amalienborg Palace and Square (a block inland, behind the fountain) is a good example of orderly Baroque planning. Queen Margrethe II and her family live in the palace to your immediate left as you enter the square from the harbor side. Her son and heir to the throne, Frederik, recently moved into the palace directly opposite his mother's. While the guards change with royal fanfare at noon only when the queen is in residence, they shower e very morning.

Leave the square on Amaliegade, heading north to Kastellet (Citadel) Park and a small museum about Denmark's World War II resistance efforts. A short stroll, past the Gefion fountain (showing the mythological story of the goddess who was given one night to carve a chunk out of Sweden to make into Denmark's main island, Zealand—which you're on) and a church built of flint and along the water, brings you to the overrated, over-fondled, and over-photographed symbol of Copenhagen, *Den Lille Havfrue—The Little Mermaid.*

You can get back downtown on foot, by taxi, or on bus #1, #6, or #9 from Store Kongensgade on the other side of Kastellet Park (a special bus may run from the *Mermaid* in summer).

Tours of Copenhagen

▲**Walking Tours**—Once upon a time, American Richard Karpen visited Copenhagen and fell in love with the city (and one of its women). He gives daily two-hour walking tours of his adopted hometown covering its people, history, and contemporary scene. His entertaining walks (there are three—each about 1.5 miles with breaks—covering different parts of the city center) leave daily at 10:30 Monday–Saturday, May–September, from in front of the TI (40 kr, kids under 12 free, pick up schedule at the TI or call Richard at tel. 32 97 14 40). All of Richard's tours, while different, complement each other and are of equal "introduction" value. Richard and local historian Helge "Jack" Jacobsen (tel. 31 51 25 90) give reasonably priced private walks and tours. Use It also offers walking tours (40 kr, 15:30 on Wednesday).

▲▲**Harbor Cruise and Canal Tours**—Two companies offer basically the same live, four-language, 60-minute tours through the city canals (2/hour, daily 10:00–17:00, later in July; runs May to mid-September). They cruise around the palace and Christianshavn area, into the wide-open harbor, and out to the *Mermaid.* Both leave from near Christiansborg Palace. It's a pleasant way to see the *Mermaid* and take a load off those weary feet. Dress warmly; boats are open-top.

The low-overhead 20-kr Netto-Bådene Tour boats (tel. 31 87 21 33) leave from Holmens Kirke across from the Borsen (stock exchange), just over Knippels Bridge. The competition, Canal Tours Copenhagen, does a 40-kr harbor tour with a hop-on-and-hop-off version. It leaves from Gammel Strand near Christiansborg Palace and the National Museum (tel. 33 13 31 05). Don't be confused. If you don't plan to get off the boat, go with Netto. There's no reason to pay double. Tour boats also start at Nyhavn.

Sights—Copenhagen

▲**Copenhagen's Town Hall (*Rådhus*)**—This city landmark, between the station/Tivoli/TI and Strøget pedestrian mall, offers private tours and trips up its 350-foot-high tower. It's draped, inside and out, in Danish symbolism. Bishop Absalon (the city's founder) stands over the door. The polar bears climbing on the rooftop symbolize the giant Danish protectorate of Greenland. The city hall is free and open to the public (Monday–Friday 10:00–15:00). Tours are given in English and get you into otherwise-closed rooms (20 kr, 45 minutes, Monday–Friday at 15:00, Saturday at 10:00). Tourists are allowed to romp up the tower's 300 steps for the best aerial view of Copenhagen (10 kr, Monday–Friday 10:00, 12:00, and 14:00; Saturday 12:00; off-season Monday–Saturday 12:00, tel. 33 66 25 82).

▲**Christiansborg Palace**—This modern *slot*, or palace, built on the ruins of the original 12th-century castle, houses the parliament, supreme court, prime minister's headquarters, and royal reception rooms. Guided 40-minute English tours of the queen's reception rooms let you slip-slide on protect-the-floor slippers through 22 rooms and gain a good feel for Danish history, royalty, and politics in this 100-year-old, still-functioning palace (35 kr, June–August daily at 11:00, 13:00, 15:00; off-season Tuesday, Thursday, and Sunday 11:00 and 15:00; tel. 33 92 64 92). For a rundown on contemporary government, you can also tour the parliament building. From the equestrian statue in front, go through the wooden door, past the entrance to the Christiansborg Castle ruins, into the courtyard, and up the stairs on the right.

▲**Christiansborg Castle ruins**—An exhibit in the scant remains of the first castle built by Bishop Absalon—the 12th-century founder of Copenhagen—lies under the palace (20 kr, daily 9:30–15:30, closed off-season Monday and Saturday, good 1-kr guide). Early birds note that this sight opens 30 minutes before other nearby sights.

▲▲▲**National Museum**—Focus on the excellent and curiously enjoyable Danish collection, which traces this civilization from its ancient beginnings. Exhibits are laid out chronologically and well-described in English. Pick up the museum map and consider the 10 kr mini-guide which highlights the top stops. Find room 1 opposite the new entrance and begin your walk following the numbers through the "prehistory" section on the ground

floor—oak coffins with still-clothed and armed skeletons from
1300 B.C., ancient and still playable lur horns, the 200-year old
Gunderstrup Cauldron of art textbook fame, lots of Viking stuff,
and a bitchin' collection of well-translated rune stones. Then go
upstairs, find room 101 and carry on—fascinating dirt on the
Reformation, everyday town life in the 16th and 17th centuries
and, in room 126, a unique "cylinder perspective" of the royal
family (from 1656) and two peep shows. The next floor takes
you into modern times (30 kr, Tuesday–Sunday 10:00–17:00,
free on Wednesday, closed Monday, enter from Ny Vestergade
10, tel. 33 13 44 11). Occasional free English tours are offered in
the summer—call first).

▲**Ny Carlsberg Glyptotek**—Scandinavia's top art gallery,
with especially intoxicating Egyptian, Greek, and Etruscan col-
lections, the best of Danish Golden Age (early 19th century)
painting, and a heady, if small, exhibit of 19th-century French
paintings (in the new "French Wing," including Géricault,
Delacroix, Manet, Impressionists, Gauguin before and after
Tahiti) is an impressive example of what beer money can do.
Linger with marble gods under the palm leaves and glass dome
of the very soothing winter garden. Designers, figuring Danes
would be more interested in a lush garden than classical art,
used this wonderful space as leafy bait to cleverly introduce
locals to a few Greek and Roman statues. (It works for tourists
too.) One of the original Rodin *Thinker*s (wondering how to
scale the Tivoli fence?) can be seen for free in the museum's
backyard. This collection is artfully displayed and thoughtfully
described—good even after a visit to Rome (15 kr, Tuesday–
Sunday 10:00–16:00, free on Wednesday and Sunday, 2-kr
English brochure/guide, classy cafeteria under palms, behind
Tivoli, Dantes Plads 7, tel. 33 41 81 41).

▲▲**Rosenborg Castle**—This impressively furnished Renais-
sance-style castle houses the Danish crown jewels and 500
years of royal knickknacks. It's musty with history (including
some great Christian IV lore . . . like the shrapnel he pulled
from his eye after a naval battle and made into earrings for his
girlfriend) and would be fascinating if anything was explained
in English. Consider purchasing the guide. The castle is surrounded by the royal gardens, a rare plant collection, and on
sunny days, a minefield of sunbathing Danish beauties and picnickers (40 kr, daily June–August 10:00–16:00; May, September, and October 11:00–15:00; there's no electricity inside, so

visit at a bright time; Richard Karpen—see Walking Tours, above—does two Rosenborg tours a week; S-train: Nørreport, tel. 33 15 32 86). There is a daily changing of the guard mini-parade from Rosenborg Castle (at 11:30) to Amalienborg Castle (at 12:00). The King's Rosegarden (across the canal from the palace) is a fine place for a picnic (for cheap open-face sandwiches to go, walk a couple of blocks to Lorraine's at the corner of Borgergade and Dronningenstværgade). The fine statue of Hans Christian Andersen in the park, actually erected in his lifetime (and approved by H.C.A.), is meant to symbolize how his stories had a message even for adults.

▲**Denmark's Resistance Museum (Frihedsmuseet)**—The fascinating story of a heroic Nazi resistance struggle (1940–1945) is well-explained in English (free, between the Queen's Palace and the *Mermaid*, daily May–mid-September 10:00–16:00, closed Monday; off-season 11:00–15:00; bus #1, #6, or #9, tel. 33 13 77 14). If prioritizing, the Resistance Museum in Oslo is more interesting.

▲**Our Savior's (Vor Frelsers) Church**—The church's bright Baroque interior is worth a look (free, daily June–August 9:00–16:30, Sunday 13:30–16:30; closes an hour early in spring and fall; closed in winter, bus #8, tel. 31 57 27 98). The unique spiral spire that you'll admire from afar can be climbed for a great city view and a good aerial view of the Christiania commune below. It's 311 feet high, claims to have 400 steps, and costs 20 kr.

Lille Mølle—This tiny intimate museum shows off a 1916 house in Christianshavn (Monday–Friday 11:00–14:00, just off south end of Torvgade, tel. 33 47 38 38). A fine café serves light lunches and dinners in its terrace garden.

Carlsberg Brewery Tour—Denmark's beloved source of legal intoxicants, Carlsberg, provides free one-hour brewery tours followed by 30-minute "tasting sessions" (Monday–Friday 11:00 and 14:00; bus #6 to 140 Ny Carlsberg Vej, tel. 33 27 13 14).

Museum of Erotica—This museum's focus: the love life of *Homo sapiens*. Better than the Amsterdam equivalents, it offers a chance to visit a porno shop and call it a museum. It took some digging, but they've documented a history of sex from Pompeii to present day. Visitors get a peep into the world of 19th-century Copenhagen prostitutes and a chance to read up on the sex lives of Martin Luther, Queen Elizabeth, Charlie Chaplin, and

Casanova. After reviewing a lifetime of *Playboy* centerfolds, visitors sit down for the arguably artistic experience of watching the "electric *tabernakel*," a dozen silently slamming screens of porn seething to the gentle accompaniment of music (worth the 49-kr entry fee only if fascinated by sex, daily May–September 10:00–23:00; 11:00–20:00 the rest of the year, a block north of Strøget at Købmagergade 24, tel. 33 12 03 11). For the real thing—unsanitized but free—wander Copenhagen's dreary little red-light district along Istedgade behind the train station.

Hovedbanegården—The great Copenhagen train station is a fascinating mesh of Scandinanity and transportation efficiency. Even if you're not a train traveler, check it out (fuller description under Orientation, above).

Nightlife—For the latest on Copenhagen's hopping jazz scene, pick up the *Copenhagen Jazz Guide* at the TI or the more "alternative" *Playtime* magazine at Use It.

Tivoli Gardens

The world's grand old amusement park—which just turned 150 years old—is 20 acres, 110,000 lanterns, and countless ice-cream cones of fun. You pay one admission price and find yourself lost in a Hans Christian Andersen wonderland of rides, restaurants, games, marching bands, roulette wheels, and funny mirrors. Tivoli is wonderfully Danish. It doesn't try to be Disney (39 kr regular admission, 30 kr entry before 13:00 and after 22:00, open daily from April–mid-September 10:00–24:00, closed off-season, tel. 33 15 10 01). Rides are 15 kr, or 1,148 kr for an all-day pass. All children's amusements are in full swing by 11:30—the rest of the amusements are open by 13:30.

Entertainment in Tivoli: Upon arrival, go right to the Tivoli Service Center (through main entry, on left) to pick up a map and events schedule. Take a moment to sit down and plan your entertainment for the evening (events on the half-hour 18:30–23:00; 19:30 concert in the concert hall can be free or cost up to 500 kr, depending on the performer). Free concerts, mime, ballet, acrobats, puppets, and other shows pop up all over the park, and a well-organized visitor can enjoy an exciting evening of entertainment without spending a single krone (though occasionally the schedule is a bit sparse). The children's theater, Valmuen, plays excellent traditional fairy tales (daily except Monday, 12:00, 13:00, and 14:00). If the Tivoli Symphony is playing, it's worth paying for. Friday evenings feature a 22:00 rock or pop show. On Wednesday and Saturday at 23:45, fireworks light up the sky. If you're taking an overnight train out of Copenhagen, Tivoli (across from the station) is the place to spend your last Copenhagen hours.

Eating at Tivoli: Generally, you'll pay amusement-park prices for amusement park quality food inside. **Søcafeen,** by the lake, allows picnics if you buy a drink. The *pølser* (sausage) stands are cheap. **Færgekroen** is a good lakeside place for a beer or some typical Danish food. The Croatian restaurant, **Hercegovina,** is a decent value (100-kr lunch buffet, 140-kr dinner buffet). For a cake and coffee, consider the **Viften** café.

Christiania

In 1971 the original 700 Christianians established squatters right in an abandoned military barracks just a ten-minute walk from the Danish parliament building. A generation later this "free city"—an ultra-human mishmash of 1,000 idealists, anarchists, hippies, dope fiends, non-materialists, and people who dream only of being a Danish bicycle seat—not only survives, it thrives. This is a communal cornucopia of dogs, dirt, soft drugs, and dazed people—or haven of peace, freedom, and no taboos, depending on your perspective. Locals will remind judgmental Americans that a society must make the choice: allow for alternative lifestyles . . . or build more prisons.

For 25 years Christiania was a political hot potato . . . no one in the Danish establishment wanted it—or had the nerve to mash it. Now that Christiania is no longer a teenager, it's making an effort to connect better with the rest of society. The community is paying its utilities and even offering daily walking tours (see below).

Passing under the city gate you'll find yourself on "Pusher Street" . . . the main drag. This is a line of stalls selling hash, pot, pipes, and souvenirs leading to the market square and a food circus beyond. Make a point of getting past this "touristy" side of Christiania. You'll find a fascinating ramshackle world of moats and earthen ramparts, alternative housing, unappetizing falafel stands, carpenter shops, hippie villas, children's playgrounds, and peaceful lanes. Be careful to distinguish between real Christianians and Christiania's uninvited guests—motley lowlife vagabonds from other countries who hang out here in the summer, skid row–type Greenlanders, and gawking tourists.

Soft Drugs: While hard drugs are out, hash and pot are sold openly (huge joints for 20 kr, senior discounts) and smoked happily. While locals will assure you you're safe within Christiania, they'll remind you that it's risky to take pot out—Denmark is required by Uncle Sam to make a token effort to snare tourists leaving the "free city" with pot. Beefy marijuana plants stand on proud pedestals at the market square. Beyond that an open-air food circus (or the canal-view perch above it, on the earthen ramparts) creates just the right ambience to lose track of time. Graffiti on the wall declares "a mind is a wonderful thing to waste."

Nitty-Gritty: Christiania is open all the time and visitors are welcome (follow the beer bottles and guitars down Prinsessegade behind Vor Frelsers' spiral church spire in Christianshavn). Photography is absolutely forbidden on Pusher Street (if you value your camera, don't even sneak a photo). Otherwise, you are welcome to snap photos, but ask residents before you photograph them. Christiania's free English/Dansk visitor's magazine, *Nitten* (available at Use It), is good reading, offering a serious explanation about how this unique community works and survives. It suggests several do-it-yourself walking tours. Guided tours leave from the front entrance of Christiania at 15:00 (daily June–August, 20 kr, in English and Danish, tel. 32 95 65 07 to confirm). Morgenstedet is a cheap and good vegetarian place (left after Pusher Street). Spiseloppen is the classy good-enough-for-Republicans restaurant (see Eating, below).

More Sights—Copenhagen

Thorvaldsen's Museum features the early 18th-century work of Denmark's greatest sculptor (free, Tuesday–Sunday 10:00–17:00, closed Monday, next to Christiansborg Palace). The noontime **changing of the guard** at the Amalienborg Palace is boring: all they change is places. **Nyhavn**, with its fine old ships, tattoo shops (pop into Tattoo Ole at #17—fun photos, very traditional), and jazz clubs, is a wonderful place to hang out. The **Round Tower**, built in 1642 by Christian IV, connects a church, library, and observatory (the oldest functioning observatory in Europe) with a ramp which spirals up to a fine view of Copenhagen (15 kr, daily 10:00–17:00, later in summer, less on Sunday, nothing to see but the ramp and the view, just off Strøget on Købmagergade).

Copenhagen's **Open Air Fol**
is a park filled with traditional D
culture (30 kr, Tuesday–Sunday
closed Monday; shorter hours (
the suburb of Lyngby, tel. 45 §
hop on the S-train to Sorgenf
walk to the museum (as you (
walk about 1 kilometer to next tra....
blocks to museum) or catch bus #184 from the ...
Nørreport station (this bus takes a circuitous through
several towns before stopping at museum).

Danes gather at Copenhagen's other great amusement
park, **Bakken** (free, daily April–August 14:00–24:00, 30 minutes by S-train to Klampenborg, then walk through the woods,
tel. 39 63 35 44).

If you don't have time to get to the idyllic island of **Ærø**
(see Central Denmark chapter), consider a trip to the tiny fishing village of **Dragør** (30 minutes on bus #30 or #33 from
Copenhagen's City Hall Square).

Shopping

Copenhagen's colorful flea market is small but feisty and surprisingly cheap (summer Saturdays 8:00–14:00 at Israels Plads)
More flea markets are listed in *Copenhagen This Week*. An
antique market enlivens Nybrogade (near the palace) every Friday and Saturday. For a streetful of shops selling "Scantiques,"
wander down Ravnsborggade from Nørrebrogade. The city's
top department stores (Illum at 52 Østergade, tel. 33 14 40 02,
and Magasin at 13 Kongens Nytorv, tel. 33 11 44 33) offer a
good, if expensive, look at today's Denmark. Both are on
Strøget and have fine cafeterias on their top floors.

Danes shop cheaper at Dælls Varehus (corner of Krystal-
gade and Fiolstræde). At UFF on Kultorvet you can buy nearly
new clothes for peanuts and support charity. Shops are open
Monday–Friday 10:00–19:00; Saturday 9:00–16:00.

The department stores and the Politiken Bookstore on the
Rådhus Square have a good selection of maps and English
travel guides.

If you buy more than 300 kr ($50) worth of stuff, you can
get 80 percent of the 25 percent VAT (MOMS in Danish)
back if you buy from a shop displaying the Danish Tax-Free
Shopping emblem. If you have your purchase mailed, the tax

...d from your bill. Call 32 52 55 66 (8:30–16:00
...ee the shopping-oriented *Copenhagen This Week*, or
...hant for specifics.

...ping in Copenhagen

...kr = about $1)
...leep Code: **S** = Single, **D** = Double/Twin, **T** = Triple, **Q** =
Quad, **b** = bathroom, **CC** = Credit Card (Visa, MasterCard,
Amex). Breakfast is often included at hotels and rarely included
with private rooms and hostels.

I've listed the best budget hotels in the center (with doubles for 400–600 kr), rooms in private homes an easy bus ride or 15-minute walk from the station (around 350 kr per double), and dormitory options (100 kr per person).

Ibsen's Hotel is a rare, simple, bath-down-the-hall, cheery, and central budget hotel, run by three women who treat you like you're paying top dollar (S-450 kr, Sb-700 kr, D-600 kr, Db-950 kr, third person-150 kr, lots of stairs, CC:VMA, Vendersgade 23, DK-1363 Copenhagen, bus #5, #7E, #16, or #40 from the station, or S-train: Nørreport, tel. 33 13 19 13, fax 33 13 19 16, e-mail: hotel@nicholls.dk).

Hotel Sankt Jørgen has big, friendly-feeling rooms with plain old wooden furnishings. Brigitte and Susan offer a warm welcome and a great value (S-375 kr, D-475 kr with this book through 1998, third person-125 kr extra, five-bed family rooms, 10 percent less in winter, breakfast served in your room, elevator, a 12-minute walk from the station or catch bus #13 to the first stop after the lake, Julius Thomsensgade 22, DK-1632 Copenhagen V, tel. 35 37 15 11, fax 35 37 11 97. Unfortunately, each room smells musty from smokers.

Webers Best Western Hotel is my best fine hotel by the train station. Just a five-minute walk down Vesterbrogade from the station, it offers breakfast in a peaceful garden courtyard (if sunny); a classy, modern but inviting interior; and generous weekend/summer rates (May–September and Friday, Saturday, and Sunday all year: Sb-695 kr, Db-995 kr, 1,095 kr, and 1,195 kr depending on size/grade of room; high season: Sb-from 1,080 kr, Db-from 1,280 kr, CC:VMA, sauna/exercise room, Vesterbrogade 11B, DK-1620 Copenhagen, tel. 31 31 14 32, fax 31 31 14 41, e-mail: webers.hotel@dk.online.dk).

Excelsior Hotel is a big, mod, normal, tour-group hotel a block behind the station, in a sleazy but safe area just half a block off the decent, bustling Vesterbrogade (small Db-770 kr, bigger Db-865 kr, CC:VMA, Colbjørnsensgade 4, DK-1652 Copenhagen, tel. 31 24 50 85, fax 31 24 50 87).

Hotel KFUM Soldaterhjem, originally for soldiers, rents eight singles and three doubles on the fifth floor, with no elevators (S-215 kr, S plus hideabed-315 kr, D-340 kr, no breakfast, Gothersgade 115, Copenhagen K, tel. 33 15 40 44). The reception is on the first floor up (weekdays 8:30–23:00, weekends 15:00–23:00) next to a budget cafeteria.

Cab-Inn is a radical innovation: 86 identical, mostly collapsible, tiny but comfy, cruise ship–type staterooms, all bright, molded, and shiny with TV, coffeepot, shower, and toilet. Each room has a single bed that expands into a twin with one or two fold-down bunks on the walls. The staff will hardly give you the time of day, but it's tough to argue with this efficiency (S-395 kr, D-495 kr, T-595 kr, Q-695 kr, breakfast-40 kr, easy parking-30 kr, CC:VMA). There are two virtually identical Cab-Inns in the same neighborhood: **Cab-Inn Copenhagen** has a bit nicer locale (Danasvej 32-34, 1910 Frederiksberg C, five minutes on bus #29 to center, tel. 31 21 04 00, fax 31 21 74 09). **Cab-Inn Scandinavia** has a bit bigger building with a bigger cafeteria. Some rooms come with a real double bed for 100 kr extra (Vodroffsvej 55, tel. 35 36 11 11, fax 35 36 11 14). E-mail either at: cabinn@inet.inu-c.dk.

Sleeping in Rooms in Private Homes

Following are a few leads for Copenhagen's best accommodations values. Most are in the lively Christianshavn neighborhood. While each TI has its own list of B&Bs, by booking direct you'll save yourself and your host the tourist-office fee. *Always* call ahead; they book in advance. Most are run by single professional women supplementing their income. All speak English and afford a fine peek into Danish domestic life. Rooms generally have no sink. Don't count on breakfast.

In Christianshavn: This area—my Copenhagen home—is a never-a-dull-moment hodgepodge of the chic, artistic, hippie, and hobo, with beer-drinking Greenlanders littering streets in the shadow of fancy government ministries. Colorful with lots of shops, cafés, and canals, it's an easy ten-minute walk to the center, and has good bus connections to the airport and downtown.

Annette and Rudy Hollender enjoy sharing their 300-year-old home with my readers. Even with a long skinny

staircase, sinkless rooms, and three rooms sharing one
toilet/shower, it's a comfortable and cheery place to call
home—which you will by day two (S-225 kr, D-300 kr,
T-400 kr, Wildersgade 19, 1408 Copenhagen K, closed
November–April, tel. 32 95 96 22, fax 31 57 24 86). Take bus
#9 from the airport, bus #8 from the station, or bus #2 from
the city hall. From downtown, push the button immediately
after crossing Knippels Bridge, and turn right off Torvegade
down Wildersgade.

Morten Frederiksen, a laid-back, ponytailed sort of guy,
rents five spacious rooms and two four-bed suites in a mod-
funky-pleasant old house. The furniture is old-time rustic but
elegant. The posters are Mapplethorpe. It's a clean, comfy,
good look at today's hip Danish lifestyle and has a great location right on Christianshavn's main drag (D-275 kr, T-375 kr,
Q-475 kr, no breakfast, two minutes from Annette's, Torvegade 36, tel. 32 95 32 73, cell phone 20 41 92 73).

Britta Krogh-Lund rents two spacious doubles in an old
Christianshavn house (S-225 kr, D-300 kr, T-400 kr, kitchen
for self-serve breakfast only, Amagergade 1, C-1423 Copenhagen K, tel. 32 95 55 85). **Loni Føgh** rents two rooms in her
modern apartment in the same area (D-300 kr, no breakfast,
Strandgade 41, third floor, tel. 32 95 44 77).

South of Christianshavn, **Gitte Kongstad** rents two
apartments, each taking up an entire spacious floor in her
flat. You'll have a kitchenette, little garden, and your own
bike (D-300 kr, family deals, no breakfast, bus #9 from airport, bus #12 or #13 from station, a ten-minute ride past
Christianshavn to Badensgade 2, 2300 Copenhagen, tel. and
fax 32 97 71 97, cell phone 20 74 21 17). While the neighborhood is inconvenient, you'll feel very at home here and
the bike ride into town is a snap.

Private Rooms in Central Copenhagen

Lone (loan-nuh) **Hardt** rents two white woody rooms, each
with a double mattress on the floor and nearly no furniture, in
a 300-year-old half-timbered building a stone's throw from the
Round Tower in the old center of town. If you want to stow
away in the very center of town, this can't be beat (D-300 kr,
no breakfast, St. Kannikestræde 5, tel. 33 14 60 79).

Solveig Diderichsen rents three rooms in her comfortable, high-ceilinged, ground-floor apartment home. She serves

no breakfast but offers kitchen facilities, and there's a good bakery around the corner. Located in a quiet embassy neighborhood next to a colorful residential area with fun shops and eateries behind the Østre Anlæg park (S-275 kr, D-325 kr, T-450 kr, bus #9 direct from the airport or three stops on the subway from the central station, to Østerport, then a three-minute walk to Upsalagade 26, 2100 Copenhagen Ø, tel. 35 43 39 58, fax 35 43 22 70, cell phone 40 11 39 58). If her place is full, she can find you a room in a B&B nearby. An avid sledder, Solveig shares her home with her sled-dog, Maya.

Annette Haugballe rents three modern, pleasant rooms in the quiet, green, residential Frederiksberg area (D-300 kr, no breakfast, easy parking, Hoffmeyersvej 33, 2000 Frederiksberg, on bus line #1 from station or City Hall Square, and near Peter Bangsvej S subway station, tel. 38 74 87 87). Her parents and her friends also rent rooms.

Near the Amalienborg Palace: This is a stately embassy neighborhood—no stress but a bit bland and up lots of stairs. You can look out your window to see the queen's palace (and the guards changing). It's a ten-minute walk north of Nyhavn and Strøget. **Puk** (pook) **De La Cour** rents two rooms in her mod, bright, and easygoing house (D-325 kr with no breakfast but tea, coffee, and a kitchen/family room available, Amaliegade 34, fourth floor, tel. 33 12 04 68). Puk's friend **Line** (lee-nuh) **Voutsinos** offers a similar deal June through September only (D-325 kr, 125 kr/extra bed, each room comes with a small double bed, no breakfast, long-term parking—5 kr/hour or 50 kr/day on street, Amaliegade 34, third floor, tel. 33 14 71 42).

Sleeping in Hostels

Copenhagen energetically accommodates the young vagabond on a shoestring. The Use It office is your best source of information. Each of these places charges about 100 kr per person for bed and breakfast. Some don't allow sleeping bags, and if you don't have your own hostel bedsheet, you'll normally have to rent one for around 30 kr. IYHF hostels normally sell noncardholders a "guest pass" for 22 kr.

The modern **Copenhagen Hostel** (IYHF) is huge, with sixty 220-kr doubles, five-bed dorms at 80 kr/bed, sheets extra, no curfew, excellent facilities, cheap meals, and a self-serve laundry. Unfortunately, it's on the edge of town: bus #10 from the

station to Mozartplads, then #37; or, daytime only, ride bus #46
direct from the station (breakfast not included, Vejlands Alle
200, 2300 Copenhagen S, tel. 32 52 29 08, fax 32 52 27 08).

The Danish **YMCA/YWCA,** open only in July and
August, is a ten-minute walk from the train station or a short
ride on bus #6 (dorm bed-65 kr, four- to ten-bed rooms,
breakfast-30 kr, Valdemarsgade 15, tel. 31 31 15 74).

The **Sleep-In** is popular with the desperate or adventur-
ous (100 kr with sheets, July–August, four-bed cubicles in a
huge 452-bed co-ed room, no curfew or breakfast, pretty wild,
lockers, always has room and free condoms; Blegdamsvej 132;
bus #1 or #6 to "Triangle" stop and look for sign, tel. 35 26 50
59). In the summer, **Jørgensens Hotel** rents beds to back-
packers in small dorms (100 kr/bed, four- to six-bed rooms, no
reservations for dorm beds, no breakfast, extra for sheets, near
Nørreport, Rømersgade 11, tel. 33 13 81 86, fax 33 15 51 05).

Eating in Copenhagen
Copenhagen's many good restaurants are well listed by category in *Copenhagen This Week*. Since restaurant prices include
25 percent tax, your budget may require alternatives. These
survival ideas for the hungry budget traveler in Copenhagen
will save lots of money.

Picnics
Irma (in arcade on Vesterbrogade next to Tivoli) and **Brugsen**
are the two largest supermarket chains. **Netto** is a cut-rate out-
fit with the cheapest prices. The little grocery store in the central station is expensive but handy (daily 8:00–24:00).

Viktualiehandler (small delis) and bakeries, found on nearly
every corner, sell fresh bread, tasty pastries (a *wienerbrød* is
what we call a "Danish"), juice, milk, cheese, and yogurt
(drinkable, in tall liter boxes). Liver paste (*leverpostej*) is cheap
and a little better than it sounds.

Smørrebrød
While virgins no longer roll around carts filled with delicate
sandwiches, Denmark's 300-year-old tradition of open-face
sandwiches survives. Open-face sandwiches cost a fortune in
restaurants, but the many smørrebrød take-out shops sell them
for 8 kr to 30 kr. Drop into one of these often-no-name,
family-run budget savers, and get several elegant OFSs to go.

The tradition calls for three sandwich courses: herring first, then meat, then cheese. It makes for a classy—and cheap—picnic. Downtown you'll find these handy local alternatives to Yankee fast-food chains: **Centrum** (open long hours, Vesterbrogade 6C, across from station), **Tria Cafe** (Monday–Friday 8:00–14:00, closed weekends, Gothersgade 12, near Kongens Nytorv), **Domhusets Smørrebrød** (Monday–Friday 7:00–14:30, Kattesundet 18), and one in Nyhavn, on the corner of Holbergsgade and Peder Skrams Gade.

The Pølse

The famous Danish hot dog, sold in *pølsevogn* (sausage wagons) throughout the city, is one of the few typically Danish institutions to resist the onslaught of our global fast-food culture. "Hot dog" is a Danish word for wienie—study the photo menu for variations. These are fast, cheap, tasty, easy to order, and almost worthless nutritionally. Even so, the local "dead man's finger" is the dog kids love to bite.

By hanging around a pølsevogn you can study this institution. Denmark's "cold feet café" is a form of social care: only people who have difficulty finding jobs, such as the handicapped, are licensed to run these wiener-mobiles. As they gain seniority they are promoted to work at more central locations. Danes like to gather here for munchies and *pølsesnak* ("sausage talk"), the local slang for empty chatter.

Inexpensive Restaurants

Riz-Raz, around the corner from Use It at Kompagnistræde 20, serves a healthy, all-you-can-eat, 49-kr Mediterranean/vegetarian buffet lunch (daily 11:30–17:00), and an even bigger 59-kr dinner buffet (until 24:00, tel. 33 15 05 75), which has to be the best deal in town. And they're happy to serve free water with your meal. Department stores serve cheery, reasonable meals in their cafeterias (such as **Illum**, an elegant top-floor circus of reasonable food under a glass dome, just past the American Express office; **Magasin**; or **Dælls Varehus**, at Nørregade 12). At **El Porron**, you'll find good Spanish tapas (Vendersgade 10, 1 block from Ibsen's Hotel).

Det Lille Apotek, the "little pharmacy," is a reasonable, candlelit place which has been popular with locals for 200 years (reasonable sandwich lunches, bigger dinners, just off Strøget, between the Frue Church and the Round Tower at

St. Kannikestræde 15, tel. 33 12 56 06). The **Chicago Pizza Factory**, next door, serves a cheap lousy pizza buffet and salad bar (49 kr).

To explore your way through a world of traditional Danish food, try a Danish *koldt bord* (an all-you-can-eat buffet). The central station's **Bistro Restaurant** is handy but touristy (154-kr dinner, served daily 11:30–21:30, tel. 33 14 12 32).

Good Eating in Christianshavn

This neighborhood is so cool, it's worth combining an evening wander with dinner even if you don't live here. **Café Wilder** serves creative and hearty dinner salads by candlelight to a trendy local clientele (corner of Wildersgade and Skt. Annæ Gade, a block off Torvegade, open until 22:00). To avoid having to choose just one of their interesting salads, try their three-salad plate (60 kr with bread). They also feature a budget dinner plate for around 75 kr and are happy to serve free water. Across the street, the **Luna Café** is also good and serves a slower-paced meal. Choose one of three good dinner salads and bread for 40 kr.

The **Ravelin Restaurant**, on a tiny island on the big road just south of Christianshavn, serves good traditional Danish-style food at reasonable prices to happy local crowds. Its lovely lakeside terrace is open on sunny days (100–170-kr dinners, Torvegade 79, tel. 32 96 20 45). A block away, at the little windmill (Lille Mølle), **Bastionen & Loven** serves Scandinavian *nouveau* cuisine on a Renoir terrace or in its Rembrandt interior (40-kr lunch specials, 50-kr dinner salads, 80–120-kr dinners, menu is small but fresh, Voldgade 54, up on the bastion off Torvegade at south end of Christianshavn, tel. 32 95 09 40).

In Christiania, the wonderfully classy **Spiseloppen** (meaning "the flea eats") serves great 100-kr vegetarian meals and 140-kr meaty ones by candlelight. Christiania is the free city/squatter town, located 3 blocks behind the spiral spire of Vor Frelser's church (restaurant open Tuesday–Sunday 17:00–22:00, closed Monday, on the top floor of an old brick warehouse, turn right just inside Christiania's gate, reservations often necessary on weekends, tel. 31 57 95 58).

Morten, who runs a local B&B, recommends: **Dhaka Town** (for good, inexpensive Bangladesh cuisine, south end of Torvegade), **Era Ora** (sophisticated Italian, south end of Torvegade), **Long Feng** (good, cheap Chinese, south end of Torvegade), and

Skipperkroen (cheap Danish, east end of Strandgade). Right on the community square you'll find a huge grocery store, fruit stands under the Greenlanders monument, and a delightful bakery (facing the square at Torvegade 45).

Transportation Connections—Copenhagen

By train to: Hillerød/Frederiksborg (40/day, 30 min), **Louisiana Museum** (Helsingør train to Humlebæk, 40/day, 30 min), **Roskilde** (16/day, 30 min), **Odense** (16/day, 2 hrs), **Helsingør** (ferry to Sweden, 40/day, 50 min), **Stockholm** (8/day, 8 hrs), **Oslo** (4/day, 10 hrs), **Växjö** (via Alvesta, 6/day, 5 hrs), **Kalmar** (6/day, via Alvesta and Växjö, 7 hrs), **Berlin** (via Gedser, 2/day, 9 hrs), **Amsterdam** (2/day, 11 hrs), **Frankfurt/Rhine** (4/day, 10 hrs). National train info tel. 33 14 17 01 International train info tel. 70 13 14 16.

Cheaper **bus trips** are listed at Use It. All Norway- and Sweden-bound trains go right onto the Helsingør–Helsingborg ferry. (You get 20 minutes to romp on the deck, eat the wind, grab a bite, and change money.) The crossing is included in any train ticket. There are convenient overnight trains from Copenhagen directly to Stockholm, Oslo, Amsterdam, and Frankfurt.

A quickie cruise from Copenhagen to Oslo: A luxurious cruise ship leaves daily from Copenhagen (departs 17:00, returns by 9:15 two days later; 16 hours sailing each way and seven hours in Norway's capital). Special packages give you a bed in a double cabin, a fine dinner, and two smørgåsbord breakfasts for around $170 in summer ($200 for single, Friday and Saturday cost more). Call DFDS Scandinavian Seaways (tel. 33 42 30 00). It's easy to make a reservation in the U.S.A. (tel. 800/5DF-DS55).

NEAR COPENHAGEN: ROSKILDE, HILLERØD, FREDERIKSBORG CASTLE, LOUISIANA, HELSINGØR, KRONBORG CASTLE

Copenhagen's the star, but there are several worthwhile sights nearby, and the public transportation system makes side-tripping a joy. Visit Roskilde's great Viking ships and royal cathedral. Tour Frederiksborg, Denmark's most spectacular castle, and slide along the cutting edge at Louisiana—a superb art museum with a coastal setting as striking as its art. At Helsingør, do the dungeons of Kronborg Castle before heading on to Sweden.

Planning Your Time

Roskilde's Viking ships and the Frederiksborg Palace are the area's essential sights. Each (an easy 30-minute commute from Copenhagen followed by a 15-minute walk) can be done in half a day. You'll find fewer tour-bus crowds in the afternoon. While you're in Roskilde, pay your respects to the tombs of the Danish royalty. By car, you can see these sights on your way in or out of Copenhagen. By train, do day trips from Copenhagen—then sleep to and from Copenhagen to heavyweight sights eight or ten hours away. Consider getting a Copenhagen Card (see Copenhagen Orientation, above), which covers your transportation and admission to all major sights.

Roskilde

Denmark's roots, both Viking and royal, are on display in Roskilde, a pleasant town 20 miles west of Copenhagen. Five hundred years ago, Roskilde was Denmark's leading city. Today, the town that introduced Christianity to Denmark in A.D. 980 is most famous for hosting northern Europe's biggest annual rock/jazz/folk festival (four days in early July). Wednesday and Saturday are flower/produce market days. Its TI, next to the cathedral, is helpful (tel. 46 35 27 00). Roskilde is an easy side trip from Copenhagen by train (30 minutes, several per hour).

Sights—Roskilde

▲▲Roskilde Cathedral—Roskilde's imposing 12th-century, twin-spired cathedral houses the tombs of 38 Danish kings and queens. It's a stately, modern-looking old church with great marble work, paintings (notice the impressive 3-D painting with Christian IV looking like a pirate, in the room behind the small pipe organ), wood carvings in and around the altar, and a silly little glockenspiel that plays high above the entrance at the top of every hour. The 20-kr guidebook is very good. (10 kr admission, open daily April–September 9:00–16:45; off-season weekdays 10:00–15:00, Saturday 9:00–12:00, Sunday 12:30–15:45, tel. 46 35 16 24.) It's a pleasant walk through a park down to the harbor and Viking ships.

▲▲▲Viking Ship Museum (Vikingeskibshallen)—
Roskilde's award-winning museum displays five different Viking ships—one is like the boat Leif Erikson sailed to America 1,000 years ago; another is like those depicted in the

Copenhagen Area

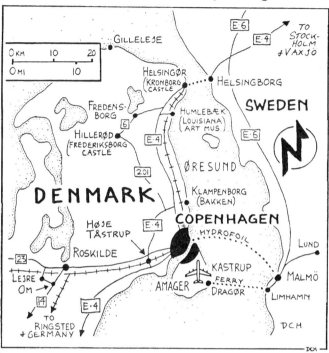

Bayeux Tapestry. The descriptions are excellent—and in English. It's the kind of museum where you want to read everything. As you enter, buy the 15-kr guide booklet and request the 15-minute English movie introduction. These ships were deliberately sunk 1,000 years ago to block a nearby harbor and were only recently excavated, preserved, and pieced together. The ships aren't as intact as those in Oslo, but the museum does a better job of explaining shipbuilding. The museum cafeteria serves a traditional smørrebrød—great after a hard day of pillage, plunder, or sightseeing (40 kr entry, open daily April–October 9:00–17:00, November–March 10:00–16:00, tel. 46 30 02 00).

Hillerød and Frederiksborg Castle
The traffic-free center of this Danishly cute town is worth a wander (just outside the gates of the mighty Frederiksborg

Castle, past the TI). The Hillerød TI can book rooms in
private homes for 125 kr per person plus a 30-kr booking fee
(tel. 48 26 28 52).

▲▲**Frederiksborg Castle**—This grandest castle in Scandinavia
is often called the Danish Versailles. Frederiksborg (built
1602–1620) is the castle of Christian IV, Denmark's great
builder king. You can almost hear the crackle of royal hoofbeats
as you walk over the moat through the stately cobbled courtyard,
past the Dutch Renaissance brick facade and into the lavish interior. Much of the castle was reconstructed in 1860, with the normal Victorian flair. The English guidebook is unnecessary, since
many rooms have a handy English information sheet and there
are often tours on which to freeload. Listen for hymns on the old
carillon at the top of each hour. The many historic paintings are
a fascinating scrapbook of Danish history. Savor the courtyard.
Picnic in the moat park, or enjoy the elegant Slotsherrens Kro
cafeteria at the moat's edge (40 kr, daily in summer 10:00–17:00,
April and October 10:00–16:00, November–March 11:00–15:00;
easy parking). From Copenhagen, take the S-train to Hillerød
and then enjoy a pleasant 15-minute walk, or catch bus #701 or
#702 (free with S-tog ticket or train pass) from the train station
(tel. 48 26 04 39).

Louisiana

This is Scandinavia's most raved-about modern art museum.
Located in the town of Humlebæk, beautifully situated on
the coast 20 miles north of Copenhagen, Louisiana is a holis-
tic place—masterfully mixing its art, architecture, and land-
scape. Wander from famous Chagalls and Picassos to more
obscure art. Poets spend days here nourishing their creative
souls with new angles, ideas, and perspectives. The views
over one of the busiest passages in the nautical world are
nearly as inspiring as the art. The cafeteria (indoor/outdoor)
is reasonable and welcomes picnickers who buy a drink
(53-kr admission or included in a special round-trip tour's
ticket—see TI, daily 10:00–17:00, Wednesday until 22:00,
tel. 49 19 07 19).

Take the train from Copenhagen toward Helsingør, and
get off (in 36 minutes) at Humlebæk. Then it's a free bus
(#388) connection or a ten-minute walk through the woods.
From Frederiksborg, there are rare Humlebæk buses, but most
will have to connect via Helsingør.

Helsingør and Kronborg Castle

Often confused with its Swedish sister, Helsingborg, just 2 miles across the channel, Helsingør is a small, pleasant Danish town with a medieval center, Kronborg Castle, and lots of Swedes who come over for lower-priced alcohol. There's a fine beachfront hostel, **Vandrerhjem Villa Moltke** (dorm bed-77 kr, D-155 kr, Db-230 kr, T-231 kr, Tb-288 kr, a mile north of the castle, tel. 49 21 16 40). I've met people who prefer small towns and small prices touring Copenhagen with this hostel as their base (two 50-min trains/hour to Copenhagen). Helsingør TI: tel. 49 21 13 33.

▲▲**Kronborg Castle**—Helsingør's Kronborg Castle (also called Elsinore) is famous for its questionable (but profitable) ties to Shakespeare. Most of the "Hamlet" castle you'll see today, darling of every big bus tour and travelogue, was built long after Hamlet died, and Shakespeare never saw the place. But there was a castle here in Hamlet's day, and a troupe of English actors worked here in Shakespeare's time (Shakespeare may have known them or even been one of them). "To see or not to see?" It's most impressive from the outside.

If you're heading to Sweden, Kalmar Castle (see the South Sweden chapter) is a better medieval castle. But you're here, and if you like castles, see Kronborg.

The royal apartments include English explanations (30 kr, daily May–September 10:30–17:00, April and October 11:00–16:00, November and March 11:00–15:00; closed Monday off-season, tel. 49 21 30 78). Don't miss the 20-minute dungeon tours that leave on the half-hour. In the basement, notice the statue of Holger Danske, a mythical Viking hero revered by Danish children. The story goes that this Danish superman will awaken if the nation is ever in danger and will restore peace and security to the land.

The free grounds between the walls and sea are great for picnics, with a pleasant view of the strait between Denmark and Sweden. If you're rushed, the view from the ferry will suffice.

Route Tips for Drivers

Copenhagen to Hillerød (45 min) to Helsingør (30 minutes) to Växjö, Sweden (3.5 hours including ferry): Just follow the town-name signs. Leave Copenhagen, following signs for E-4 and Helsingør. The freeway is great. "Hillerød" signs lead to the Frederiksborg Castle (not to be confused with the nearby Fredensborg *slot* (palace) in the pleasant town of

Hillerød. Follow signs to Hillerød C (for "center"), then "slot" (for "castle"). While the E-4 freeway is the fastest, the "Strandvejen" coastal road (152) is pleasant, going past some of Denmark's finest mansions (including that of Danish writer Karen Blixen, a.k.a. Isak Dinesen of *Out of Africa* fame, in Rungstedlund, which is now a museum, 30 kr, daily May–September 10:00–17:00, less-off season, tel. 42 57 10 57).

The freeway leads right onto the ferry to Sweden (follow the signs to Helsingborg, Sweden). Boats leave every 20 minutes. Buy your ticket as you roll on board (255 kr one-way for car, driver, and up to five passengers; round-trip gives you the return at less than half-price). Reservations are free and smart (tel. 49 26 26 81 and wait out the obnoxious tune). If you arrive before your time, you can probably drive onto any ferry.

The 30-minute Helsingør–Helsingborg ferry ride gives you just enough time to enjoy the view of the Kronborg "Hamlet" castle, be impressed by the narrowness of this very strategic channel, and change money. The ferry exchange desk's rate is decent, and its 5-kr-per-check fee beats Sweden's standard 40-kr minimum fee for traveler's checks. In Helsingborg, follow signs for E-4 and Stockholm. The road's good, traffic's light, and towns are all clearly signposted. You can change money at the post office in the pleasant town of Markaryd's (just off the road, open late). At Ljungby, road 25 takes you to Växjö and Kalmar. Entering Växjö, skip the first Växjö exit and follow the freeway into "Centrum," where it ends. It's about a six-hour drive from Copenhagen to Kalmar.

CENTRAL DENMARK: ÆRØ AND ODENSE

The sleepy isle of Ærø is the cuddle after the climax. It's the perfect time-passed world in which to wind down, enjoy the seagulls, and take a day off. Get Ærø-dynamic and pedal a rented bike into the essence of Denmark. Stop for lunch in a traditional *kro* (country inn). Settle into a cobbled world of sailors, who, after someone connected a steam engine to a propeller, decided that maybe building ships in bottles was more their style.

On your way to (or from) Ærø, drop by the bustling city of Odense, home of Hans Christian Andersen and a fine open-air folk museum.

Planning Your Time
Odense is a transportation hub, the center of the island of Funen. It is an easy stop, worth half a day on the way to or from Ærø. More out of the way, Ærø is a well-worthwhile headache to get to. Once there, you'll want two nights and a day to properly enjoy it.

ISLAND OF ÆRØ
This small (22-by-6-mile) island on the south edge of Denmark is salty and sleepy as can be. Tombstones here say things like, "Here lies Christian Hansen at anchor with his wife. He'll not weigh until he stands before God." It's the kind of island where baskets of strawberries sit in front of houses—for sale on the honor system. Since it's about 10 miles across the water

Central Denmark

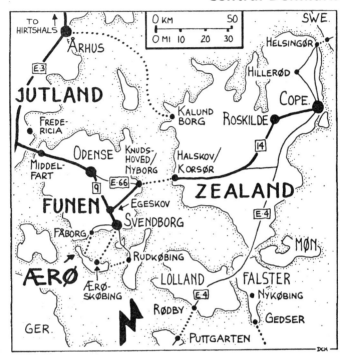

from Germany, you'll see plenty of smug Germans who return regularly to this peaceful retreat.

Ærøskøbing

Ærøskøbing is Ærø's town in a bottle. The government, recognizing the value of this amazingly preserved little town, prohibits modern building anywhere in the center. It's the only town in Denmark protected in this way. Drop into the 1680s, when Ærøskøbing was the wealthy home port of more than 100 windjammers. The many Danes who come here for the tranquillity—washing up the cobbled main drag in waves with the landing of each boat—call it the fairy-tale town. The Danish word for "cozy" is *hyggelig* (hew-glee), and that describes Ærøskøbing well.

Ærøskøbing is just a pleasant place to wander. Stubby little porthole-type houses lean on each other like drunk, sleeping

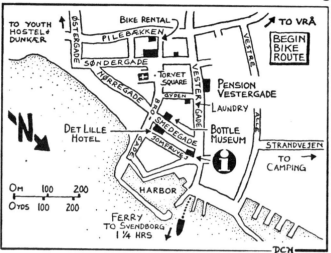

sailors, with their birthdates displayed in proud decorative
rebar. Wander under flickering old-time lampposts. The harbor
now caters to holiday yachts, and on midnight low tides you can
almost hear the crabs playing cards. Snoop around town. It's
OK. Notice the many "snooping mirrors" on the houses.
Antique locals are following your every move.

The town economy, once rich with the windjammer trade,
hit the rocks in the 20th century. Outside of tourism, there are
few jobs. Kids 15 to 18 years old go to a boarding school in
Svendborg; many don't return. It's an interesting discussion:
Do the island folk pickle their culture in tourism or forget
about the cuteness and get modern?

Orientation

The town of Ærøskøbing is tiny. Everything is just a few cobbles from the ferry landing.

Tourist Information: The TI is straight ahead as you
get off the ferry (Monday–Friday 9:00–17:00, shorter hours
Saturday, Sunday, and off-season, tel. 62 52 13 00, fax 62 52
14 36, web site: www.194.19.145.26/f_boye@wwwaeroe.htm).
They can find you a 220-kr double in a private home (for
no charge).

Ferries: If you're driving, plan ahead. When you arrive in Ærø, reserve a spot on the ferry for your departure (telephone hours: Monday–Friday 8:00–16:00, less on weekends, tel. 62 52 40 00).

Sights—Ærøskøbing

▲**"Bottle Peter" Museum**—This fascinating house has 750 different bottled ships. Old Peter Jacobsen, who made his first bottle at 16 and his last at 85, bragged that he drank the contents of each bottle, except those containing milk. He died in 1960 (most likely buried in a glass bottle), leaving a lifetime of tedious little creations for visitors to squint and marvel at (20 kr, daily May–September 10:00–17:00; off-season Monday–Thursday 13:00–17:00, Sunday 10:00–13:00; on Smedegade).

▲**Hammerich House**—These 12 funky rooms in three houses are filled with 200-to-300-year-old junk (15 kr, daily June–August 11:00–15:00, closed off-season). The third sight in town, the Ærø Museum, is nowhere near as interesting as the Hammerich House.

▲▲**Ærøskøbing Evening Walk**—With the sun low, the shadows long, and the colors rich, join the locals in an evening stroll. Start at the harbor. Facing the ferry landing, head right past the smoked-fish joint. Wander out the breakwater to see what the yachters are barbecueing and to see the historic wooden boats coming in. The dreamy-looking island immediately across the way is a natural preserve and a resting spot for birds making their huge journey from north to south. In the winter, when the water freezes, locals love to slip and slide over for a visit. Continue down the peaceful Molestyen Lane— peaceful beach on left, a row of much-loved houses and gardens on your right. (If you continue on the trail along the water you'll come to a place where fishermen pull out their boats and tidy up their nets.) From the end of Molestyen, cut back into town along Nørregade. Peek into living rooms. Catch snatches of Danish life. Ponder the beauty of a society with such a keenly developed sense of civic responsibility that fishing permits commit you "to catch only what you need." At Brogade you can detour left to the town square (Torvet) or continue straight back to Vestergade.

▲▲**Beach Bungalow Sunset Stroll**—For the actual sunset, stroll in the other direction. Facing the ferry dock, go left, following the harbor. Upon leaving the town you'll pass a children's playground and see a row of tiny, Monopoly-like huts past the wavy wheat field. This is the Vestre Strandvej, facing the sunset. And these tiny huts are little beach escapes. Each is different and many are filled with locals enjoying themselves Danish-style. It's a fine walk out to the end of Urehoved, as this spit of land is called.

The Ærø Island Bike Ride (or Car Tour)

While serious biking maps take you on more involved routes, this 18-mile trip shows you the best of this windmill-covered island's charms. While the highest point on the island is only 180 feet, the wind can be strong, and the hills seem long. This ride is good exercise. If your hotel can't loan you a bike (ask), rent one from the Energi Station (40 kr for three-speeds, 15 kr for worthwhile "*cykel*" map; Monday–Friday 8:00–17:30, Saturday 9:00–14:00, Sunday 10:00–14:00; go through the door at the Søndergade end of the Torvet, past the garden to the next road, Pilebækken 7, tel. 62 52 11 10). The hostel and the campground also rent bikes (later hours). On Ærø there are no deposits and few locks.

Ready to go? May the wind be always at your back. Leave Ærøskøbing to the west on the road to Vrå (Vråvejen). You'll see the first of many U-shaped farms, typical of Denmark. The three sides block the wind and are used for storing cows, hay, and people. *Gaard* (farm) shows up on many local names. Until the old generation's gone, you'll see only sturdy old women behind the wheelbarrows. Bike along the coast in the protection of the dike that made the once-salty swampland to your left farmable. At the T-junction take a right turn to Borgnæs. You'll see a sleek modern windmill, and soon, a pleasant cluster of mostly modern summer cottages called Borgnæs. (At this point, you can take a shortcut by turning left directly to Vindeballe.)

Keep to the right, following sign (behind bushes) toward "Ø. Bregninge," pass another Vindeballe turnoff, go along a secluded beach, and then climb uphill over the island's 180-foot summit to Bregninge. Unless you're tired of thatched and half-timbered cottages, turn right and roll through Denmark's "second longest village" to the church. Peek inside. (Great pulpit for frustrated preachers and photo hams, public WC in the churchyard.) Then roll back through Bregninge past many more U-shaped gaards, heading about a mile down the main road towards Vindeballe, taking the Vodrup turnoff

Ærø Island Bike Route

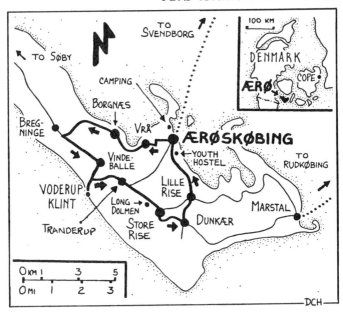

to the right. (The Vindeballe Kro is a traditional inn serving fine food.)

A straight road leads you downhill (with a jog to the right) to a rugged bluff called Vodrup Klint. If I were a pagan, I'd worship here—the sea, the wind, the chilling view. Notice how the land slipped in long chunks to make terraces stepping down to the sea. Hike down to the foamy beach. While the wind can drag a kite-flier at the top, the beach can be ideal for sunbathing.

Then it's on to Tranderup. You'll roll past the old farm full of cows, a lovely pond, and left past a row of wind-bent stumps. (Care to guess the direction of the prevailing wind?) Follow the sign to Tranderup, stay parallel to the big road through the town, past a lovely farm (that does bed and breakfast) and the potato stand, and finally to the main road. Turn right. At the Ærøskøbing turnoff, just before the tiny little white house, turn left to the big stone (commemorating the return of the island to Denmark from Germany in 1750). Seattle-ites should be sure to visit Claus Clausen's rock (in the picnic area), a memorial to an extremely obscure Washington state pioneer.

Return to the big road, pass the little white house, and head toward Store Rise, the next church spire in the distance. Just after the Stokkeby turnoff, follow the very rough tree-lined path on your right to the Langdysse (Long Dolmen) Tingstedet, just behind the church spire. Here you'll see a 5,000-year-old early Neolithic burial place. Ærø had more than 100 of these prehistoric tombs, but few survive.

Carry on down the lane to the Store Rise church. Inside, notice the little ships hanging in the nave, the fine altarpiece, and Martin Luther keeping his Protestant hand on the rudder in the stern. Can you find anyone buried in the graveyard whose name doesn't end in "sen"? Continue down the main road with the impressive—and hopeful—forest of modern windmills on your right, until you get to Dunkær.

For the home stretch, take the small road, signed "Lille Rise," past the topless windmill. Except for the Lille Rise, it's all downhill from here, as you coast past great sea views and the hostel back home to Ærøskøbing.

Still rolling? Bike out past the campground, along the Urehoved *strand* (beach) to poke into the coziest little beach houses you'll never see back in the "big is beautiful" U.S.A. This is Europe, where the concept of sustainability is neither new nor subversive.

Sleeping in Ærøskøbing
(7 kr = about $1)

Sleep Code: **S** = Single, **D** = Double/Twin, **T** = Triple, **Q** = Quad, **b** = bathroom, **CC** = Credit Card (Visa, MasterCard, Amex). The TI books B&Bs for no charge.

Pension Vestergade is a pleasantly quirky old place (built for a sea-captain's daughter in 1784) located right on the main street in the town center. Susanna Greve and her daughters Henrietta and Celia speak the queen's English and take very good care of their guests, with six big homey rooms (S-200 kr, D-300 kr, breakfast-40 kr, Vestergade 44, 5970 Ærøskøbing, tel. 62 52 22 98). This is your ideal home on Ærø. Picnic in the backyard. Call well in advance for a place here.

Det Lille Hotel, a former 19th-century captain's home, is as warm, tidy, and modern as a sailboat. It's one street off the harbor next to the cutest house in town, (S-325 kr, D-465 kr, 140 kr per extra bed, includes huge breakfast, CC:VM, Smedegade 33, 5970 Ærøskøbing, tel. & fax 62 52 23 00, run by Heidi).

Hotel Ærøhus is big and sprawling, the closest thing to a grand hotel in this capital of quaint (33 rooms, D-400 kr, Db-650 kr, fancy Db with a terrace-680 kr, 15 percent less from September through May, CC:VMA, on Vestergade 2 blocks up from ferry, tel. 62 52 10 03, fax 62 52 21 23).

All of the following places are clean, comfortable, and modern homes with wonderful gardens. They each rent two or three rooms in quiet residential areas along the edge of town, a five-to-ten-minute walk from the ferry: **Margit Kruse** (small D-220 kr, breakfast-35 kr, Moseager 6, tel. 62 52 24 70, a little English spoken); the **Hoffmann home** (S-150 kr, D-220 kr, breakfast-35 kr, Søtoften 3, tel. 62 52 12 31, no English spoken); and **Mrs. Pedersen** (D-220 kr, no breakfast, Sygehusvejen 4, just 3 blocks from the ferry landing, tel. 62 52 23 09).

If you have a car, you may want to try one of the many B&Bs in the countryside. **Julie and Aksel Hansen's Graasten B&B** is a kid-friendly dairy farm 300 meters from the sea (D-250 kr, breakfast-40 kr, evening meals-80 kr, bike rental-40 kr, kitchenette for guests, off-season discounts, Østermarksvej 20, 7 km from Ærøskøbing toward Marstal, tel. and fax 62 52 24 25, English spoken).

The **Ærøskøbing Youth Hostel** is a glorious place, equipped with a fine living room, a members' kitchen, and family rooms with two or four beds (80 kr each, D-200 kr, T-270 kr, no breakfast, Smedevejen 15, 500 yards out of town, tel. 62 52 10 44, fax 62 52 16 44). The place is packed in July and closed October through March.

The three-star **campground**, on a fine beach, offers a lodge with fireplace, campsites (42 kr per person), and cottages (295–335 kr, sheets-10 kr, May–September; facing the water, follow waterfront to the left, a short walk from the center, tel. 62 52 18 54.

Eating in Ærøskøbing

Ærøskøbing has only a handful of eateries and each has a different character: starting at the ferry dock you'll find a grocery store and **Lille Claus Cafe** (a Danish Denny's without the class, young crowd, cheap). Facing the harbor a wonderful little snack joint serves fresh smoked fish. Heading up Vestergade, past the pink and popular Vaffelbageriet (homemade waffles and ice cream), you'll find another burger joint and the classy **Greta's Restaurant** (fine cooking, a bit pricey). At the top of

Vestergade, **Restaurant Pileboekken** serves probably the best reasonable daily special (100 kr for the meal of the day, 55 Vestergade, tel. 62 52 19 91). **Det Lille Hotel** serves a good 100-kr *dagens rett* in a pleasant dining room or garden (next to photogenic "littlest house" and across from the ship-in-a-bottle museum). **MUMM's** candlelit ambience is occasionally blown out by the German yachting crowd, but the food is fine—if expensive (Søndergade 12). There's a **pizzeria** on the main square (Torvet). The **bakery** (top of Vestergade) serves home-made bread, cheese, a tin of liver paste, and liter boxes of drink-able yogurt. The liveliest bar in town is the **Arrebo Pub** near the ferry landing at the bottom of Vestergade.

Transportation Connections—Ærøskøbing

Ærøskøbing is accessible by ferry from **Svendborg**. It's a pleasant 70-minute crossing (245-kr round-trip per car and driver, 110-kr round-trip per person; you can leave the island via any of the three different Ærø ferry crossings; you'll save a little money with round-trip tickets).

Svendborg–Ærø ferry: Departures from Svendborg daily at 7:30, 10:30, 13:30, 16:30, 19:30, and 22:30, no early depar-ture on Saturday or Sunday mornings. Departures from Ærøskøbing daily at 6:00, 9:00, 12:00, 15:00, 18:00, 21:00, no early departure on weekend mornings. While walk-ons always make it on board, cars need reservations (tel. 62 52 40 00). A ferry/bus combo ticket gives you the whole island with stopovers.

Trains connecting with Svendborg–Ærø ferry: There is a train scheduled to arrive in Svendborg within 15 minutes of each boat crossing. From the train station, it's a 4-block walk to the ferry dock. Head downhill to the harbor and look right for the "Ærø" sign. And within 15 minutes of each ferry arrival in Svendborg, a train is leaving for Copenhagen (via Odense). Copenhagen–Svendborg is about 2.5 hours (with a 30-minute wait for a connection in Odense).

ODENSE

Founded in 988, named after Odin (the Nordic Zeus), Odense is the hometown of storyteller Hans Christian Andersen. He once said, "Perhaps Odense will one day become famous because of me. Today Odense (OH-then-za) is one of Denmark's most visited towns. Denmark's third-largest city, with 183,000 people,

is big and industrial. But its old center retains some of the fairy-
tale charm it had in the days of H.C.A.

Tourist Information: The TI, in the town hall right
downtown, runs a "Meet the Danes" program (open in summer Monday–Saturday 9:00–19:00, Sunday 11:00–19:00; off-
season Monday–Friday 9:30–16:30, Saturday 10:00–13:00,
closed Sunday, tel. 66 12 75 20). For a quick visit, all you need
is the free map/guide from the Hans Christian Andersen Hus.
(Note: The Danes call him "Hoe See," for "H. C." Andersen.)

Sights—Odense

▲**Den Fynske Landsby Open-Air Museum**—This sleepy
gathering of 26 old buildings preserves the 18th-century culture of this region. There are no explanations in the buildings,
because the many school groups who visit play guessing
games. Pick up the 15-kr guidebook. (25-kr admission, daily
June–August 10:00–19:00; April–May and September–October
10:00–17:00, tel. 66 13 13 72.) From mid-July to mid-August,
there are H. C. Andersen musicals (in Danish) in the theater
daily at 16:00. The 50-kr play ticket includes admission 90
minutes early (not before 14:30) to see the museum.

▲▲**Hans Christian Andersen Hus**—This museum is packed
with mementos from the writer's life, his letters and books, and
hordes of children and tourists. It's fun if you like his tales (25 kr,
daily in summer 9:00–18:00, less off-season, Hans Jensens
Stræde 37, tel. 66 13 13 72 ext. 4662). You'll find good descriptions in English, so the guidebook is unnecessary (but pick up
the free city guide). The garden fairy-tale parade, with pleasing
vignettes, thrills kids daily (late June–early August) in the
museum garden at 11:00, 13:00, and 15:00. Across the street is a
shop full of mobiles and Danish arts and crafts. Just around the
corner is Flensted Uromagerens Hus (mobile-maker's house).

▲**Møntergarden Urban History Museum**—Very close to
the H.C.A. Hus, this fun little museum (15 kr, daily
10:00–16:00) offers Odense history, early photos, a great coin
collection, and the cheapest coffee in Denmark.

Sleeping in Odense
(7 kr = about $1)
Radisson H.C.A. Hotel has a deal July–mid-August (06-675 kr,
with breakfast, regular price Db-1,135 kr, CC:VMA, tel. 66 14
78 00, fax 66 14 78 90). **Jytte (u-ter) Gamdrup** rents two rooms

in her 17th-century home a few doors down from the H.C.A. Museum (Ramsherred 17, 5000 Odense C).

Transportation Connections—Odense
By train to: **Copenhagen** (hrly, 1.5 hrs), **Århus** (hrly, 2 hrs), **Svendborg** (hrly, 1 hr, to Ærø ferry), **Roskilde** (hrly, 1 hr).

Route Tips for Drivers
Århus or Billund to Ærø: The freeway takes you over a suspension bridge on the island of Fyn. At Odense take Highway 9 south to Svendborg. Figure about two hours to drive from Billund to Svendborg.

Leave your car in Svendborg (at the easy long-term parking lot 2 blocks from the ferry dock) and sail for Ærø. It's an easy 70-minute crossing (245-kr round-trip per car and driver, 110-kr round-trip per person). There are only six boats a day (7:30, 10:30, 13:30, 16:30, 19:30, and 22:30; no early departures on Saturday and Sunday; confirm times; cars need reservations; call 62 52 40 00). A ferry/bus combo ticket gives you the whole island with stopovers.

Ærø to Copenhagen via Odense: Catch the 6:00 ferry to Svendborg (tel. 62 52 40 00). Reservations for walk-ons are never necessary. On weekends, there are no early trips. By 7:40, you'll be driving north on Highway 9; follow signs first to Fåborg, past the Egeskov Castle to Odense. For the folk museum, leave Route 9 just south of town at Højby, turning left toward Dalum and the Odense Campground (on Odensevej). Look for "Den Fynske Landsby" signs (near the train tracks, south edge of town). If you're going directly to H. C. Andersen Hus follow the signs.

Until June 1, 1998, you'll still ride a ferry to connect Odense and Copenhagen. It's a 30-minute drive from Odense to the ferry (follow signs for Nyborg/Knudshoved). Call 53 57 15 77 for a free reservation (2/hr, 60 min, 270 kr one-way for car, driver and up to 4 passengers). In June 1998, the bridge will save you an hour but cost drivers about the same (tel. 58 35 01 00, exhibition center in Halsskov). Then head for København (Copenhagen). At Ringsted, signs take you to Roskilde. Aim toward twin church spires, follow signs to Vikingskibene—Viking ships.

Copenhagen is 30 minutes from Roskilde. If you're heading to the airport, stay on the freeway to the end, following signs to København C, then to Dragør/Kastrup Airport.

JUTLAND: LEGOLAND AND ÅRHUS

Jutland, the part of Denmark that juts up from Germany, is a land of sand dunes, Lego toys, moated manor houses, and fortified old towns. Make a pilgrimage to the most famous land in all of Jutland: the pint-sized kid's paradise, Legoland. In Århus, the lively capital of Jutland, wander the pedestrian street of this busy port, tour its boggy prehistory, and visit centuries-old Danish town life in its open-air museum.

Planning Your Time

Jutland (Jylland in Danish) is worth two days on a three-week trip through Scandinavia. On a quick trip, drivers coming from Norway might take the overnight boat from Kristiansand to Hirtshals. By noon you'll be in Århus. Den Gamle By (Old Town museum) is worth an afternoon. Spend the next morning at Legoland, on the way to Funen and Ærø. Speedier travelers could make Århus an afternoon stop only and drive to Legoland that evening (which is free if you enter late).

LEGOLAND

Legoland is Scandinavia's top kids' sight. If you have a child (or think you might be one), it's a fun stop. This huge park is a happy combination of rides, restaurants, trees, smiles, and 33 million Lego bricks creatively arranged into such wonders as Mt. Rushmore, the Parthenon, "Mad" Ludwig's castle, and the Statue of Liberty. It's a Lego world here, as everything is cleverly related to this very popular toy. Surprisingly, the restaurants don't serve Legolamb.

The indoor "museum" features the history of the company, high-tech Lego creations, a great doll collection, and a toy museum full of mechanical wonders from the early 1900s, many ready to jump into action as soon as you push the button. There's a Lego playroom for hands-on fun—and a campground across the street if your kids refuse to move on (110-kr entry, 100 kr for kids ages 3–13, 70 kr for kids over 60; gets you on all the rides; open daily April 1–October 31 from 10:00 to 20:00; until 21:00 in summer; closed off-season, tel. 75 33 13 33). The gates are unguarded, but don't worry: Legoland doesn't charge in the evening (free after 19:00 in July and late August, otherwise after 18:00). Activities close an hour before the park, but it's basically the same place after dinner as during the day—with fewer tour groups.

Legoland is located in the unremarkable town of Billund. The TI in Legoland, (tel. 75 33 19 26) can arrange rooms for about 300 kr for a double. (See Sleeping, below.)

Sights—Near Legoland

Jelling—I know you've always wanted to see the hometown of the ancient Danish kings Gorm the Old and Harald Bluetooth. And this is your chance. Jelling is a small village (12 miles from Legoland, just off the highway near Vejle) with a small church that has Denmark's oldest frescoes and two old runic stones in its courtyard—often called "Denmark's birth certificate."

▲**Ribe**—A Viking port 1,000 years ago, Ribe is the oldest, and possibly loveliest, town in Denmark. It's an entertaining mix of cobbled lanes and leaning old houses, with a fine church (7 kr, modern paintings under Romanesque arches). A smoky, low-ceilinged, atmospheric inn, the Weis' Stue, rents a few rooms and serves good meals across the street from the church (tel. 75 42 07 00). Drop by the TI for its handy walking-tour brochure, or better yet, catch a guided town walk (35 kr, Monday–Friday in summer at 11:30, Torvet 3, tel. 75 42 15 00).

Sleeping near Legoland, in Billund
(7 kr = about $1)

Sleep Code: **S** = Single, **D** = Double/Twin, **T** = Triple, **Q** = Quad, **b** = bathroom, **CC** = Credit Card (Visa, MasterCard, Amex). Prices include breakfast unless otherwise noted.

Jutland: Legoland and Århus

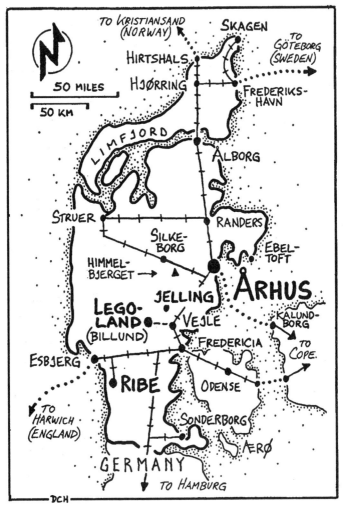

The **Legoland Hotel** adjoins Legoland (1,025 kr for a family-of-four room including discounted admission to the park, CC:VMA, tel. 75 33 12 44, fax 75 35 38 10). **Hotel Svanen** is nearby in Billund (Sb-645 kr, Db-695 kr, extra bed-125–140 kr, CC:VMA, Nordmarksvej 8, tel. 75 33 28 33, fax 75 35 35 15).

Private rooms are the key to a budget visit here. **Erik and Mary Sort** have four doubles and a great setup in a forest just outside of town. Their guests enjoy a huge living room, a kitchen, lots of Lego toys, and a kid-friendly yard (D-280 kr, discounts for kids; leave Billund on the Grindsted road, turn right on Stilbjergvej after the Shell station, about a half-mile down the road on the right at Stilbjergvej 4, tel. 75 33 23 27).

Billund Youth Hostel is brand-new with 85-kr dorm beds in ten-bed rooms (D-300 kr, sheets-40 kr, one night membership-25 kr, breakfast not included, Ellehammers Alle 2, 7190 Billund; bus #912 or #44 from Vejle train station stops nearby; tel. 75 33 27 77, fax 75 33 28 77).

ÅRHUS

Denmark's second-largest city, with a population of 280,000, Århus (OAR-hoos) is Jutland's capital and cultural hub. Its Viking founders, ever conscious of aesthetics, chose a lovely, wooded, where-the-river-hits-the-sea setting. Today it bustles with a lively port and an important university. It's well worth a stop.

Tourist Information: Visit the TI in the town hall to get the helpful Århus brochure and map (mid-June to mid-September Monday–Friday 9:30–18:00, Saturday 9:30–17:00, Sunday 9:30–13:00; shorter hours off-season and closed Sunday, tel. 86 12 16 00, fax 86 12 95 90). They run a fine city introduction bus tour (daily in summer from the TI at 10:00 for 2.5 hours, 45 kr, which also gives you 24 hours of unlimited city bus travel). For a longer visit, consider getting the two-day Århus Passet (110 kr), which covers all sights, the city introduction bus tour, and transportation.

Getting Around Århus: City buses easily connect the center and train station with the open-air and prehistory museums.

Sights—Århus

▲▲▲**Den Gamle By**—The Old Town open-air folk museum puts Århus on the touristic map. Seventy half-timbered houses and crafts shops are wonderfully furnished just as they were back in Hans Christian Andersen's day. The Mayor's House (from 1597) is the nucleus and reason enough to visit. Unlike other Scandinavian open-air museums that focus on rural folk life, Den Gamle By re-creates old Danish town life (50 kr, daily June–August 9:00–18:00; May and September 9:00–17:00; shorter

Århus

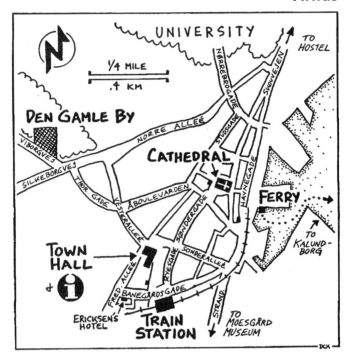

hours off-season; there are some English descriptions inside; take bus #3, #14, or #25, or walk 15 minutes from the train station to Viborgvej 2, tel. 86 12 31 88). Ask about walking tours in English (two/day in summer) and pick up the schedule of tours. After hours, the buildings are locked but the peaceful park is open. There's a fine botanical garden next door.

▲**Forhistorisk Museum Moesgård**—This prehistory museum at Moesgård, just south of Århus, is famous for its incredibly well-preserved Grauballe Man. This 2,000-year-old "bog man" looks like a fellow half his age. You'll see his skin, nails, hair, and even the slit in his throat given him at the sacrificial banquet. The museum has fine Stone, Bronze, Iron, and Viking Age exhibits (35 kr, daily 10:00–17:00; off-season 10:00–16:00 and closed Monday, Moesgård Alle 20, tel. 89 42 11 00). Take bus #6 from the Århus station to the last stop. Behind the museum, a prehistoric open-air museum ("trackway," good 10-kr guide booklet) stretches 2 miles down to a fine beach from which, in the summer, bus #19 takes you back downtown. The museum cafeteria sells picnics-to-go.

Århus Cathedral—This late Gothic church (from 1479) is Denmark's biggest—over 300 feet long and tall (Monday–Saturday 9:30–16:00; off-season 10:00–15:00).

Other Århus Attractions—Århus has a great pedestrian street that stretches at least two ice-cream cones from the cathedral to the train station (Søndergade/Clements Torv). There's lots more to see and do in Århus, including an art museum (Århus Kunstmuseum, 30 kr, Tuesday–Sunday 10:00–17:00, closed Monday, shorter hours off-season, buses #1 and #6 from train station, tel. 86 13 52 55), a Viking museum (free, in a bank basement across from the cathedral), and a "Tivoli" amusement park.

Sleeping in Århus
(7 kr = about $1)

Sleep Code: **S** = Single, **D** = Double/Twin, **T** = Triple, **Q** = Quad, **b** = bathroom, **CC** = Credit Card (**V**isa, **M**asterCard, **A**mex). All accommodations are centrally located near the train station and TI. The TI can set you up in a private home for 150 kr per person in a double room, and they also have summer deals on ritzy hotels (Db-700 kr).

Eriksen's Hotel is a shipshape, friendly, creative little place with showers down the hall and cheap meals (S-330 kr, D-480 kr, less without breakfast, CC:VM, Banegårdsgade 6-8, tel. 86 13 62 96, fax 86 13 76 76).

Plaza Hotel is 100 meters from the station and a good value (Db-690–880 kr depending on big/small/old/new, includes breakfast, CC:VMA, sauna, Banegardspladsen 14, tel. 86 12 41 22, fax 86 20 29 04).

The basic **City Sleep In** is open 24 hours a day year-round (dorm beds-85 kr, D-200 kr, Db-250 kr, sheets-30 kr, no breakfast, Havnegade 20, tel. 86 19 20 55).

The **hostel** with 80-kr beds and plenty of two- and four-bed rooms, is near the water 2 miles out of town (Marien-lundsvej 10, bus #1 to the end, follow signs, tel. 86 16 72 98).

Eating in Århus

Det Gronne Hiorne at Frederiksgade offers an ethnic all-you-can-eat buffet (50 kr before 16:00, 70 kr after). **Restaurant**

Italia is reasonable (corner of Mindebrogade and Åboulevarden). **Munkestuen** has good 120-kr meals (Klostertorvet 5, tel. 86 12 95 67). At **Dee Dee's Sandwiches & Salads,** nothing costs more than 40 kr (just across from the train station). Try the brunch at cozy **Café Jorden** (11:00–14:00, Badstuegade 3). The area around Klostertorvet/Klostergade offers great cafés and people-watching. The park in front of Musikhuset concert hall is good for picnics.

Transportation Connections—Århus

By train to: Hirtshals (16/day, 2.5 hrs), **Odense** (16/day, 2 hrs), **Copenhagen** (hrly, 4.5 hrs), **Hamburg** (3/day, 5.5 hrs).

Ferries: Day and night, ferries sail between Hirtshals, Denmark, and Kristiansand, Norway. On board, you'll find a decent smørgåsbord, music, duty-free shopping, and a bank (no fee). The crossing takes four hours (overnight, six) and the cost ranges wildly from 98 kr to 360 kr (July and weekends are priciest). The charge for a car is 180 kr to 500 kr; a "car package" deal lets five in a car travel for 1,390 kr (summer, Monday–Thursday). The overnight boat offers varying levels of comfort and privacy (40 kr for a reclining seat, 65 kr for a simple curtained couchette, 110–130 kr for a bed in a four-berth room, or 130–260 kr for a bed in a private double with shower). Call Color Line for information and reservations (Monday–Saturday 8:00–22:00, Sunday 8:00–21:00, tel. 99 56 19 77 in Denmark; in the U.S.A. tel. 212/319-1300, fax 212/319-1390). If you've got a car or want a room, make a reservation and pay when you arrive at the dock.

Route Tips for Drivers

From the ferry dock at Hirtshals to Århus to Billund:
From the dock in Hirtshals, drive E-45 south (signs to Hjørring, Ålborg). It's about a 2.5-hour drive even on the scenic road 507 from Ålborg (signs to Hadsund). E-45 takes you into Århus. (To skip Århus, skirt the center and follow E-45 south). To get to downtown Århus, follow signs to the center, then Domkirke. Park in the pay lot across from the cathedral. Signs all over town direct you to the open-air folk museum, Den Gamle By. From Århus, continue south on E-45 (leave on Skanderborg Road; signs to Vejle, Kolding). For Legoland, take the Vejle S (after Vejle N) exit sign for Billund.

NORWAY

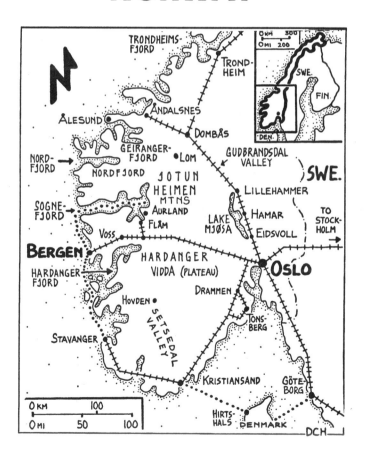

OSLO

Oslo is the smallest and least earthshaking of the Nordic capitals, but this brisk little city offers more sightseeing thrills than you might expect. Sights of the Viking spirit—past and present—tell an exciting story. Prowl through the remains of ancient Viking ships and marvel at more peaceful but equally gutsy modern boats like the *Kon-Tiki*, *Ra*, and *Fram*. Dive into the country's folk culture at the open-air folk museum and get stirred up by Norway's heroic spirit at the Nazi resistance museum.

For a look at modern Oslo, browse through the new yuppie-style harbor shopping complex, tour the striking city hall, take a peek at sculptor Vigeland's people pillars, and climb the towering Holmenkollen ski jump.

Situated at the head of a 60-mile-long fjord, surrounded by forests, and populated by more than 500,000 people, Oslo is Norway's cultural hub and an all-you-can-see smørgåsbord of historic sights, trees, art, and Nordic fun.

Planning Your Time

Oslo offers an exciting two-day slate of sightseeing thrills. Ideally, arrive on the overnight train from Stockholm, spend two days, and leave on the night train to Copenhagen or on the scenic train to Bergen the third morning. Spend the two days like this:

Day 1: Set up. Visit the TI. Tour the Akershus Castle and Norwegian Resistance Museum. Take a picnic on the ferry to Bygdøy and enjoy a view of the city harbor. Tour the *Fram*, *Kon-Tiki*, and Viking ships. Finish the afternoon at the Norwegian Open Air Folk Museum. Boat home. For evening culture, consider the folk music and dance show (20:30 Monday and Thursday).

Day 2: At 10:00 catch the city hall tour, then browse through the National Gallery. Spend the afternoon at Vigeland Park and at the Holmenkollen ski jump and museum. Browse Karl Johans Gate (all the way to the station) and Aker Brygge harbor in the early evening for the Norwegian *paseo*. Consider munching a fast-food dinner on the harbor mini-cruise.

Orientation

Oslo is easy to manage, with nearly all its sights clustered around the central "barbell" street (Karl Johans Gate, with the Royal Palace on one end and the train station on the other), or in the Bygdøy district, a ten-minute ferry ride across the harbor.

Tourist Information

The **Norwegian Information Center** displays Norway as if it were a giant booth at a trade show (on the waterfront between the city hall and Aker Brygge, daily 9:00–20:00, shorter hours off-season, tel. 22 83 00 50). Stock up on brochures for Oslo and all of your Norwegian destinations, especially the *Bergen Guide*. Pick up the free Oslo map, Sporveiskart transit map, *What's on in Oslo* monthly (for the most accurate listing of museum hours and special events), *Streetwise* magazine (hip, fun to read, and full of offbeat ideas), and the free annual *Oslo Guide* (with plenty of details on sightseeing, shopping and eating). Consider buying the Oslo Card (unless your hotel provides it for free, see below). The info center has a rack of free pages on contemporary Norwegian issues and life (near the door); a 30-minute "multi-vision" slideshow taking you around Norway (free, top of the hour, in theater in the back); a 30-minute video called *Look to Norway* that runs all day; a handy public toilet; and rooms showcasing various crafts and ways you can spend your money. The tourist information window in the central station is much simpler and deals only with Oslo but can handle your needs just as well (daily in summer 8:00–23:00, less off-season).

Use It is a hardworking youth information center, providing solid, money-saving, experience-enhancing information to young, student, and vagabond travelers (mid-June–mid-August Monday–Friday 7:30–18:00, Saturday 9:00–14:00, closed Sunday; Monday–Friday 11:00–17:00 the rest of the year, Møllergata 3, tel. 22 41 51 32, web site: www.unginfo.oslo.no). They have telephones and e-mail, and can find you the cheapest beds in town for no fee. Read their free *Streetwise* magazine for ideas on eating and sleeping cheap, good nightspots, best beaches, and so on.

The **Oslo Card** gives you free use of all city public transit and boats, free entry to all sights, a free harbor mini-cruise tour, free parking, and many more discounts—and is also a handy handbook (24 hours-130 kr, 48 hours-200 kr, or 72 hours-240 kr). Almost any two-day visit to Oslo will be cheaper with the Oslo Card (which costs less than three Bygdøy museum admissions, the ski jump, and one city bus ride). Students with an ISIC card may be better off without the Oslo Card. The TI's special Oslo Package hotel deal (described under Sleeping, below) includes this card with your discounted hotel room.

Arrival in Oslo

Oslo S, the modern central train station, is slick and helpful, with a late-hours TI (daily in summer 8:00–23:00, less off-season), room-finding service, late-hours bank (fair rates, normal fee), supermarket (daily 6:30–23:30), and an **Interrail Center** that offers any traveler with a train pass 15-kr showers, free rucksack storage racks, a bright and clean lounge, cheap snacks, a bulletin board for cheap sleeping deals, and an information center (daily mid-June–September 7:00–23:00). Pick up information leaflets on the Flåm and Bergen Railway.

Getting Around Oslo

By Public Transit: Oslo's transit system is made up of buses, trams, ferries, and a subway. Tickets cost 18 kr and are good for one hour of use on any combination of the above. Flexi-cards give eight rides for 105 kr. Buy tickets as you board (bus info tel. 22 17 70 30, daily 8:00–23:00). **Trafikanten**, the public transit information center, is under the ugly tower immediately in front of the station. Their free "Sporveiskart for Oslo" transit map is the best city map around and makes the transit

Oslo Center

❶ CITY HOTEL
❷ RAINBOW HOTEL ASTORIA
❸ RAINBOW HOTEL SPECTRUM
❹ COCH'S PENSJONAT
❺ VEGETA VERTSHUS

system easy. The similar but smaller "Visitor's Map Oslo" (available at TI) is easier to use and also free. The **Dagskort Tourist Ticket** is a 40-kr, 24-hour transit pass that pays for itself on the third ride. The Oslo Card (see Tourist Information, above) gives you free run of the entire transit system. Note how gracefully the subway lines fan out after huddling at Stortinget. Take advantage of the way they run like clockwork, with schedules clearly posted and followed.

By Bike: Oslo is a good biking town, especially if you'd like to get out into the woods or ride a tram uphill out of town and coast for miles back. Vestbanen organizes tours and rents bikes (three hours/90–130 kr, six hours/140–180 kr depending on bike, in-line skates 100 kr/3 hours, 20 percent discount for readers of this book; May–September weekdays 7:00–22:00, weekends 10:00–18:00, closes earlier off-season; on the harbor next to the Norway Information Center; tel. 23 11 51 00).

Helpful Hints
To get a taxi, call 22 38 80 70, then dial 1. To get on the Internet, try the new cyber café in the east hall of the train station

and the Velvet café nearby (10 kr per hour, Monday–Thursday
14:00–20:00, Friday 14:00–18:00, Nedre Slottsgate 2). Jern-
banetorgets Apotek is a 24-hour pharmacy directly across from
the train station (on Jernbanetorget, tel. 22 41 24 82). Kilroy
Travel is everyone's favorite for student and discounted air tickets (Nedre Slottsgate 23, tel. 23 10 23 10).

Sights—Downtown Oslo

Note: Because of Norway's passion for minor differences in
opening times from month to month, I've generally listed only
the peak-season hours. Assume opening hours shorten as the
days do. The high season in Oslo is mid-June to mid-August.
(I'll call that "summer" in this chapter.)

▲▲**City Hall**—Construction on Oslo's richly decorated
Rådhuset began in 1931. Finished in 1950 to celebrate the
city's 900th birthday, Norway's leading artists (including
Edvard Munch) all contributed to what was an avant-garde
thrill in its day. The interior's 2,000 square yards of bold and
colorful "socialist modernism" murals (which take you on a
voyage through the collective psyche of Norway, from its
simple rural beginnings through the scar tissue of the Nazi
occupation and beyond) are meaningful only with the excellent, free guided tours (20 kr, tours offered Monday–Friday at
10:00, 12:00, and 14:00; open Monday–Saturday 9:00–17:00,
Sunday 12:00–17:00, until 16:00 in off-season, entry on the
Karl Johans side, tel. 22 86 16 00). Ever notice how city halls
rather than churches are the dominant buildings in the your-
government-loves-you northern corner of Europe? The main
hall of Oslo's city hall actually feels like a temple to good
government (the altar-like mural celebrates "work, play, and
civic administration"). The Nobel Peace Prize is awarded
each December in this room.

▲**Akershus Fortress Complex**—This park-like complex of
sites scattered over Oslo's fortified center is still a military base.
But dodging patrolling guards and vans filled with soldiers you'll
see war memorials, the castle, prison, Nazi resistance museum,
armed forces museum, and cannon-strewn ramparts affording
fine harbor views and picnic perches. Immediately inside the
gate is an information center with an interesting exhibit on
medieval Oslo's fortifications. In summer, free 45-minute tours
of the grounds leave from the center (10:00, 12:00, 14:00, 16:00,
daily but not Sunday morning, tel. 23 09 39 17). There's a small

changing of the guard daily at 13:30. The prison, which is visited on the guided walk, will open as a museum in 1998.

Akershus Fortress—One of the oldest buildings in town, this castle overlooking Oslo's harbor is mediocre by European standards. The big, empty rooms remind us of Norway's medieval poverty. Behind the chapel altar, steps lead down to the tombs of some Norwegian kings. The castle is interesting only with the tour (20 kr for castle entry, May to mid-September Monday–Saturday 10:00–16:00, Sunday 12:30–16:00; open Sunday only in spring and fall; closed in winter; free 50-minute English tours offered in summer from Monday–Saturday at 11:00, 13:00, and 15:00, Sunday at 13:00 and 15:00; tel. 22 41 25 21).

▲▲Norwegian Resistance Museum (Norges Hjemmefrontmuseum)—A stirring story about the Nazi invasion and occupation is told with wonderful English descriptions. This is the best look in Europe at how national spirit endured total German occupation (20 kr, Monday–Saturday 10:00–17:00, Sunday 11:00–17:00, closes one hour earlier off-season, next to castle in building overlooking the harbor, tel. 23 09 31 38).

Armed Forces Museum—Across the fortress parade ground, a large museum traces Norwegian military from Viking days to post-WWII. The early stuff is very sketchy but the WWII story is fascinating (free, Monday–Friday 10:00–18:00, weekends 11:00–16:00, shorter hours September–May, tel. 22 40 35 82).

▲National Gallery—Located downtown, this easy-to-handle museum gives you an effortless tour back in time and through Norway's most beautiful valleys, mountains, and villages, with the help of its romantic painters (especially Dahl). The gallery also has several Picassos, a noteworthy Impressionist collection, some Vigeland statues, and a representative roomful of Munch paintings, including the famous *Scream*. His paintings here make a trip to the Munch museum unnecessary for most. For an entertaining survey of 2,500 years of sculpture, go through the museum gift shop and down the stairs to the right for a room filled with plaster copies of famous works (free, Monday, Wednesday, Friday 10:00–18:00; Thursday 10:00–20:00; Saturday 10:00–16:00; Sunday 11:00–15:00; closed Tuesday; Universitets Gata 13, tel. 22 20 04 04).

▲▲Browsing—Oslo's pulse is best felt along and near the central Karl Johans Gate (from station to palace), between the city hall and the harbor, and in the trendy new harborside

Greater Oslo

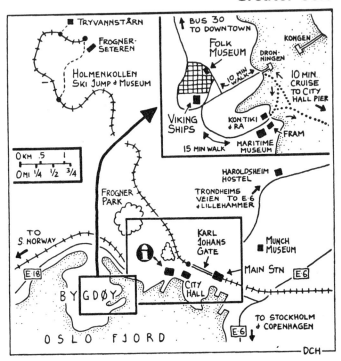

Aker Brygge Festival Market Mall—a glass-and-chrome collection of sharp cafés and polished produce stalls just west of the city hall (trams #10 and #15 to/from train station). The buskers are among the best in Europe. Aker Brygge is very lively late evenings.

▲▲▲**Vigeland Sculptures and the Vigeland Museum in Frogner Park**—The 75-acre park contains a lifetime of work by Norway's greatest sculptor, Gustav Vigeland. From 1924 through 1942, he sculpted 175 bronze and granite statues—each nude and unique. Walking over the statue-lined bridge you'll come to the main fountain. Trace the story of our lives in the series of humans intertwined with trees around the fountain. The maze in the pavement around the fountain starts opposite the monolith and comes out, 3 kilometers later, closest to the monolith. Try following it . . . you can't go wrong. Vigeland's 60-foot-high tangled tower of 121 bodies called "the

monolith of life" is the centerpiece of the park. While it seems
the lower figures are laden with earthly concerns and the higher
ones are freed to pursue loftier, more spiritual adventures,
Vigeland gives us permission to interpret it any way we like.
Pick up the free map from the box on the kiosk wall as you
enter. The park is more than great art. It's a city at play. Enjoy
its urban Norwegian ambience. Then visit the Vigeland
Museum to see the models for the statues and more in the
artist's studio. Don't miss the photos on the wall showing the
construction of the monolith (20 kr for museum, Tuesday–
Saturday 10:00–18:00, Sunday 12:00–19:00, closed Monday;
off-season Tuesday–Sunday 12:00–16:00 and free, tel. 22 44 11
36). The park is always open and free. Take T-bane #2, bus #20
or #45, or tram #12 or #15 to Frogner Plass.

Oslo City Museum—Located in the Frogner Manor farm in
Frogner Park, this museum tells the story of Oslo. A helpful free
English brochure guides you through the exhibits (20 kr,
Tuesday–Friday 10:00–18:00, Saturday and Sunday 11:00–17:00,
closed Monday; shorter hours off-season, tel. 22 43 06 45).

▲▲Edvard Munch Museum—The only Norwegian painter
to have had a serious impact on European art, Munch (monk) is
a surprise to many who visit this fine museum. The emotional,
disturbing, and powerfully expressionist work of this strange
and perplexing man is arranged chronologically. You'll see
paintings, drawings, lithographs, and photographs. Don't miss
The Scream, which captures the fright many feel as the human
"race" does just that (50 kr, daily 10:00–18:00; off-season closes
as early as 16:00 and all day Monday; take the T-bane from the
station to "Tøyen," tel. 22 67 37 74). If the price or location is a
problem, you can see a roomful of Munch paintings in the free
National Gallery downtown.

Sights—Oslo's Bygdøy Neighborhood

▲▲▲Bygdøy—This exciting cluster of sights is on a park-like
peninsula just across the harbor from downtown. To get to
Bygdøy, either take bus #30 from the station and National
Theater or, more fun, catch the ferry from City Hall (18 kr,
free with transit pass or Oslo Card, 3/hour, 8:30–21:00). The
Folk Museum and Viking ships are a ten-minute walk from the
ferry's first stop, Dronningen. The other museums are at the
second stop, Bygdøynes. (See Bygdøy inset in "Greater Oslo"
map in this chapter.) All Bygdøy sights are within a 15-minute

walk of each other. While a handy tourist train shuttles visitors around Bygdøy (3/hour, 20 kr for an all-day pass) the *Fram*-Viking ships walk gives you a fine feel for rural Norway.

▲▲**Norwegian Folk Museum**—Brought from all corners of Norway, 150 buildings have been reassembled on these 35 acres. While Stockholm's Skansen was the first to open to the public, this museum is a bit older, starting in 1885 as the king's private collection. You'll find craftspeople doing their traditional things; security guards disguised in cute, colorful, and traditional local costumes; endless creative ways to make do in a primitive log-cabin-and-goats-on-the-roof age; a 12th-century stave church; and a museum filled with toys and fine folk costumes. The place hops in the summer but is dead off-season. Catch the free one-hour guided walks at 10:00, 12:00, and 14:00 (call to confirm schedule). Otherwise, glean information from the 10-kr guidebook and the informative attendants who look like Rebecca Boone's Norwegian pen pals (50 kr, daily June–August 9:00–18:00; off-season 10:00–17:00 or less). For folk dance performances, tour, and crafts demonstration schedules, call 22 12 37 00.

▲▲**Viking Ships**—Three great ninth-century Viking ships are surrounded by artifacts from the days of rape, pillage, and—ya sure, yu betcha—plunder. There are no museum tours, but everything is well described in English, and it's hard not to hear the English-speaking bus tour guides. There was a time when much of a frightened Europe closed every prayer with "And deliver us from the Vikings, Amen." Gazing up at the prow of one of these sleek, time-stained vessels, you can almost hear the screams and smell the armpits of those redheads on the rampage (30 kr, daily summer 9:00–18:00, off-season 11:00–15:00, tel. 22 43 83 79). To miss the tour-group crowds, come early, late, or at lunchtime.

▲▲**The *Fram***—This great ship took modern-day Vikings Amundsen and Nansen deep into the Arctic and Antarctic, farther north and south than any ship before. For three years the *Fram* was part of an Arctic ice drift. The exhibit is fascinating. Read the ground-floor displays, then explore the boat (20 kr, daily summer 9:00–18:45, shorter hours off-season). You can step into the lobby and see the ship's hull for free. The **Polar Sloop *Gjøa*** is dry-docked next to the ferry dock. This is the boat Amundsen and a crew of six used from 1903 to 1906 to "discover" the Northwest Passage (*Fram* ticket gets you aboard).

▲▲The *Kon-Tiki* Museum—Next to the *Fram* are the *Kon-Tiki* and the *Ra II*, the boats Thor Heyerdahl built and sailed 4,000 and 3,000 miles, respectively, to prove that early South Americans could have sailed to Polynesia and Africans could have populated Barbados. Both are well-displayed and described in English. A short "adventures of Thor Heyerdahl" movie plays constantly (25 kr, daily 9:30–17:45, off-season 10:30–16:45).

▲Norwegian Maritime Museum—If you like the sea, this museum is a salt lick, providing a fine look at Norway's maritime heritage (30 kr, 60 kr for a family, daily 10:00–19:00, off-season 10:30–16:00 and sometimes later). Consider viewing the wide-screen nature film on Norway's coast called *The Ocean, A Way of Life* (free, 20 minutes, on the half-hour).

Other Oslo Sights and Activities
▲Henie-Onstad Art Center—Norway's best private modern art collection, donated by the famous Norwegian Olympic skater/movie star Sonja Henie (and her husband), combines modern art, a stunning building, a beautiful fjordside setting, and the great café/restaurant Pirouetten. Don't miss her glittering trophy room near the entrance of the center (40 kr, Monday 11:00–17:00, Tuesday–Friday 9:00–21:00, weekends 11:00–19:00, tel. 67 54 30 50). It's in Høvikodden, 8 miles southwest of Oslo (catch bus #151, #153, #251, or #252 from the Oslo train station or from Universitets Plass by the National Theater).

▲▲Holmenkollen Ski Jump and Ski Museum—Overlooking Oslo is a tremendous ski jump with a unique museum of skiing. The T-bane #1 gets you out of the city, into the hills and forests that surround Oslo, and to the jump. After touring the history of skiing in the museum, ride the elevator and climb the 100-step stairway to the thrilling top of the jump for the best possible view of Oslo—and a chance to look down the long and frightening ramp that has sent so many tumbling into the agony of defeat. The **ski museum** is a must for skiers—tracing the evolution of the sport from 4,000-year-old rock paintings, to crude 1,500-year-old skis, to the slick and quickly evolving skis of our century (50 kr, ski jump and museum open daily 9:00–20:00 in June, 9:00–22:00 in July and August, closes earlier off-season).

For a special thrill, step into the **Simulator** and fly down the French Alps in a Disneyland-style downhill ski-race simulator. My legs were exhausted after the four-minute terror.

This stimulator, parked in front of the ski museum, costs 35 kr. (Japanese tourists, who wig out over this one, are usually given a free ride after paying for four.)

To get to the ski jump, ride the T-bane line #1 to the Holmenkollen stop and hike up the road ten minutes. For a longer walk, ride to the end of the line (Frognerseteren) and walk ten minutes down to the **Frognerseteren Hovedrestaurant**. This classy, traditional old place, with a terrace that offers a commanding view of the city, is a popular stop for apple-cake and coffee or a splurge dinner (daily 11:00–22:30, tel. 22 14 37 36). From the restaurant it's a 30-minute walk downhill through the woods on a gravel path that runs generally parallel to Holmenkollenveien.

The nearby **Tryvannstårnet observatory tower** offers a lofty 360-degree view of Oslo in the distance, the fjord, and endless forests, lakes, and soft hills. It's impressive but not necessary if you climbed the ski jump, which gives you a much better view of the city (daily 10:00–19:00 in June, 9:00–22:00 in July, and 9:00–20:00 in August, less off-season, ten-minute walk from Voksenkollen T-bane stop, tel. 22 14 67 11).

Forests, Lakes, and Beaches—Oslo is surrounded by a vast forest dotted with idyllic little lakes, huts, joggers, bikers, and sun-worshipers. Mountain-bike riding possibilities are endless (as you'll discover if you go exploring without a guide or good map). For a quick ride, you can take the T-bane (with your bike; it needs a ticket too) to the end of line #1 (Frognerseteren, 30 minutes from the National Theater, gaining you the most altitude possible) and follow the gravelly roads (mostly downhill but with some climbing) past several dreamy lakes to Sognsvann at the end of T-bane line #3 (a one-hour ride, not counting time lost). Farther east, from Maridalsvannet, a bike path follows the Aker River all the way back into town. For plenty of trees and none of the exercise, ride the T-bane #3 to Sognsvann (with a beach towel rather than a bike) and join in the lakeside scene. Other popular beaches (such as Bygdøy Huk—direct boat from city hall pier, and others on islands in the harbor) are described in Use It's *Streetwise* magazine.

Harbor and Fjord Tours—Several tour boats leave regularly from Pier 3 in front of the city hall. A relaxing and scenic 50-minute mini-cruise with a boring three-language commentary departs hourly and costs only 70 kr (free with Oslo Card, daily 11:00–20:00, tel. 22 20 07 15). They won't scream if you bring something to Munch. The cheapest way to enjoy the scenic Oslo fjord is to simply ride the ferries that regularly connect the nearby islands with downtown (free with the Oslo Card or transit pass).

▲▲▲**Folk Entertainment**—A group of amateur musicians and dancers (called "Leikarringen Bondeungdomslaget"— Oslo's country youth society) gives a sweet, caring, and vibrant 90-minute show at the Oslo Concert Hall. Several traditional instruments are explained and demonstrated. While folk dancing seems hokey to many, if you think of it as medieval flirting set to music and ponder the complexities of village social life back then, the experience takes you away (140–180 kr, Monday and Thursday from July through early September at 20:30; tel. 22 83 45 10 or 81 53 31 33). Look for the big, brown, glassy overpass on Munkedamsveien; the recommended Vegata Vertshus restaurant is just up the street. For their off-season concert schedule (different locales), call 22 41 40 70.

Tusenfryd/Vinkinglandet—A giant amusement complex just out of town offers a world of family fun—sort of a combo Norwegian Disneyland/Viking Knott's Berry Farm. It's one big company. While the Tusenfryd entry includes the Vikings, you can do just the Viking park if you like. Tusenfryd offers more than 50 rides, plenty of entertainment, family fun, and restaurants. Vikinglandet is a Viking theme park. A coach shuttles fun-seekers to the park from behind the train station (20 kr, 2/hr, 20-minute ride). The entry, 180 kr, is not covered by the Oslo Card (daily 10:30–19:00 in summer, closed in winter). For Viking Land only, tickets cost 95 kr (55 kr for kids under 4'7", tel. 64 94 63 63).

Wet Fun—Oslo offers lots of water fun for about 35 kr (kids half-price). In Frogner Park, the Frognerbadet has a sauna, outdoor pools, high dives, a cafeteria, and lots of young families (free with Oslo Card, daily mid-May–late August 11:00– 17:45, Middelthunsgate 28, tel. 22 44 74 29). Kriskis and Svettis (tel. 22 83 25 40) organize free community exercise sessions at Frognerpark. Toyenbadet is a modern indoor pool complex with mini-golf and a 100-yard-long water slide (free with Oslo Card, open at odd hours throughout the year, Helgengate 90, a ten-minute walk from Munch Museum, tel. 22 68 24 23). Oslo's free botanical gardens are nearby. (For more ideas on swimming, pick up *Streetwise* magazine.)

Nightlife—They used to tell people who asked about nightlife in Oslo that Copenhagen was only an hour away by plane. Now Oslo has sprouted a nightlife of its own. The scene is always changing. The tourist office has information on Oslo's many cafés, discos, and jazz clubs. It is the best source of information for local hot spots.

Shopping—For a great selection (but high prices) in sweaters and other Norwegian crafts, shop at Husfliden, the retail center for the Norwegian Association of Home Arts and Crafts (Sunday–Friday 10:00–17:00, Saturday until 15:00, Den Norske Husflidsforening, Møllergata 4, behind the cathedral, tel. 22 42 10 75). Shops are generally open 10:00 to 18:00. Many stay open until 20:00 on Thursday and close early on Saturday and all day Sunday.

Sleeping in Oslo
(7 kr = about $1)
Sleep Code: **S** = Single, **D** = Double/Twin, **T** = Triple, **Q** = Quad, **b** = bathroom, **CC** = Credit Card (**V**isa, **M**asterCard, **A**mex).

Yes, Oslo is expensive. In Oslo, the season dictates the best deals. In low season (July–mid-August, and Friday, Saturday, and Sunday the rest of the year), fancy hotels are the best value for softies, with 600 kr for a double with breakfast. In high season (business days outside of summer), your affordable choices are dumpy-for-Scandinavia (but still nice by European standards) doubles for around 500 kr in hotels and 350 kr in private homes. For experience and economy (but not convenience), go for a private home. Oslo's new Albertine hostel (see below) is well-located and normally has space available (100 kr per bed, 300-kr doubles).

Like those in its sister Scandinavian capitals, Oslo's hotels are designed for business travelers. They're expensive during our off-season (fall through spring), full in May and June for conventions (get reservations), and empty otherwise. Only the TI can sort through all the confusing hotel "specials" and get you the best deal possible on a fancy hotel—push-list rooms at about half-price. Half-price is still 600 kr to 700 kr, but that includes a huge breakfast and a lot of extra comfort for a few extra kroner over the cost of a cheap hotel. Cheap hotels, whose rates are the same throughout the year, are a bad value in summer but offer real savings in low season.

The TI's **Oslo Package** advertises 700-kr discounted doubles in business-class (normally priced at 1,200 kr) rooms and includes a free Oslo Card (worth 130 kr/day). The Oslo Package is a good deal for couples and an incredible deal for families with children under 16 who are traveling in late-June through mid-August or on weekends. Two kids under 16 sleep free, breakfast included, and up to four family members get Oslo Cards, covering free admission to sights and all public transportation. The clincher is that the cards are valid for four days, even if you only stay at the hotel for one night (technically, you should stay two nights, but this is not enforced). Buy this through your travel agent at home, ScanAm World Tour at 800/545-2204, or, easier, upon arrival in Oslo (at the tourist information office).

Use the TI only for these push-list deals, not for cheap hotels or private homes. Some of the cheaper hotels (my listings) tell the TI (which gets a 10 percent fee) they're full when they're not. Go direct. A hotel getting 100 percent of your payment is more likely to have a room. July and early August are easy, but June can be crammed by conventions and September can be tight.

Sleeping in Hotels near the Train Station

Each of these places is within a five-minute walk of the station, in a neighborhood your mom probably wouldn't want you hanging around in at night. The hotels themselves, however, are secure and comfortable. Leave nothing in your car. The Paleet parking garage is handy but not cheap—120 kr per 24 hours.

City Hotel, clean, basic, very homey, and with a wonderful lounge, originated 100 years ago as a cheap place for Norwegians to sleep while they waited to sail to their new homes in America. It now serves the opposite purpose with good if well-worn rooms and a great location (S-380 kr, Sb-495 kr, D-550 kr, Db-680 kr, includes breakfast, CC:VMA, Skippergata 19, enter from Prinsens Gate, tel. 22 41 36 10, fax 22 42 24 29).

Rainbow Hotel Astoria is a comfortable, modern place, and part of the quickly growing Rainbow Hotel chain that understands which comforts are worth paying for. There are umbrellas, televisions, telephones, and full modern bathrooms in each room. Ice machines! Designed for businessmen, the place has mostly singles. Most "twins" are actually "combi" rooms with a regular bed and a fold-out sofa bed (Sb-395–595 kr,

Twin/Db-540–695 kr, Db-640–795 kr, rates vary with season, included buffet breakfast, CC:VMA, 3 blocks in front of the station, 50 yards off Karl Johans Gate, Dronningensgate 21, 0154 Oslo, tel. 22 42 00 10, fax 22 42 57 65).

Rainbow Hotel Spectrum is also conveniently located and a good value (discounted prices Friday, Saturday, Sunday, and throughout July: "combi" Twin/b-570–695 kr, full doubles—actually two twins shoved together—100 kr more, CC:VMA, 4 blocks to the right as you leave the station on Lilletorget, Brugata 7, 0186 Oslo, tel. 22 17 60 30, fax 22 17 60 80). **Rainbow Hotel Terminus** is similar and closer to the station, but has a less exciting low-season deal (Friday, Saturday, or Sunday anytime or reservations within 48 hours any day during the May–August period: Sb-420 kr, small bed Db-580 kr, Db-680 kr, regular Db rate-810 kr, includes breakfast, Stenersgate 10, tel. 22 05 60 00, fax 22 17 08 98).

Sleeping in the West End

Cochs Pensjonat has 68 plain rooms (plus nine remodeled doubles) with fresh paint and stale carpets. It's right behind the palace (S-310 kr, Sb-390 kr, D-420 kr, Db-530–580 kr, all Dbs have kitchenettes, no breakfast, CC:VM, tram #11, #13, #17, or #18 to Parkveien 25, tel. 22 60 48 36, fax 22 46 54 02).

Ellingsen's Pensjonat has no lounge, no breakfasts, and dreary halls. But its rooms are great, with fluffy down comforters. It's located in a residential neighborhood 4 blocks behind the Royal Palace (a lot of S-240 kr, S with extra bed-340 kr, D-380 kr, Db-470 kr, extra bed-100 kr, call well in advance for doubles, Holtegata 25, 0355 Oslo 3, tel. 22 60 03 59, fax 22 60 99 21). Located near the Uranienborg church, it's #25 on the east side of the street (T-bane #19 from the station).

Sleeping in Rooms in Private Homes

The TI can find you a 300-kr double for a 20-kr fee (minimum two-night stay). My listings are pretty funky, but full of memories.

Mr. Naess offers big, homey old rooms overlooking a park, and the use of a fully-equipped kitchen. This is a flat in a big ramshackle building, in a borderline-rough neighborhood with workaday shops and eateries nearby (special prices for two or more nights: S-150 kr, D-250 kr, T-375 kr, add 40 kr extra per person for one night stay, no breakfast, plenty of stairs, Toftegate 45, tel. & fax 22 37 58 94). Walk 20 minutes from the station, or take bus #30 from the tower in front of the station to Olaf Ryes Plass (five stops). Three people (or two with lots of luggage) should take a taxi.

Marius Meisfjord, a retired teacher deeply interested in imparting Norse culture, rents rooms behind the palace. Beds are 145 kr per person in a house stuffed with ancient furniture and pictures of European royalty. This eccentric place feels more like a museum than a B&B, and friendly Mr. Meisfjord looks more like Ibsen than a B&B host (breakfast extra, take tram #12 or #15 to Elisensbergveien, walk 2 blocks to Thomas Heftes Gate 46, tel. 22 55 38 46).

The **Caspari family** rents four comfortable rooms in their home (D-280 kr, breakfast-45 kr). Loosely run, it's set in a lush green yard in a peaceful suburb behind Frogner Park, a quick T-bane ride away (get off at Borgen and walk 100 yards more on the right-hand side of the tracks, Heggelbakken 1, tel. 22 14 57 70).

Sleeping in Hostels

Albertine Hostel, a huge student dorm newly opened to travelers of any age, offers the best cheap doubles in town. It feels like a bomb shelter but each room is spacious, simple, and clean. There are kitchens, free parking, and elevators (Sb-225 kr, Db-300 kr, beds in quads-125 kr, beds in six-bedded rooms-95 kr, sheets-35 kr, towel-15 kr, breakfast-45 kr; catch tram #11, #12, #15, or #17, or bus #27 or #30 from the station; Storgata 55, N-0182 Oslo, tel. 22 99 72 00, fax 22 99 72 20, web site: www.anker.oslo.no/Anker/turist/Engelsk/turistuk.html). In winter they use the adjacent Anker hotel reception desk.

Haraldsheim Youth Hostel (IYHF), a huge, modern hostel, is open all year, situated far from the center on a hill with a grand view, laundry, and self-service kitchen. Its 270 beds (four per room) are often completely booked. Beds in the new fancy quads with private showers and toilets are 175 kr per person, including buffet breakfast. (Beds in simple quads-155 kr, includes breakfast, sheets-35 kr, guest membership-25 kr; tram #10 or #11 from station to Sinsen, 4 km out of town, five-minute uphill hike; Haraldsheimveien 4; tel. 22 15 50 43, fax 22 22 10 25.) Eurailers can train (2/hour, to Gressen) to the hostel for free.

YMCA Sleep-In Oslo, located near the train station, offers the cheapest mattresses in town in three large rooms with 15 to 30 mattresses each, plus a left-luggage room, kitchen, and piano lounge (earplugs for sale). It's as pleasant as a sleep-in can be (100 kr, no bedding provided, you must bring a sleeping bag, reception open daily 8:00–11:00 and 17:00–24:00 July to mid-August only, Møllergata 1, entry from Grubbegata, 1 block beyond the cathedral behind Use It, tel. 22 20 83 97). They take no reservations, but call to see if there's a place.

Sleeping on the Train

Norway's trains offer 100-kr beds in triple compartments and 200-kr beds in doubles. Eurailers who sleep well to the rhythm of the rails have several very scenic overnight trips to choose from (it's light until midnight for much of the early summer at Oslo's latitude). If you have a train pass, use the station's service center (across from the ticket windows) and avoid the long lines.

Eating in Oslo

My strategy is to splurge for a hotel that includes breakfast. A 50-kr Norwegian breakfast is fit for a Viking. Have a picnic for lunch or dinner, using one of the many grocery stores. Basements of big department stores have huge first-class supermarkets with lots of picnic dinner-quality alternatives to sandwiches. The little yogurt tubs with cereal come with a collapsible spoon. The train station has a late-hours grocery.

Oslo is awash with clever little budget eateries (modern, ethnic, fast food, pizza, department store cafeterias). Here are three places for those who want to eat like my Norwegian grandparents:

Kaffistova is an alcohol-free cafeteria serving simple, hearty, and typically Norwegian (read "bland") meals for the best price around. You'll get your choice of an entrée (meatballs) and all the salad, cooked vegetables, and "flat bread" you want (or, at least, need) for around 80 kr (open Monday–Friday 12:00–20:30, until 17:00 Saturday and 18:00 Sunday in summer, closes earlier off-season, 8 Rosenkrantzgate).

Norrøna Cafeteria is another traditional budget-saver (70-kr *dagens rett*, before 14:00 you'll get the same thing for 60 kr with a cup of coffee tossed in; Monday–Friday until 18:00, later off-season; central at 19 Grensen). For a classier traditional meal with a grand view, consider the Frogner-seteren restaurant (described above with the ski jump).

Vegeta Vertshus, which has been keeping Oslo vegetarians fat, happy, and low on the food chain for 60 years, serves a huge selection of hearty vegetarian food that would satisfy even a hungry Viking. Fill your plate once (small plate-73 kr, large plate-83 kr) or eternally for 114 kr. How's your balance? One plate did me fine (daily 11:00–23:00, no smoking, no meat, Munkedamsveien 3B, near top of Stortingsgata between palace and city hall, tel. 22 83 42 32).

The **Aker Brygge** (harborfront mall) development isn't cheap, but it has some cheery cafés, classy delis, open-'til-22:00 restaurants, and markets.

For a grand and traditional breakfast, consider the elegant spread at the **Bristol Hotel** (90 kr, a block off Karl Johans Gate behind the Grand Hotel).

Transportation Connections—Oslo

For train info, call 81 50 08 88 (7:00–23:00, phone tree, press 1 and wait).

By train to Bergen: Oslo and Bergen are linked by a spectacularly scenic seven-hour train ride. Reservations (20 kr) are required on all long and IC (express) trains. Departures are roughly at 7:45, 10:45, 14:45, 16:00, and 23:00 daily in both directions (500 kr, or 380 kr if you buy a day early and don't travel at peak times like Friday or Sunday). For more info, see "The Oslo–Bergen Train" section in the Fjords, Mountains, and Valleys chapter.

By boat to Copenhagen: Consider the cheap quickie cruise that leaves daily from Copenhagen (departs 17:00, returns 9:15 two days later; 16 hrs sailing each way and seven hrs in Norway's capital). See Copenhagen chapter for specifics.

By plane: Oslo's new Gardermoen Airport opens in 1998. Unlike the old airport, this one is far from town (30 miles to the north) but will be connected by a slick shuttle train to the central train station.

FJORDS, MOUNTAINS, AND VALLEYS

While Oslo and Bergen are the big touristic draws, Norway is essentially a land of natural beauty. There is a certain mystique about the "land of the midnight sun," but you'll get the most scenic travel thrills per mile, minute, and dollar by going west rather than north.

Leave Oslo and meander across the center of the country along an arc of tradition-steeped valleys, myth-inspiring Mountains, and troll-thrilling fjords. This chapter describes two ways to cover Norway's greatest natural charms:

1. A series of dramatic train, boat, and bus rides called "Norway in a Nutshell," which takes a day. Do it from Oslo (or from Bergen) or en route between Oslo and Bergen.

2. For those with a car and more time, the powerfully scenic arc up Gudbrandsdalen Valley, over the Jotunheimen Mountains, and down Norway's greatest fjord, Sognefjord.

Both routes cover the great Aurlandsfjord branch of Sognefjord.

FJORD COUNTRY AND "NORWAY IN A NUTSHELL"

Norway's greatest claims to scenic fame are her deep, lush fjords. A series of well-organized and spectacular bus, train, and ferry connections, appropriately called "Norway in a Nutshell," lays Norway's beautiful fjord country spread-eagled on a scenic platter. This is the seductive Sognefjord—tiny but tough ferries, towering canyons, and isolated farms and villages

Fjords, Mountains, and Valleys

marinated in the mist of countless waterfalls. You're an eager Lilliputian on the Norwegian Gulliver of nature.

Today the region enjoys mild weather for its latitude, thanks to the warm Gulf Stream. But 3 million years ago, an Ice Age made this land as inhabitable as the center of Greenland. Like the hairline on Dick Clark, the ice slowly receded. As the last glaciers of the Ice Age cut their way to the sea, they gouged out long grooves—today's fjords. Since the ice was thicker inland and only a relatively thin lip at the coast, the gouging was deeper inland. The average fjord is 4,000 feet deep far inland and only around 600 feet deep where it reaches the open sea.

The entire west coast is slashed by stunning fjords, but the Sognefjord, Norway's longest (120 miles) and deepest (over a mile), is tops. Anything but Sognefjord is, at best, foreplay. This is it, the ultimate natural thrill Norway has to offer.

Aurland, a good home base for your exploration, is on Aurlandsfjord, a remote, scenic, and accessible arm of the Sognefjord. The local weather is actually decent, with about

24 inches of rain per year, compared to more than 6 feet annually in nearby Bergen.

Planning Your Time

Even the blitz tourist needs a day for the "Norway in a Nutshell" trip. This is easily done as a long day trip from Oslo or Bergen. (All connections are designed for tourists, explained in English, convenient, and easy—see below.) Ideally, break the trip with an overnight in Flåm or Aurland, carry on into Bergen, and enjoy a day in Bergen before sleeping on the night train (past all the scenery you saw westbound) back to Oslo. Those with a car and only one day should take the train from Oslo. With more time, drivers can improve on the "Nutshell" by following the more time-consuming and thorough version of this scenic smørgåsbord explained in the second half of this chapter.

Norway in a Nutshell

The most exciting single-day trip you could make from Oslo or Bergen is this circular train/boat/bus/train jaunt through this spectacular chunk of fjord country. Rushed travelers zip in and out by train from Oslo or Bergen. Those with more time do the Nutshell segments at their leisure. It's famous, everybody does it, and if you're looking for the scenic grandeur of Norway, so should you.

Tourist offices have souvenir-worthy brochures with photos, descriptions, and exact times. The all-day trip starts by train every morning from Oslo and Bergen. It's a good day trip or an exciting way to connect the two cities. Here's the route in a nutshell: ride the Oslo–Bergen train to Myrdal (MIUR-doll); take the scenic Myrdal–Flåm train; hop on the Flåm–Gudvangen cruise; and then take the Gudvangen–Voss bus. (It's easy. Just follow the crowds.) At Voss, jump on the Oslo–Bergen train, and head west for Bergen or east for Oslo. The Nutshell trip is possible all year. Some say it's most beautiful in winter (but not possible as a day trip from Oslo).

Sample "Norway in a Nutshell" Schedules

Confirm all times. Nutshell connections are made even if trains/boats/buses are running late.

Oslo–Bergen: Train departs Oslo 7:42, arrives Myrdal 12:28, departs Myrdal 12:30, arrives Flåm 13:22, boat from Flåm

Norway in a Nutshell

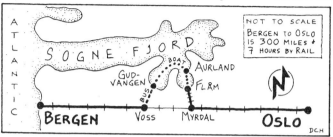

14:40, arrives Gudvangen 16:40, bus from Gudvangen 17:15, arrives Voss 18:30, train from Voss 19:00, arrives Bergen 20:18.

Day Trip from Oslo: Same as above through the arrival in Flåm, boat from Flåm 14:00, arrives Gudvangen 15:15, bus from Gudvangen 15:20, arrives Voss 16:40, train from Voss 16:48, arrives Oslo 22:21.

Bergen–Oslo: Train departs Bergen 8:30, arrives Voss 9:43, bus from Voss 10:00, arrives Gudvangen 11:25, boat from Gudvangen 11:30, arrives Flåm 13:40, train from Flåm 15:53, arrives Myrdal 16:50, train from Myrdal 17:33, arrives Oslo 22:21.

Day Trip from Bergen: Same as above through Flåm, train from Flåm 15:35, arrives Myrdal 16:16, departs Myrdal 16:23, arrives Bergen 18:33. There is also a fast boat from Flåm-to-Bergen return option. Tickets and info: Bergen tel. 55 96 69 00 or 81 50 08 88.

Sights—Norway in a Nutshell

▲▲**The Oslo–Bergen Train**—This is simply the most spectacular train ride in northern Europe. The scenery crescendos as you climb over Norway's mountainous spine. After a mild three hours of deep woods and lakes you're into the barren, windswept heaths, and glaciers. The line was started in 1894 to link Stockholm and Bergen. But Norway won its independence from Sweden in 1905 so the line served to link the two main cities in the new country.

The railway, an amazing engineering feat completed in 1909, is 300 miles long, peaks at 4,266 feet (which at this Alaskan latitude is far above the tree line), goes under 18 miles of snow sheds, trundles over 300 bridges, and passes through 200 tunnels in just under seven hours. (About 500 kr, second class one-way, 100 kr cheaper if you buy a day early and don't travel on Friday or Sunday, departures roughly 7:40, 10:45, 14:45, 16:00, and 23:00 daily in both directions, reservations required.) Nutshell travelers get off the Oslo–Bergen train at Myrdal and rejoin it later at Voss.

Leaving Oslo you pass through a 6-mile-long tunnel and stop in Drammen, Norway's fifth-largest town. The scenery stays mild and woodsy up Hallingdal valley until you reach Geilo, a popular ski resort. Then you enter a land of big views and tough little cabins. Finse, at about 4,000 feet, is the highest point on the line. From here, you enter the longest high mountain stretch of railway in Europe. Much of the line is protected by snow tunnels. The scenery is most dramatic the hour before and after Myrdal. Just before Myrdal look to the right, down into Flåm Valley (Flåmsdalen) where the 12-mile-long branch line winds its way down to the fjord.

▲▲Myrdal–Flåm Train—This little 12-mile spur line leaves the Oslo–Bergen line at Myrdal (2,800 feet, nothing but a scenic train junction with a decent cafeteria). From Myrdal, the train winds down to Flåm (sea level) in 50 thrilling minutes (90-kr ticket or 50-kr supplement for Eurail and Scanrail passholders). It's party time on board, and the conductor even stops the train for photos at the best waterfall. This line has 20 tunnels (more than 3 miles' worth) and is so steep that the train has five separate braking systems.

▲Flåm—On the Norway in a Nutshell route, this scenic, touristy transit junction at the head of the Aurlandsfjord is little more than a train station, ferry landing, grocery store, souvenir shop (overpriced reindeer pelts—cheaper in Bergen), cluster of hotels and hostels, and a helpful tourist office (daily June–September 8:30–20:30, then shorter hours, tel. 57 63 21 06). For accommodations, see Sleeping, below, or better yet, stay in nearby Aurland (see below). Nightlife in Flåm is sparse. A walk on the sandy beach is fine at twilight, if it's not too windy. Pubs include the more touristy and older Furnkroa at the ferry dock and Heimly Marina's pub, which serves pizza and beer and caters to a younger crowd.

▲▲▲Flåm–Gudvangen Fjord Cruise—At Flåm, if you're doing the Nutshell Suite, follow the crowds and hop on the sightseeing boat. Boats leave Flåm daily at 9:00, 11:05, 14:00, and 14:40, stopping at the town of Aurland, then continuing to Gudvangen (125 kr one-way, 63 kr for those with an ISIC card, no railpass discounts; couples ask for the "family" discount that lets the spouse go for half-price). The boat takes you right into the mist of the many fjord waterfalls and close to the goats, sheep, and awesome cliffs.

You'll cruise up the lovely Aurlandsfjord and hang a left at the stunning Nærøyfjord. It's a breathtaking voyage no matter what the weather does. For 90 glorious minutes, camera-clicking tourists scurry around the drool-stained deck like nervous roosters, scratching fitfully for a photo to catch the magic. Waterfalls turn the black rock cliffs into bridal veils, and you can nearly reach out and touch the Nærøyfjord's awesome sheer cliffs. The ride is the ultimate fjord experience. It's one of those fine times, like when you're high on the tip of an Alp, and a warm camaraderie spontaneously combusts between all the strangers who came together for the experience.

You can request a stopover in Undredal (see below) or Styvi (which has a farm museum, 20 kr). There's an idyllic 6-kilometer shoreline along the 17th-century postal road from Styvi to Bleikindli (ask if the boat stops there, but you'll likely have to walk back to Styvi for a ferry pickup to Gudvangen). If you do get off the boat, you can let the next boat know that you'd like to be picked up by turning on a signal light.

Gudvangen–Voss Bus—Gudvangen is little more than a boat dock and giant tourist kiosk. Norway Nutshellers get off the boat at Gudvangen and catch a bus (60 kr, about a one-hour ride, buses depart 12/day including each ferry landing) up the Nærøydalen (Narrow Valley) to Voss. Try to catch a bus taking the extra-scenic route via Stalheim. At the end of Nærøydalen the bus climbs a corkscrew series of switchbacks before stopping at the Stalheim Hotel for a last grand view back into fjord country.

Voss—A plain town in a lovely lake-and-mountain setting, Voss does have an interesting folk museum (daily June–August 10:00–19:00, closes earlier off-season), a 13th-century church, and a few other historic sights, but it's basically a home base for summer or winter sports. At Voss, the bus drops you at the train station (on the Oslo–Bergen train line). Drivers should zip right through. You can spend the night, but I wouldn't. **Kringsja Pension** is nice with a lake view (D-480 kr, Db-640 kr with breakfast, tel. 56 51 16 27) and the **Voss Youth Hostel** is luxurious (tel. 56 51 20 17). **Voss Camping**, on the lake, has huts, bikes, and rowboats (tel. 56 51 15 97). TI tel. 56 51 17 16.

More Fjord Sights

▲▲**Flåm Valley Bike Ride**—While the Myrdal–Flåm train is scenic, the ride doesn't do the view justice. For the best single-day's activity from Flåm, take the train to Myrdal, then hike or mountain bike the gravelly construction road back down to Flåm (four hours, great mountain scenery but no fjord views). Bring a picnic and extra film. The Flåm TI rents bikes (25 kr/hour, 125 kr/day for mountain bikes; costs 50-kr to take bike up to Myrdal on train). You could just hike the best two hours from Myrdal to Berekvam, where you can catch the train into the valley.

▲▲**Aurland**—A few miles north of Flåm, Aurland is more of a town and less of a tourist depot. Nothing exciting, but it's a good, easygoing fjord-side home base (see Sleeping, below). You can hike up the valley or tour the electrical works (public tours show visitors the source of most of Oslo's electricity from July to mid-August, Monday–Friday at 11:00 and 13:00). The harborside public library is a pleasant refuge and the 800-year-old church is worth a look.

The local *geitost* (goat's cheese) is sweet and delicious. Aurland has as many goats as people (1,900). The one who runs the tourist office speaks English (mid-June–August weekdays 9:00–19:00, weekends 10:00–17:00, shorter hours off-season, tel. 57 63 33 13, fax 57 63 32 80). Pick up the English-language Bergen guide.

Note: Every train (except for the late-night one) arriving in Flåm connects with a bus or boat to Aurland. Fifteen buses and at least four ferries link the towns daily. The Flåm–Gudvangen boat stops at Aurland en route, so it's easy to continue the Nutshell route from Aurland without backtracking to Flåm.

▲**Undredal**—This almost impossibly remote community of 52 families was accessible only by boat until 1985, when the road from Flåm was opened. Undredal has Norway's smallest still-used church (built in the 12th century, holds up to 40 people). The 15-minute drive from Flåm is mostly through a new tunnel. There's not much in the town, which is famous for its goat cheese and church, but I'll never forget the picnic I had on the ferry wharf. If you want the ferry to stop, turn on the blinking light (though some express boats will not stop). You'll sail by Undredal on the Flåm–Gudvangen boat. **Undredal Brygge** (the harborfront cafeteria) rents four modern, woody rooms (comfortable but on a back street with little character, Db-580 kr, Tb-680 kr, includes breakfast, N-5746 Undredal, tel. & fax 57 63 17 45).

▲▲**Sognefjord Scenic Express Boat**—Boats speed between Flåm and Bergen through the Sognefjord. Boats depart Bergen at 8:00 and arrive in Flåm at 13:30; depart Flåm at 15:30 and arrive in Bergen at 20:45 (675 kr, 520 kr round-trip if you return by train, discounted with ISIC card, daily in June, July, and August; all stop in Aurland, tel. 55 32 40 15).

Sleeping on Sognefjord
(7 kr = about $1)
Sleep Code: **S** = Single, **D** = Double/Twin, **T** = Triple, **Q** = Quad, **b** = bathroom, **CC** = Credit Card (**V**isa, **M**asterCard, **A**mex).

Sleeping in Flåm
Heimly Lodge is doing its best to go big time in a small-time town. It's clean, efficient, and the best normal hotel in town (25 rooms in hotel, seven in annex, S-450 kr, Sb-590 kr, D-650 kr, Db-800 kr, includes breakfast, CC:VMA, bike rental, N-5743 Flåm, tel. 57 63 23 00, fax 57 63 23 40). Their pricing is soft and complex. You can save by sleeping in their annex, providing your own sheets and skipping breakfast. Their cheap basic deal for a room in the hotel (if available), or in the annex, is: D-250 kr, Db-300 kr, add 50 kr per person for sheets and 75 kr per person for breakfast. Sit on the porch with new friends and watch the clouds roll down the fjord. Located 400 yards along the harbor from the station, they will pick up and drop off at the station/dock for 10 kr round-trip.

Flåm Youth Hostel and Camping Bungalows, recently voted Scandinavia's most beautiful campground, has the cheapest beds in the area. On the river just behind the Flåm train station, the Holand family offers dorm beds in four-bed hostel rooms (85 kr per bed with kitchenette, 35 kr for sheets, 25 kr extra if not a hostel member). They also have some doubles for 300 kr with bedding, four-bed cabins for 300 kr without sheets, and a deluxe cabin for 500 kr (tel. 57 63 21 21, fax 57 63 23 80). Note that the season is boom or bust here, and it can be crowded in July and August.

Sleeping in Aurland
The **Aabelheim Pension/Vangen Motel** complex, dominating the old center of Aurland, is run from one reception desk (CC:V, tel. 57 63 35 80, fax 57 63 35 95, Astrid). **Aabelheim**

Pension is far and away Aurland's best cozy-like-a-farmhouse place. "Cozy" is *koselig*, a good Norwegian word (six D-360 kr, 70-kr breakfasts are served in a wonderfully traditional dining room, fine old-time living room, open mid-June to early September). **Vangen Motel**, nestled between Aabelheim and the fjord, is a simple old hotel offering basic rooms, a big self-serve kitchen, and a dining and living area (Ds-450 kr, 350 kr when you BYO sheets, breakfast-70 kr, open all year). The motel has four-bed cabins right on the water for 350 kr without sheets.

 Aurland Fjord Hotel is big, modern, friendly, and centrally located, with more comfort (sauna, steam bath, TV) and less traditional coziness (30 rooms, Db-900 kr with breakfast, attached restaurant, CC:VMA, tel. 57 63 35 05, fax 57 63 36 22).

 At the farmhouse **Skahjem Gård**, Aurland's deputy mayor, Nils Tore, rents out family apartments (one 300-kr hut, five newer 500-kr huts, with private bath and kitchenettes, 35 kr extra per person for sheets, 2.5 km up the Oslo road from Aurland, tel. 57 63 33 29). It's a 20-minute walk from town, but Nils will pick up and drop off travelers at the ferry. This is best for families who are driving.

 Lunde Camping offers 14 cabins overlooking the river a mile out of Aurland (at the Aurland exit off the big road). Each cabin has four beds in two bunks, a kitchenette and river view (350 kr for up to four people in July, 300 kr the rest of the year, 40 kr extra per person for sheets, open April–October, generally full from June 20–August 20, tel. 57 63 34 12, fax 57 63 31 65, Jens Lunde).

 Eating in Aurland: The Vangen Motel runs the **Duehuset** pub (long hours, 70–180-kr dinners). For cheap eats on dockside picnic benches, gather a picnic at the late hours grocery story next to the Vangen Motel (9:00–22:00).

GUDBRANDSDALEN VALLEY

This in-depth look at scenic Norway is best for drivers with more time. Gudbrandsdalen Valley is the country of Peer Gynt, the Norwegian Huck Finn. This romantic valley of timeworn hills, log cabins, and velvet farms has connected northern and southern Norway since ancient times.

 Lillehammer, with Norway's best folk museum, provides an excellent introduction. You might spend the night in a log-and-sod farmstead-turned-hotel, tucked in a quiet valley under Norway's highest peaks.

Next, Norway's highest mountain pass takes you on an exhilarating roller-coaster ride through the heart of Jotunheimen (the "giant's home"), which bristles with Norway's most gigantic mountains.

The road then hairpins down into fjord country, a softer world of fjords full of medieval stave churches, peely fishing boats, and brightly painted shiplap villages.

Planning Your Time

While you could enjoyably spend five or six days in this area, on a three-week Scandinavian rampage, this slice of the region is worth three days. By car, I'd spend them like this:

Day 1: Leave Oslo early, spend midday at the Maihaugen Open-Air Folk Museum for a tour and picnic. Drive up Gudbrandsdalen Valley, making a short stop at the Lom church. Evening in Jotunheimen country.

Day 2: Drive out of the mountains, along Lustrafjord, over Hornadalen Pass, and into Aurlandsfjord. Sleep in Aurland.

Day 3: Cruise the Aurland and Nærøy fjords (round-trip) before carrying on to Bergen.

Sights—Gudbrandsdalen Valley

▲**Lillehammer**—This pleasant winter and summer resort town of 23,000 was the smallest town ever to host the winter Olympics (1994). At Håkon Hall, the 1994 Ice Hockey arena, you can try a bobsled simulator, visit a museum showcasing Olympics history, and see the "world-famous egg" from the Lillehammer opening ceremonies (15 kr, daily 9:00–19:00, less on weekends and off-season, 15-minute walk from the station towards Maihaugen, tel. 61 25 11 40). Lillehammer has a happy old wooden pedestrian zone and several interesting museums, including a popular transportation museum and the Maihaugen Open-Air Folk Museum (see below). Lillehammer's TI is right in the colorful pedestrian shopping zone (9:00–19:00, less on Sundays and off-season, tel. 61 25 92 99). For accommodations, see Sleeping, below.

▲▲▲**Maihaugen Open-Air Folk Museum**—Located in Lillehammer, this wonderfully laid-out look at the local culture provides an excellent introduction to the Gudbrandsdalen Valley. Anders Sandvig, a "visionary dentist," started the collection in 1887. The outdoor section has 150 old buildings from the Gudbrandsdalen region, with plenty of free English tours, crafts in action, and even people living there from ages ago (Williamsburg-style, July only).

Indoors, the "We won the land" exhibit gives a look at local life during the Ice Age, the Vikings, the plague, the Industrial Revolution, etc. The indoor museum also has the original shops of 40 crafts- and tradespeople (such as a hatter, cooper, bookbinder, and Dr. Sandvig's old dental office). There's a thorough English guidebook (50 kr), English descriptions at each house, and free 45-minute guided tours daily in English (11:00, 13:00, 15:00, and sometimes 17:00 or on request if you call in advance).

The museum welcomes picnickers and has a café and an outdoor cafeteria (60 kr, daily June–mid-August 9:00–18:00, shoulder season 10:00–17:00, in winter the park is open but the houses are closed, tel. 61 28 89 00; call to be sure you arrive for a tour, especially off-season). Ask on arrival about special events, crafts, or music, and don't miss the indoor museum. Maihaugen is a steep 30-minute walk or short bus ride from the Lillehammer train station.

▲**Eidsvoll Manor**—During the Napoleonic period, Denmark was about to give Norway to Sweden. This ruffled the patriotic feathers of Norway's Thomas Jeffersons and Ben Franklins, and in 1814, Norway's constitution was written and signed in this stately mansion (in the town of Eidsvoll Verk, north of Oslo). It's full of elegant furnishings and stirring history (2 kr, daily mid-June–mid-August 10:00–17:00, 12:00–14:00 in winter, tel. 63 95 13 04).

Scenic Drives—Two side trips give visitors a good dose of the wild beauty of this land. Peer Gyntveien is a 30-kr toll road that leaves E-6 at Tretten, looping west for 25 miles and rejoining E-6 at Vinstra. This trip sounds romantic, but it's basically a windy, curvy dirt road over a high desolate heath and scrub-brush plateau with fine mountain views: scenic, but so is E-6. The second scenic side trip, which is lesser known but more rewarding, is the Peer Gynt Seterveg.

▲**Lom**—This isn't much of a town—except for its great stave church, which causes the closest thing to a tour-bus jam this neck of the Norwegian woods will ever see. Drop by the church; you'll see its dark spire just over the bridge (20 kr, daily mid-June–mid-August 9:00–21:00, shorter off-season and during funerals, fine 5-kr leaflet, check out the little footbridge over the waterfall) and take advantage of the tourist information office (in

summer, Monday–Saturday 9:00–21:00, Sunday 10:00–19:00,
shorter hours off-season, tel. 61 21 12 86). I wouldn't sleep in
Lom, but if you would, see Sleeping, below.

Sleeping in Gudbrandsdalen Valley
(7 kr = about $1)
Gudbrandsdalen Valley is a very popular vacation valley for
Norwegians, and you'll find loads of reasonable small hotels and
campgrounds with huts (*hytter* means "bungalow," *rom* is "private room," and *ledig* means "vacancy") for those who aren't
quite campers. These huts normally cost around 200 kr and can
hold from four to six people. Although they are simple, you'll
have a kitchenette and access to a good WC and shower. When
available, sheets rent for an extra 40 kr per person. Local TIs can
find you rooms. Only in the middle three weeks of July will
finding a bed without a reservation prove difficult.

Sleeping in Lillehammer
The town's best budget hotel, with a great view of the valley, is
the **Gjestehuset Ersgaard** (13 rooms, D-490 kr, Db-590–
650 kr with breakfast, CC:VMA, 2 km east and above town at
Nordseterveien 201, tel. 61 25 06 84, fax 61 25 31 09). **Som-
merstuene** rents three rooms with kitchenettes (300–500 kr,
25 kr extra for sheets, family rooms, Kirkegata 6, 2600 Lillehammer, tel. 61 25 79 29). For cheap beds, try the **GjesteBu** private
hostel (eight-bed dorms, 60 kr per bed, D-250 kr and up, sheets
40 kr extra, Gamleveien 110, 3 blocks from TI, reserve in
advance, tel. 61 25 43 21) or the **IYHF hostel** in the train/bus
station (bed in quad-165 kr for members, sheets extra).

Sleeping in Kvam
The **Kirketeigen Ungdomssenter**, literally "Church Youth
Center," welcomes travelers all year long. They have camping places (80 kr per tent or van), huts (220 kr per four-
person hut), and very simple four-bed rooms (220 kr for two
to four people with sheets, CC:V). Sheets and blankets
(60 kr) can be rented (2650 Kvam i Gudbrandsdalen, located
behind the town church, tel. 61 29 40 82, fax 61 29 40 76,
call in advance). One hundred meters away is the **Sinclair
Vertshuset Motel**, which has an inexpensive pizzeria (Db-
590 kr with breakfast but no personality, cheaper off-season,
tel. 61 29 40 24, fax 61 29 45 55). The motel was named after

a Scotsman who led a band of adventurers into this valley,
attempting to set up their own Scottish kingdom. They
failed. (All were kilt.)

Sleeping in Lom
About 10 miles north of Røisheim, Lom has plenty of accommodations, such as the rustic **Strind Gard**. This 150-year-old
farmhouse offers rooms in sod-roofed huts and in the main
house (D-150–200 kr, T-230 kr, Quint-300 kr, great valley
views, 3 km outside Lom on Route 55 towards Sogndal, tel. 61
21 12 37).

JOTUNHEIMEN MOUNTAINS

Sights—Jotunheimen Mountains
▲▲**Sognefjell**—Norway's highest mountain crossing (4,600
feet) is a thrilling drive through a cancan line of northern
Europe's highest mountains. In previous centuries, the farmers
of Gudbrandsdalen took their horse caravans over this difficult
mountain pass on their necessary treks to Bergen. Today the
road (Route 55) is still narrow, windy, and otherworldly (and
usually closed from mid-October to May). The ten hairpin
turns between Turtagrø and Fortun are white-knuckle exciting. Be sure to stop, get out, look around, and enjoy the lavish
views. Treat each turn as if it were your last.
Scenic Drives and Hikes—From the main road near Bøverdal
and Røisheim, you have several options springing from three
toll roads. The Bøverdal hostel has good information and a
fine 1:150,000 hiking map.

  Spiterstulen: From Røisheim, this 18-km toll road (60 kr)
takes you to the Spiterstulen mountain hotel/lodge (1,100
meters). This is the best destination for serious all-day hikes to
Norway's two mightiest mountains: Glittertinden (2,470
meters) and Galdhøpiggen (a four-hour hike up and a three-
hour hike down, doable without a guide).

  Juvasshytta: This toll road, starting from Bøverdal, takes
you the highest you can drive and the closest you can get to
Galdhøpiggen by car (1,840 meters). At the end of the 50-kr
toll road, there are daily guided six-hour hikes across the
glacier to the summit and back (60 kr, 10:00 and 11:30 in the
summer, 6 km each way, hiking shoes a good idea, easiest
ascent but very dangerous without a guide). You can sleep in

the Juvasshytta lodge (D-400 kr, D without sheets-350 kr, 130 kr beds in quads, sheets-20 kr, breakfast-75 kr, dinner-140 kr, tel. 61 21 15 50).

Leirvassbu: This 18-km, 30-kr toll road is most scenic for "car hikers." It takes you to a lodge (owned by the Elvesæter Hotel people, see Sleeping, below) at 1,400 meters with great views and easy walks. A serious (four-hour round-trip) hike goes to the lone peak, Kyrkja (2,030 meters).

Besseggen: This ridge offers an incredible opportunity to hike between two lakes separated by 5 feet of land and a 1,000-foot cliff. To get to the trailhead, drivers detour down road #51 after Otta south to Maurvangen. Turn right to Gjendsheim to park your car. From Gjendesheim, catch the boat to Memurubu. The path starts at the boat dock. Hike along the ridge with a blue lake on one side and a green lake on the other, and keep your balance. The six-hour trail leads back to Gjendesheim. (This is a thrilling but potentially dangerous hike, and it's a major detour: Gjendesheim is about an hour, or 55 miles, from Røisheim.)

▲▲Jostedalsbre's Nigardsbreen Glacier Hike—Jostedalsbre is the most accessible branch of mainland Europe's largest glacier (185 square miles), and the Nigardsbreen Glacier Hike is a good chance for a hands-on glacier experience. It's an easy drive up Jostedal from Lustrafjord.

From Gaupne, drive up road #604 for 23 miles just past Gjerde, where the private 20-kr toll road continues 2 miles to the lake. Before the toll road (and 2.5 km past Gjerde), look for Breheimsenteret, an information center on the glacier and its history, at the entrance to the Nigard Glacier valley (daily in summer 9:00–19:00, May and September 10:00–17:00, tel. 57 68 32 50). From here take the special boat (15 kr round-trip, two 15-minute rides/hr, mid-June–mid-August 10:00–18:00) to within a 20-minute walk of the glacier.

The walk is steep and slippery. Follow the red marks. There are 90-minute guided "family" walks of the glacier (80 kr, 40 kr for kids, daily departures from 12:00 to 14:30 depending on demand, minimum age 5, I'd rate them PG-13 myself, you get clamp-on crampons). Tougher glacier hikes are also offered (starting at 175 kr including boots, real crampons, and more, daily 10:30 and 13:00, four hours, but you'll need to be at the Glacier Center nearly two hours early to buy tickets and pick up your gear, book by telephone the day before).

Respect the glacier. It's a powerful river of ice, and fatal accidents are not uncommon. The guided walk is the safest, and exciting enough. Use the Gaupne TI to confirm your plans (tel. 57 68 15 88). If this is your first glacier, it's worth the time and hike even without the tour. If glaciers don't give you tingles and you're feeling pressed, it's not worth the long drive.

Sleeping in Jotunheimen
(7 kr = about $1)

Røisheim and Elvesæter are just hotel road stops in the wild. Bøverdal, 2 miles up the road, is a tiny village with a hostel.

Røisheim, in a marvelously remote mountain setting, is a storybook hotel comprised of a cluster of centuries-old, sod-roofed log farmhouses. Filled with antiques, Norwegian travelers, and the hard work of its owners, Røisheim is a cultural end in itself. Each room is rustic but elegant (Db-900–1,200 kr without breakfast, CC:VM, Lars and Christina Aanes). Some rooms are in old log huts with low ceilings and heavy beams. Gilded-lily breakfasts are 125 kr, and a full three-course traditional dinner (one that Norway's royalty travels far to eat) is served at 19:00 (375 kr). Call ahead so they'll be prepared. (Open mid-May–September, 6 miles south of Lom on the Sognefjell Road 55 in Bøverdalen, tel. 61 21 20 31, fax 61 21 21 51.)

Elvesæter Hotel is as Old World romantic as Røisheim but cheaper and less impressed with itself (Db-550 kr with breakfast, wonderful 150-kr buffet dinners, open June–September, CC:VMA, a few minutes farther up Road 55, just past Bøverdal, tel. 61 21 20 00, fax 61 21 21 01). They also offer apartments with kitchens and all bedding (three to six people, 500–850 kr without breakfast). The Elvesæter family has done a great job of retaining the historic character of their medieval farm, even though the place is big enough to handle large tour groups. They have the dubious distinction of being, as far as I know, the only hotel in Europe that charges for its advertising flier (5 kr). It's scenic—but not that scenic.

Bøverdalen Youth Hostel, just a couple of miles from Røisheim, is in another galaxy price-wise (75 kr per bed in four- to six-bed rooms, D-190 kr, the usual extra for sheets and nonmembers, hot and self-serve meals, open mid-May–September, tel. & fax 61 21 20 64). It's in the center of a little community (store, campground, and toll road up to Galdhopiggen area). The hostel is a comfortable budget value. An added advantage is that you'll be encountering real hikers rather than car tourists.

LUSTRAFJORD

Sights—Lustrafjord

This arm of the famous Sognefjord is rugged country. Only 2 percent of this land is fit to build or farm on. Lustrafjord is ringed with tiny villages where farmers sell cherries and giant raspberries. Urnes, perched on the east bank of Lustrafjord, has an ancient stave church and a less ancient ferry dock (ferries connect with sleepy Solvorn on the west bank, car crossings at the bottom of each hour 10:00–17:50, pedestrian ferries more often, ten-minute ride, 30 kr round-trip).

▲▲**Urnes Stave Church**—A steep but pleasant 20-minute walk takes you from the town of Urnes to Norway's oldest stave church (b. 1150) and the most important artistic and historic sight in the region (40 kr, daily early June–late August 10:30–17:30, ask for an English tour).

Solvorn—Ten miles east of Sogndal, on the west bank of the Lustrafjord, Solvorn is a sleepy little Victorian town. Its tiny fjerry crosses the fjord regularly to Urnes (ten-minute ride, 40 kr round-trip). For accommodations, see Sleeping, below.

Sogndal—About a ten-minute drive from the Mannheller ferry, Sogndal is the only sizable town in this region. It's big enough to have a busy shopping street and a helpful tourist information office (tel. 57 67 30 83). See Sleeping, below.

Honorable Mention—As you drive along Lustrafjord, check out these towns and sights. Skjolden, a village at the north tip of Lustrafjord, has a helpful tourist office (tel. 57 68 67 50) with advice on fjord ferries and glacier hikes, and a cozy youth hostel on the river (85 kr per bed, D-200 kr, open mid-May–mid-September, tel. 57 68 66 15). From the little town of Nes on the west bank of the Lustrafjord, look across the fjord at the impressive Feigumfoss Waterfall. Drops and dribbles come from miles around for this 200-yard tumble. Viki Fjord Camping, located directly across from Feigumfoss Waterfall, has great fjord-side huts (tel. 57 68 64 20). Dale, a village on the west bank, boasts a 13th-century stone Gothic church with 14th-century frescoes. It's unique and worth a peek.

Kaupanger–Gudvangen by Car Ferry—Ferries take tourists through an arm and elbow of the Sognefjord. Marvel at the staggering Nærøyfjord. Boats leave Kaupanger daily at 9:20, 12:05, 16:00, and 18:50 (two-hour trip, ferry info tel. 57 74 62 00 or 94 50 65 20). Kaupanger is a ferry landing set on the scenic Sognefjord, and little more. The little stave-type church at the edge of Kaupanger merits a look.

▲▲**Sogndal/Mannheller/Fodnes/Lærdal/Hornadalen/Aurland Scenic Drive**—This drive takes you over an incredible mountain pass, offers classic aerial fjord views, and winds into the pleasant fjord-side town of Aurland. Near Sogndal, catch the Mannheller–Fodnes ferry (15-minute ride, 2/hour, no reservations so arrive early in summer) and drive through the tunnel to Lærdal. While work is in progress on a 24-kilometer- long tunnel from Lærdal under Hornadalen to Aurland (this will be the world's longest tunnel when it opens in 2000), the scenic route over the pass is worth the messy pants. Leave E-68 at Erdal (just west of Lærdal) for the breathtaking 90-minute drive to Aurland over 4,000-foot-high Hornadalen. This summer-only road passes remote mountain huts and terrifying mountain views before its 12-hairpin zigzag descent into the Aurlandsfjord. Stop at the first fjord viewpoint as you begin your descent; it's the best.

Short-cut scenically and directly from Kaupanger to Gudvangen by ferry (4/day, 185 kr for car and driver, 53 kr per adult passenger) to get a quick taste of all this fjord scenery

Sleeping on Lustrafjord
(7 kr = about $1)

Sleeping in Solvorn
Walaker Hotel, a former inn and coach station, has been run by the Walaker family for 307 years (that's a lot of pressure on the next generation). In the main house, tradition drips like butter through the halls and living rooms. The rooms are simple but good, a warm family feeling pervades, and there are only patriotic hymns on the piano. The Walaker, set right on the Lustrafjord (in the perfect garden to get over a mental breakdown), is open mid-April to mid-October. Oda and Hermod Walaker are a wealth of information, and they help serve fine food (D-660 kr, Db-980 kr with breakfast, dinners are worth the 260-kr splurge, CC:VM, tel. 57 68 42 07, fax 57 68 45 44).

Sleeping in Sogndal
For budget rooms, try the home of **Bjarne and Ella Skield-estad** (150 kr per person, kitchenette, on the main drag at Gravensteinsgate 10, tel. 57 67 21 83), the **Loftenes Pensjonat** (D-550 kr, Db-600 kr with breakfast, CC:VM, near the water, tel. 57 67 15 77), or the excellent **youth hostel** (beds in three- and four-bed rooms for 90 kr, S-160 kr, D-210 kr, sheets and guest membership extra, breakfast-50 kr, members' kitchen—bring your own pots; at fork in the road as you enter town, closed 10:00–17:00 and mid-August to mid-June, tel. 57 67 20 33).

Transportation Connections
Cars are better, but if you're without wheels: **Oslo to Lillehammer** (11 trains/day, 2.5 hrs), **Lillehammer to Otta** (4 trains/day); a bus meets the train for travelers heading on to **Lom** (1 hr, 60 kr), **Lom to Sogndal** (2 buses/day).

Route Tips for Drivers
Oslo across Norway to Jotunheimen: It's 2.5 hours from Oslo to Lillehammer and four hours after that to Lom. Wind out of Oslo following signs for E-6 (not to Drammen, but for several yards to Stockholm and then to Trondheim). In a few minutes you're in the wide-open pastoral countryside of eastern Norway. Norway's Constitution Hall is a five-minute detour off E-6, a couple of miles south of Eidsvoll in Eidsvoll Verk (follow the signs to Eidsvoll Bygningen). Then E-6 takes you along Norway's largest lake (Mjosa), through the town of Hamar, over a toll bridge (15 kr), and past more nice lake scenery into Lillehammer. The old E-6 stays east of the lake, is only marginally slower, and avoids the toll bridge. Signs direct you uphill from downtown Lillehammer to the Maihaugen museum. There's free parking near the pay lot (10 kr) above the entrance. Then E-6 enters the valley of Gudbrandsdalen. From Lillehammer, cross the bridge again and follow signs to E-6/Dombås and Trondheim. At Otta, exit for Lom.

   Mountain driving tips: Use low gears and lots of patience both up (to keep it cool) and down (to save your brakes). Uphill traffic gets the right-of-way, but drivers, up or down, considerately dive for the nearest fat part whenever they meet. Ask backseat drivers not to scream until you've actually been hit or have left the road.

Ferry travel: Car ferries and express boats connect towns along the Sognefjord and Bergen. Ferries cost roughly $4 per hour for walk-ons and $14 per hour for a car, driver, and passenger. Reservations are generally not necessary (and sometimes not possible), but in summer, especially on Friday and Sunday, I'd get one to be safe (free and easy, tel. 55 32 40 15).

From Gudvangen to Bergen (85 miles): From Gudvangen, drive up the Nærøydalen (Narrow Valley) past a river bubbling excitedly about the plunge it just took. You'll see the two giant falls just before the road marked "Stalheimskleiva." Follow the sign (exiting left) to the little Stalheimskleiva road. This incredible road doggedly worms its way up into the ozone. My car overheated in a few minutes. Take it, but take it easy. (The main road gets you there easier—through a tunnel and 1.3 km back up a smaller road.) As you wind up, you can view the falls from several turnouts. At the top, stop for a break at the friendly but very, very touristy Stalheim Hotel. This huge eagle's-nest hotel is a stop for just about every tour group that ever saw a fjord. Here, genuine trolls sew the pewter buttons on the sweaters, and the priceless view is free.

The road continues into a mellower beauty, past lakes and farms, toward Voss. Tvindefossen, a waterfall with a handy campground/WC/kiosk picnic area right under it, is worth a stop. Unless you judge waterfalls by megatonnage, this 150-yard-long fall has nuclear charms. The grassy meadow and flat rocks at its base were made especially for your picnic lunch.

The highway takes you through Voss and into Bergen. From Monday through Friday, 6:00 to 22:00, drivers pay a 5-kr toll to enter Bergen. (If you plan to visit Edvard Grieg's home and the nearby Fantoft stave church, now is the ideal time since you'll be driving right by. Both are overrated but almost obligatory, a headache from downtown, and open until 17:30.)

BERGEN

Bergen has a rugged charm, permanently salted with robust cobbles and a rich sea-trading heritage. Norway's capital in the 12th and 13th centuries, Bergen's wealth and importance were due to its membership in the heavyweight medieval trading club of merchant cities called the Hanseatic League. Bergen still wears her rich maritime heritage proudly.

Famous for its lousy weather, Bergen gets an average of 80 inches of rain annually (compared to 30 inches in Oslo). A good year has 60 days of sunshine. With 221,000 people, Bergen has its big-city tension, parking problems, and high prices. But visitors stick mainly to the old center.

Enjoy her salty market, then stroll the easy-on-foot old quarter. From downtown Bergen, a funicular zips you up a little mountain for a bird's-eye view of this sailors' town. And as Bergen gets ready for its reign as Europe's City of Culture in the year 2000, it will be more inviting than ever.

Planning Your Time

Bergen can be enjoyed even on the tail end of a day's scenic train ride from Oslo before returning on the overnight train. But that teasing taste will make you wish you had more time. On a three-week tour of Scandinavia, Bergen is worth a whole day. Start that day at the harborfront fish market and spend the rest of the morning in the Bryggen quarter (the tour is a must).

Bergen, a geographic dead end for most, is an efficient place to end your Scandinavian tour. Consider flying home from here. (Ask your travel agent about the economic feasibility of this "open jaws" option.)

Orientation

The action is on the waterfront. Virtually everything in this chapter is within a few minutes' walk of the fish market. The busy Torget (market square and fish market) is at the head of the bay. Facing the sea from here, Bergen's TI and historic "Hanseatic" quarter (Bryggen) line the harbor on the right, and boats from Flåm and Stavanger tie up at the left side of the harbor. Two blocks from the market square or Torget (behind Bryggen), a funicular stands ready to whisk you to the top of Mount Fløyen.

Tourist Information

On the harborfront in the old town, this TI covers Bergen and West Norway. They change money at 4 percent less than the banks, but they don't charge the typical 15-kr-per-check fee for traveler's checks or cash; they're OK if you're exchanging less than $100 or if you're stuck with small checks in Norway. The TI also has information and tickets for tours and concerts and a daily events board (May–September Monday–Saturday 8:30–21:00, Sunday 10:00–19:00; off-season 9:00–16:00, closed Sunday; a ten- to 15-minute walk from the train station, tel. 55 32 14 80). From late May through late August, there's also a TI at the train station (daily 7:15–23:00). Pick up a free *Bergen Guide*, which lists all sights, hours, and special events and has a fine map. The **Bergen Card** gives you 24 hours of city buses, the Mount Fløyen funicular, and admission to many sights for 120 kr (48 hours for 190 kr). But check carefully to see if it will pay off for you, as it doesn't cover the Hanseatic Museum or Troldhaugen.

Arrival in Bergen

By Train or Bus: Bergen's train and bus stations are on Strømgaten, facing a park-rimmed lake. Walk around the lake to Ole Bulls Plass, then take a right on the wide street called Torgelmenning, which leads down to Torget (a ten- to 15-minute walk from the station), where you'll find Bergen's famous and fragrant fish market and the waterfront.

By Plane: The SAS bus runs between Bergen's Flesland Airport and downtown Bergen, stopping at the SAS hotel in

Bergen and Harbor

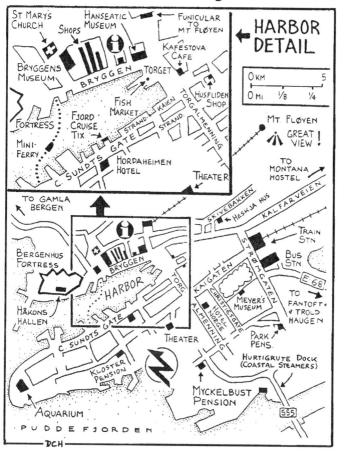

Bryggen, Hotel Norge, and the bus station at platform 17 (40 kr, 40 min). Taxis take up to four people and cost about 200 kr for the 30-minute ride. SAS info tel. 55 99 75 90 or 81 00 33 00.

Getting Around Bergen

Most sights are walkable. Buses cost 15 kr per ride or 90 kr for a 48-hour Tourist Ticket (purchase as you board). The best buses for a city joyride are #1 (along the coast) and #4 (into the hills). The *Beffen*, a little orange ferry, chugs across the harbor every half-hour (8 kr, Monday–Friday). This three-minute "poor man's cruise" has great harbor views. Bikes are rented at the bus station and at the TI (only 50-kr/day but only four bikes so pay the day before to reserve). For a taxi call 55 99 70 00.

Sights—Bergen's Hanseatic Quarter

Called "the German wharf" until WWII, now just called "the wharf," or "Bryggen" (BREW-gun), this is Bergen's old German trading center. From 1370 to 1754, German merchants controlled Bergen's trade. In 1550, it was a German city of 2,000 workaholic merchants—walled and surrounded by 8,000 Norwegians. Bryggen, which has burned down several times, is now gentrified and boutiquish but still lots of fun. Explore. You'll find plenty of sweater shops, restaurants, planky alleys, leaning old wooden warehouses, good browsing, atmospheric eating, and two worthwhile museums within a five-minute walk of each other.

 ▲▲▲**Walking Tour**—Local guides take visitors on an excellent 90-minute walk through the old Hanseatic town (30 minutes in Bryggens Museum, 30-minute walk through old quarter and Schøtstuene, and 30 minutes in Hanseatic Museum). This is a great way to get an understanding of Bergen's 900 years of history. Tours cost 60 kr and leave from the Bryggens Museum (next to the big modern SAS Hotel). When you consider that the tour cost includes entry tickets to the Hanseatic and Bryggens Museums and the medieval assembly rooms called the Schøtstuene (worthwhile only with a guide), the tour is virtually free (daily at 11:00 and 13:00 June–August; you can re-enter museums; tel. 55 31 67 10).

▲▲**Hanseatic Museum**—This wonderful little museum is in an atmospheric old merchant house furnished with dried fish, old ropes, an old oxtail (used for wringing spilled cod-liver oil back into the bucket), sagging steps, and cupboard beds from the early 1700s, one with a medieval pinup (35 kr, daily in summer 9:00–17:00; off-season weekdays 11:00–14:00, Saturday 12:00–15:00, and Sunday 12:00–16:00, good guided tours, tel. 55 31 41 89).

▲▲**Bryggens Museum**—This modern museum on the archaeological site of the earliest Bergen (1050–1500), with interesting temporary exhibits upstairs, offers little English information. To understand the exhibits you can borrow the museum guidebook, take the free 30-minute Walkman tour, or join the guided walk explained above. You can see the actual excavation for free from the window just below St. Mary's Church (20 kr, 10:00–17:00, less off-season, tel. 55 31 67 10). The museum has a good, inexpensive cafeteria with soup-and-bread specials.

St. Mary's Church—Dating from about 1150, this is Bergen's oldest building and one of Norway's finest churches (10 kr, summer Monday–Friday 11:00–16:00).

▲▲**Fish Market**—This famous, bustling market has become touristy but still offers lots of smelly photo fun (Monday–Friday 7:00–16:00, Saturday until 15:00). Don't miss it. This could be the only outdoor fish market that accepts credit cards.

More Sights—Bergen

▲**Håkon's Hall/Rosenkrantz Tower**—These reminders of Bergen's medieval importance sit barren and boldly out of place on the harbor just beyond Bryggen. Håkon's Hall was a royal residence 700 years ago when Bergen was the political center of Norway. Tours of both start in Håkon's Hall and leave on the hour (15 kr, May–September 10:00–16:00, 45-minute tours, last tour at 15:00 daily, shorter hours off-season, tel. 55 31 60 67). There's a great harbor view from the tower's rooftop.

▲▲**Fløibanen**—Just 2 blocks up from the fish market, ride the funicular to the top of "Mount" Fløyen (1,000 feet up in eight minutes) for the best view of the town, surrounding islands, and fjords all the way to the west coast. The top is a popular picnic or pizza-to-go dinner spot (Peppe's Pizza is a block away from the base of the lift) and the jumping off point for many peaceful hikes. Sunsets are great here. It's a pleasant walk back down into Bergen. But to save your knees, you can get off at the "Promsgate" stop halfway down and then wander through the delightful cobbled and shiplap lanes (30 kr round-trip, departures each way on the half-hour and often on the quarter-hour until 23:00). This is actually used by locals commuting into and out of downtown.

▲▲**Wandering**—Bergen is a great strolling town. The harborfront is a fine place to kick back and watch the pigeons mate. Other good areas to explore are Klostergate, Marken, Knosesmanet, Ytre Markevei, and the area behind Bryggen. The modern town also has a pleasant ambience, especially around Ole Bulls Plass.

▲▲**Aquarium**—Small but great fun if you like fish, this aquarium, wonderfully laid out and explained in English, claims to be the second-most-visited sight in Norway. A pleasant 20-minute walk from the center, it has a cheery cafeteria with fresh fish sandwiches (45 kr, daily 9:00–20:00, off-season 10:00–18:00, feeding times 11:00, 14:00, and 18:00, bus #4, tel. 55 23 85 53).

▲**Old Bergen**—Gamle Bergen is a Disney-cute gathering of 40 18th- and 19th-century shops and houses offering a cutesy, cobbled look at "the old life." The town is free, and some of the buildings are art galleries and gift shops. English tours departing on the hour (40 kr) get you into the 20 or so museum buildings (daily mid-May–August 11:00–17:00, with English guided tours on the hour, tel. 55 25 78 50). Take bus #9, #20, or #22 from Bryggen (direction Lonborg) to Gamle Bergen (first stop after the second tunnel).

▲▲**Art Museums**—If you need to get out of the rain (or want to see more of Dahl, the realist Krogh, Munch, and other Norwegian painters), check out Rasmus Meyer's Collection (35 kr, 7 Rasmus Meyers Alle). The Stenersen Collection next door has some interesting modern art, including Munch and Picasso (35 kr). Both are free with the Bergen Card.

▲**Various City Tours**—The tourist information center sells tickets to several tours, including a daily 90-minute introduction at 17:00 (90 kr) and a daily two-hour tour at 14:30 (125 kr). These tours, which leave from the TI, are barely worthwhile for a quick orientation. More fun and very informative, if you're into city tours, are the harbor tours (14:30, from the fish market, aboard the *White Lady*, tel. 55 25 90 00) and the tacky tourist train with English-language headphone tours. Both cost 70 kr for 50 minutes and leave on the hour from the harborfront.

▲**Fantoft Stave Church**—The huge, preserved-in-tar, most-touristy-stave-church-in-Norway burned down in 1992. It was rebuilt and reopened in 1997, but it can never be the same. Situated in a quiet forest next to a mysterious stone cross, this 12th-century wooden church is bigger, but no better, than others covered in this book. But it's worth a look if you're in the neighborhood, even after hours, for its evocative setting (30 kr, daily 10:30–13:30, 14:00–17:30 in season).

▲**Edvard Grieg's Home, Troldhaugen**—Norway's greatest composer spent his last 22 years here (1885–1907), soaking up inspirational fjord beauty and composing many of his greatest works. In a very romantic Victorian setting, the ambience of the place is pleasant, even for non-fans, and essential to anyone who knows and loves Grieg's music. The house is full of memories, and his little studio hut near the water makes you want to sit down and modulate. Unfortunately, it gets the "Worst Presentation for a Scandinavian Historical Sight" Award, since it's mobbed with tour groups, offers nothing in English, and uses no imagination in mixing Grieg's music with the house (40 kr, daily May–September 9:00–18:00, tel. 55 91 17 91). Ask the tourist office about concerts in the concert hall at the site (100 kr, plus 50 kr for the shuttle bus from the TI, Wednesday and Sunday at 19:30, Saturday at 14:00 in late July and August; arrive one hour early for tickets).

The TI's free "Bergen Guide" pamphlet gives bus directions to Troldhaugen (the bus leaves you with a 30-minute walk). The daily three-hour bus tour (10:00, 180 kr) is worthwhile for the very informative guide and the easy transportation. If you've seen other stave churches and can't whistle anything by Grieg, skip them.

Shopping—The Husfliden Shop (just off the market at 3 Vågsalmenning) is a fine place for handmade Norwegian sweaters and goodies (good variety and quality but expensive). Like most shops, it's open Monday through Friday 9:00 to 16:30, Thursday until 19:00, Saturday 9:00 to 14:00. Major shops are closed on Sunday, but shop-til-you-drop tourists manage to find plenty of action even on the day of rest.

Folk Evenings—The "Fana Folklore" show is Bergen's most advertised folk evening. An old farm hosts this very touristy collection of cultural clichés, with food, music, dancing, and colorful costumes. While many think it's too gimmicky, and many think it's lots of fun, *nobody* likes the meager dinner (200 kr includes the short bus trip and the meal; most nights June–August 19:00–22:30; tel. 55 91 52 40).

The **Bergen Folklore show** is a smaller, less gimmicky program, featuring a good music-and-dance look at rural and traditional Norway. Performances are downtown at the Bryggens Museum (Tuesday and Thursday evenings at 21:00, June to August, tickets for the one-hour show are 95 kr at the TI or at the door, tel. 55 31 95 50).

Scenic Boats and Trains from Bergen—The TI has several brochures on tours of the nearby Hardanger and Sogne fjords. There are plenty of choices. For all the specifics on "Norway in a Nutshell," a scenic combination of buses, ferries, and trains, that can be done in a day from Bergen (7:33–16:16 or

8:30–18:33, reservation required), see the Fjords, Mountains, and Valleys chapter.

Sleeping in Bergen
(7 kr = about $1)

Sleep Code: **S** = Single, **D** = Double/Twin, **T** = Triple, **Q** = Quad, **b** = bathroom, **CC** = Credit Card (**V**isa, **M**asterCard, **A**mex).

There are two kinds of demands on the hotel scene in Bergen: business travelers fill up the fancy hotels outside of summer and weekends, and tourists take the budget places from July through mid-August. If you want a simple, comfy place in summer, reservations are advisable. If you just show up in summer, unless you're unlucky and hit some convention, you'll get a great deal on a business-class hotel. While Bergen lacks the great summer discounts found in other big Nordic cities, if you can handle showers down the hall and cooking breakfast yourself in the communal kitchens, several pensions offer better rooms with homey atmospheres and fine central locations for half the hotel prices.

The private homes I list are cheap, central, and quite professional. The cheapest dorm/hostel-style beds don't cost much less than the private homes, and unless the shoestring you're traveling on is really frazzled or you like to hang out with other vagabonds and hostelers, I'd stick with the private rooms. The tourist office is helpful in finding the least expensive rooms (for a 20-kr fee).

Consider the **Bergen Package**, giving you a bed, big breakfast, and Bergen Card (worth 120 kr) for from 325 kr per person (double occupancy) depending on the fancy hotel you choose (good only on Friday, Saturday, or Sunday or from mid-June–mid-August, purchase through your hometown travel agent or upon arrival). The arithmetic: Db + card for 650 kr. If you'd each buy a card anyway, that gives you an 800-kr double with buffet breakfast for about 410 kr . . . wow.

Laundromat: Jarlens Vaskeri (Monday–Friday 10:00–18:00, Saturday 9:00–15:00, closed Sunday, Lille Ovregate 17, near Korskirken, tel. 55 32 55 04).

Sleeping in Hotels and Pensions

If you must have a uniformed person behind the key desk, the prestigious old **Hotel Hordaheimen** is central, just off the harbor, and a good budget-hotel bet (Db-995 kr, 650 kr on off-season weekends, or 800 kr in summer with reservations no more than 48 hours in advance, CC:VMA, C. Sundts Gate 18, tel. 55 23 23 20, fax 55 23 49 50). Run by the same alcohol-free, give-the-working-man-a-break organization that brought you Kaffistova restaurants, their cafeteria, open late, serves traditional, drab, inexpensive meals.

Rainbow Hotel Bristol, a big, modern, all-the-comforts place in the center of town, is one of a chain of hotels which offer less character but more comfort for the krone (three price tiers—regular: Sb-775 kr, Db-1,090 kr; Friday/Saturday/Sunday night mid-September–mid-May: Sb-480 kr, Db-680 kr; and booked within 48 hours mid-June–mid-August only: Sb-510 kr, Db-725 kr, includes breakfast, extra bed-150 kr, a block off Ole Bulls Plass at Torglamenningen 11, N-5014 Bergen, tel. 55 23 23 44, fax 55 23 23 19). **Hotel Bryggen Orion** beyond Bryggen near Håkon's Hall offers similar comfort, location, and value (Bradbenken 3, tel. 55 31 80 80, fax 55 32 94 14).

Mycklebust Pension, a family-run explosion of homey-ness, offers better rooms than the Hordaheimen but provides pension rather than hotel services. It's friendly and central (a five-minute walk to market), with your own kitchen and laundry service, and showers down the hall (six rooms, D-470 kr, Db-520 kr, extra bed-100 kr, breakfast-25 kr, Rosenberggate 19, tel. 55 90 16 70, fax 55 23 18 01).

Kloster Pension, in a funky cobbled neighborhood 4 blocks off the harbor, has basic doubles including breakfast (S-300 kr, D-450 kr, Db-600 kr, Strange Hagen 2, tel. 55 90 21 58, fax 55 23 30 22). **Fagerheim Pension** offers some of the cheapest doubles in town (S-220 kr, D-400 kr, breakfast extra, up King Oscar's Gate half a mile, Kalvedalsveien 49A, tel. 55 31 01 72). **Park Pension** is classy, nearly a hotel, and in a wonderful neighborhood—central but residential. People who have the money for a cheap hotel but want Old World lived-in elegance love this place (40 rooms, 20 of them in the classy old hotel, 20 in a nearby annex, Sb-610 kr, D-620 kr, Db-750 kr, includes breakfast, summer and weekend discounts, CC:VMA, Harald Hårfagres Gate 35, tel. 55 32 09 60, fax 55 31 03 34).

Sleeping in Rooms in Private Homes

Since the Bergen hotel owners don't quite understand the magic of the marketplace, there are more private homes opening up to travelers than ever. While (for a price) the TI would love to help you out, here are several you can book direct. They are cheap, quite private, and lack a lot of chatty interaction with your hosts. The first two are the most central.

Alf and Elisabeth Heskja are a young couple with four doubles, one shared shower/WC, and a kitchen. This is my home in Bergen, and far better than the hostel for budget train travelers (D-280 kr, 17 Skivebakken, 5018 Bergen, reserve in advance, tel. 55 31 30 30, fax 55 31 30 90, e-mail: heskja@online.no). It's located five minutes from the train station (down King Oscar's Gate, uphill on D. Krohns Gate, up the stairs at the end of the block) on Skivebakken, the steep, cobbled, "most painted street in Bergen." The Heskjas also rent rooms out of a building at Veiten 2b (a block off Ole Bull Plass, farther from station but closer to the city action, bigger rooms, not quite as cute but still a fine deal).

The **Olsnes' home** is nearby (S-160 kr, Sb-180 kr, D-270 kr, Db-320 kr, 24 Skivebakken, tel. 55 31 20 44, run by Yngve).

Skansen Pensjonat rents seven rooms out of a classy old house situated a steep but scenic five-minute climb above the entrance to the Fløibanen lift overlooking the fish market (S-300–350 kr, D-450 kr, fancy D on corner with view and balcony-600 kr, includes breakfast, a bit cheaper off-season, two showers on ground floor, sinks in rooms, homey family room with TV, one parking place, look for bed symbol above the Fløibanen station, Vetrlidsalmenning 29, N-5014 Bergen, tel. 55 31 90 80, run by Alvaer family).

The **Vågenes family** has six doubles in a large, comfortable house on the edge of town (D-270 kr, Db-320 kr, breakfast-35 kr, big rooms with kitchens, easy parking, J.L. Mowinckelsvei 95, tel. 55 16 11 01). It's ten minutes from downtown on bus #60. Driving from downtown, cross the Puddefjordsbroen bridge (Road 555), go through the upper tunnel on Road 540, and turn left 200 meters after tunnel on J.L. Mowinckelsvei until Helge-plasset Street, just past the Hagesenter on right.

Sleeping in Hostels

For 100 kr at the **YMCA Interrail Center,** you get a bed in 12- to 70-person rooms (one for women, one for men, the others mixed) 2 blocks off the fish market. If you don't have a sleeping bag, you can rent sheets and blankets for 30 kr (mid-June–mid-September 7:00–01:00, always a place available, lots of budget travel activities organized, five minutes from the station, near the center, Nedre Korskirke alm #4, tel. 55 31 72 52, fax 55 31 35 77).

Montana Youth Hostel (IYHF) is one of Europe's best hostels, but its drawbacks are the remote location and relatively high price. Still, the bus connections (#4, 15 minutes from the center) and the facilities (modern five-bed rooms, classy living room, no curfew, huge parking lot, members' kitchen) are excellent (150 kr per bed in quints with a big breakfast, sheets-30 kr, nonmembers pay 25 kr extra, 30 Johan Blydts Vei, tel. 55 29 29 00).

Eating in Bergen

Eating in Bryggen
All of these places are in the old Hanseatic quarter (with rarely a street number but always a sign). They serve traditional Norsk food in candlelit old Norsk ambience (meals 150 kr to 220 kr, as usual, more potatoes are yours on request). If you're in the mood for a little Donner or Blitzen, look no farther. To avoid a wait, you may want to call in a reservation.

Bryggestuene and Loft, actually one restaurant with one menu on two levels with two different styles, offers good (but smoky) atmosphere and seafood and traditional meals. Except in summer, they offer a 70-kr *dagens* menu (daily 11:00–23:30, #11 in the Bryggen harborfront, tel. 55 31 06 30). If there's a line downstairs, go upstairs.

Bryggen Tracteursted serves moderately-priced Norwegian food in the oldest pub in town (daily from noon, deep in the atmospheric center of Bryggen, follow signs from front street, tel. 55 31 40 46).

Enhjørningen, or "The Unicorn," serves some of Bergen's best seafood dinners and offers its 150-kr seafood lunch buffet (available Monday–Saturday 12:00–16:00) to readers of this book for 100 kr. For this deal no reservations are taken, but it's easy to find a seat after 14:00 (200 kr for lavish seafood dinners, look for the anatomically correct unicorn on the old wharf facade, tel. 55 32 79 19.)

Facing the Harbor
Perhaps the tastiest and most memorable cheap meal in Bergen would be a seafood picnic picked up right at the **Fisketorvet**

(fish market). The stalls are bursting with salmon sandwiches, fresh shrimp, and fish cakes. And for dessert, Baker Brun is right there with *skillingsbolle* (cinnamon rolls) still warm out of the oven. For small, cozy, and untouristy places with the best prices, walk around the Korskirken (church) 2 blocks off the market square and check out the four or five little no-nonsense eateries.

Zachariasbryggen is a restaurant complex filling a pier at the head of the harbor (on Torget). It thrives with eateries all day and is a lively nightspot. You'll find **Baker Brun** (open from 9:00, fresh pastries, sandwiches, seating around back or take-away), Chinese, Italian, and great Mexican food (**Skibet Tex-Mex**, daily 12:00–23:00, 150-kr dinners, upstairs inside, great harbor view seats, tel. 55 55 96 50). **Freddie's**, a piano bar, is open late and popular with locals.

Kaffistova til Ervingen Cafeteria, overlooking the fish market (in the building with the Eskimo on top), is a good basic food value with fine Norwegian atmosphere in its first-floor self-service cafeteria (50-kr breakfasts, 80-kr dinners, Monday–Friday 8:00–21:00, Saturday 8:00–17:00, Sunday 11:00–18:00, closed earlier off-season, second floor, 2 Strandkaien, tel. 55 32 30 30). The **Kafe Bergenhus**, next door, offers similar food and prices (10:00–17:00). For old Norwegian fare, eat at the borderline-dreary cafeteria in the **Hordaheimen Hotel**, offering cheap 49-kr meals and lots of *lefse*.

From Ole Bull's Square up to the Theater

Bergen's "in" cafés are stylish, cozy, small, and open very late—great places to experience the local yuppie scene. The trendy **Café Opera** is good (80-kr dinners, 37-kr soup-and-bread specials, live music many Fridays and Saturdays, live locals nightly, English newspapers, chess, across from theater, Engen 18, tel. 55 23 03 15). **Kjøttbørsen**, literally "meat market," is a splurge local carnivores enjoy (hearty servings, 200-kr meals, closed Sunday, Vaskerelven 6, tel. 55 23 14 59). **På Folkemunne** is pricey but popular with locals (170-kr meals, Ole Bulls Plass 9). A good place for a drink is **Dickens** on Ole Bulls Plass, packed on Friday and Saturday nights.

Radisson SAS/Hotel Norge's "Koltbord" buffet, offered by Bergen's ritziest hotel, is a daily all-you-can-eat buffet in a classy Ole Bull restaurant—hot dishes, seafood, and desserts rich in both memories and calories (170-kr lunch, enter 12:00–16:00; tel. 55 21 01 00).

Hotel Neptun has the highest-rated restaurant in town (one Michelin star). Its **Bistro Pascal** serves fine food out of the same restaurant at a more affordable price (between the harbor and the theater at Valkansdorfsgata 8, tel. 55 30 68 00). Students and budget travelers carbo-load at **Pasta Sentral** (50-kr meals, open late, near the station at Vestre Strømkai 6).

Transportation Connections—Bergen

Bergen is conveniently connected to **Oslo** only by train (departing Bergen roughly at 7:30, 8:30, 10:20, 15:00, 15:45, 23:00, arriving Oslo seven scenic hours later, 20-kr reservation required). Train info tel. 55 96 69 00.

To get to **Stockholm**, **Copenhagen**, or even **Trondheim**, you'll be going via Oslo unless you fly. Before buying any long train ticket from Bergen, look into cheap flights. **Kilroy Travels** has a handle on cheap flights for youths and older (Parkveien 1 in Student Sentret, tel. 55 32 64 00). **British Midland** airlines has a cheap ($139) flight between Bergen and London.

By bus to Kristiansand: If you're heading to Denmark, you'll take the ferry from Kristiansand. Catch the Haukeli express bus #181 departing Bergen at 7:20. After a two-hour lay-over in Haukeligrend, take bus #221 at 15:20, arriving at 19:30 in Kristiansand (520 kr, cheaper for students with ISIC cards, tel. 81 54 44 44), easily in time for the overnight ferry to Denmark.

By boat to Newcastle, England: The Color Line sails from Bergen to Newcastle, England, on Tuesday, Friday, and Sunday, June through August (tel. 55 54 86 60). The cheapest peak-season crossing for the 22-hour trip is 880 kr on Tuesday or Sunday for a reclining chair ("sleeperette"). Cars with up to four passengers cost about 2,700 kr.

By boat to Stavanger: FlaggRuten catamarans sail to Sta-vanger (2–4/day in four hours, 450 kr, 50 percent discount for students or Scanrail passholders, tel. 55 23 87 80). From Sta-vanger trains run to Kristiansand and Oslo (overnight possible).

By boat to the Arctic: Hurtigrute coastal steamers depart daily in summer at 22:30 for the seven-day trip north up the scenic west coast to Kirkenes on the Russian border. Cabins should be booked well in advance. Call Bergen Lines in the U.S.A. at 212/319-1300. Deck space and seats are usually avail-able with short or no notice (info in Bergen, tel. 55 55 72 00, reservations 77 64 81 00). For most, the ride is great one way but a flight back south is a logical last leg.

SOUTH NORWAY'S SETESDAL VALLEY

Welcome to the remote—and therefore very traditional—Setesdal Valley. Probably Norway's most authentic cranny, the valley is a mellow montage of sod-roofed water mills, ancient churches, derelict farmhouses, yellowed recipes, and gentle scenery. The locals practice fiddles and harmonicas, rose painting, whittling, and gold- and silverwork. The famous Setesdal filigree echoes the rhythmical design of the Viking era and Middle Ages.

The Setesdal Valley joined the 20th century with the construction of the valley highway in the 1950s. All along the valley you'll see the unique two-story storage sheds called *stabburs* (the top floor stored clothes; the bottom, food) and many sod roofs. Even the bus stops have rooftops the local goats love to munch.

In the high country, just over the Sessvatn summit (3,000 feet), you'll see goat herds and summer farms. If you see an "*Ekte Geitost*" sign, that means genuine homemade goat cheese is for sale. (It's sold cheaper and in more manageable sizes in grocery stores.) To some it looks like a decade's accumulation of ear wax. I think it's delicious. Remember, *ekte* means all-goat—real strong. The more popular and easier-to-eat regular goat cheese is mixed with cow's-milk cheese.

Each town in the Setesdal Valley has a weekly rotating series of hikes and activities for the regular, stay-put-for-a-week visitor. The upper valley is dead in the summer but enjoys a bustling winter. This is easygoing sightseeing—nothing earthshaking. Let's just pretend you're on vacation.

Setesdal Valley

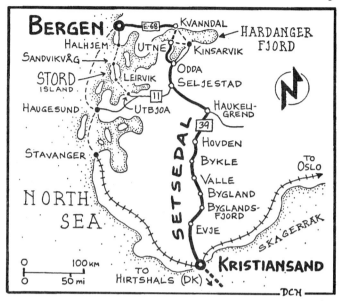

Planning Your Time

Frankly, without a car, Setesdal is not worth the trouble. There are no trains, bus schedules are as sparse as the population, and the sights are best for joyriding. If you're driving in Bergen and want to get back to Denmark, this route is more interesting than repeating Oslo. On a three-week Scandinavian trip, I'd do it in one long day, as follows: 6:00, leave Bergen; 8:00, catch the Kvanndal ferry to Utne; 9:00, say good-bye to the last fjord at Odda; 12:00, lunch in Hovden at the top of Setesdal Valley; 13:00, frolic south with a few short stops in the valley; 18:00, arrive in Kristiansand—dinner and a movie?; 23:00· board boat for overnight crossing to Denmark.

Sights—Setesdal Valley

These sights are listed from north to south.

Odda—At the end of the Hardanger fjord, just past the huge zinc and copper industrial plant, you'll hit the industrial town of Odda (well-stocked TI for whole region and beyond, tel. 53 64 12 97). Odda brags that Kaiser Wilhelm came here a lot, but he's dead and I'd drive right through. If you want to visit the tongue of a glacier, drive to Buar and hike an hour to Buarbreen. From Odda, drive into the land of boulders. The many, mighty waterfalls that line the road seem to have hurled huge rocks (with rooted trees) into the rivers and fields. Stop at the giant double waterfall (on the left, pull out on the right, drive slowly through it if you need a car wash).

Røldal—Continue over Røldalsfjellet and into the valley below, where the old town of Røldal is trying to develop some tourism. Drive straight through. Its old church isn't worth the time or money. Lakes like frosted mirrors make desolate huts come in pairs. Haukeliseter, a group of sod-roofed buildings filled with cultural clichés and tour groups, offers pastries, sandwiches, and reasonable (65–85-kr) hot meals in a lakeside setting. Try the traditional *rømmegrøt* porridge.

Haukeligrend—The TI is open 10:00 to 18:00 late June through early August (tel. 35 07 03 67). If you plan to stay here, **Haukelid Turistheim Pensjonat** offers quaint old rooms (in the quaint old half of the building), a feel-at-home Old World living room, a Ping-Pong table, and no breakfast but a reasonable cafeteria (D-300 kr, at the junction of Roads 39 and 11 in Haukeligrend, about six hours out of Bergen, 30 minutes before Hovden, tel. 35 07 01 26). Haukeligrend is a bus/traffic junction, with daily bus service to/from Bergen and to/from Kristiansand.

Hovden—At the top of the Setesdal Valley, Hovden is a ski resort (2,500 feet high), barren in the summer and painfully in need of charm. Locals come here to walk and relax for a week. Good walks offer a chance to see reindeer, moose, arctic fox, and wabbits—so they say. Tuesday, Thursday, and Saturday a chair lift takes summer visitors to its nearby 3,700-foot peak. The Hegni Center, on the lake at the south edge of town, rents canoes for 30 kr an hour. A new super indoor spa/pool complex, the Hovden Badeland (100 kr, daily 11:00–19:00 in summer) provides a much-needed way to spend an otherwise dreary (and very likely) drizzly early evening here. The TI is open all year (Monday–Friday 9:00–16:00, and summer Saturdays 10:00–14:00, tel. 37 93 96 30).

   Hovdehytta Hostel is a big old ski chalet with an inviting ski-lodge atmosphere (large dining room and open fire in the living room), offering clean, modern bunk-bed doubles with a large breakfast for 340 kr (50 kr extra for sheets and 25 kr for those without a hostel card). Good 80-kr dinners must be ordered by 15:00, dinner at 18:00 (open June–September, tel. 37 93 95 22). Built in 1911, this is the oldest place in town with the only cozy and reasonable accommodations in this booming winter resort of sprawling ranch-style ski hotels.

▲**Dammar Vatnedalsvatn**—Just south of Hovden is a 2-mile side trip to a 400-foot-high rock-pile dam. Great view, impressive rockery. This is one of the highest dams in northern Europe. Read the chart. Sit out of the wind a few rows down the rock pile and ponder the vastness of Norwegian wood.

▲**Bykle**—The most interesting folk museum and church in Setesdal are in the teeny town of Bykle. The 17th-century interior has two balconies—one for men and one for women (10 kr, mid-June–mid-August weekdays 10:00–18:00, weekends 12:00–18:00).

The **Huldreheimen Museum**, a wonderful little open-air museum, is a typical 800-year-old seterhouse used when the cattle spent the summer high in the mountains. Follow the sign up a road to a farm high above the town, park, then hike a steep 150 yards into Norway's medieval peasant past—fine view, six houses filled with old stuff, and a good English brochure (15 kr, mid-June–mid-August weekdays 10:00–18:00, weekends 12:00–18:00).

Grasbrokke—On the east side of the main road (at the "Grasbrokke" sign) you'll see an old water mill (1630). A few minutes farther south is a "Picnic and WC" sign. Exit onto that little road. You'll pass another old water mill with a fragile rotten-log sluice. At the second picnic turnout (just before this roadlet returns to the highway, you'll find a covered picnic table for rainy lunches), turn out and frolic along the river rocks.

Flateland—One mile east, off the main road, is the Setesdal museum (Rygnestadtunet), offering more of what you saw at Bykle (20 kr, two buildings, daily mid-June–mid-August 11:00–17:00). Unless you're a glutton for culture, I wouldn't do both.

▲**Valle**—This is Setesdal's prettiest village (but don't tell Bykle). In the center, you'll find fine silver- and goldwork, traditional dinners in the cozy Bergtun Hotel (130–180 kr, summer only), homemade crafts next to the TI, old-fashioned *lefse* cooking demonstrations (in the small log house by the campground), and a fine suspension bridge for kids of any age who still like to bounce (and for anyone interested in a great view over the river of the strange mountains that look like polished, petrified mud slides). European rock climbers, tired of the over-climbed Alps, often entertain spectators with their sport.

Is anyone climbing? (TI open mid-June–mid-August, weekdays 10:00–17:00, Saturday 10:00–14:00, closed Sunday except in July 10:00–14:00, less off-season, tel. 37 93 73 12.)

If you stay in Valle, try the **Bergtun Hotel**. Run by Halvor Kjelleberg, it's a real folksy, sit-a-spell Setesdal lodging full of traditional furniture, paintings, and carvings in each charming room (open mid-June–mid-August, D-500 kr, some rooms have bunks, extra bed-100 kr, includes breakfast, Valle i Setesdal, tel. 37 93 77 20, fax 37 93 74 37).

Nomeland—Sylvartun, the silversmith with the valley's most aggressive publicity department, demonstrates the Setesdal specialty in a 17th-century traditional log cabin and a free little gallery/museum. He also gives a free 30-minute fiddle concert weekdays in July at 13:00. On Monday and Thursday at 14:30, you can see a 30-minute folk-dancing show (40 kr).

Grendi—The Ardal Church (1827) has a rune stone in its yard, and 300 yards south of the church is a 900-year-old oak tree.

Evje—A huge town by Setesdal standards (3,500 people), Evje is famous for its gems and mines. Fancy stones fill the shops here. Only rockhounds would find the nearby mines fun; for a small fee you can hunt for gems. The super-for-rockhounds new Setesdal Mineral Park is on the main road, 3 kilometers south of town. For modern, bright, functional doubles in Evje, stay with the **Haugen family** (two-bunk rooms for 200 kr, 280 kr with sheets, a pleasant garden, a kitchenette, and a huge stuffed moose in the garage) on the Arendal Road (last house on the left, look for "Rom" sign, tel. 37 93 08 88, fax 37 93 01 14).

KRISTIANSAND

This "capital of the south" has 67,000 inhabitants, a pleasant grid-plan Renaissance layout (Posebyen), a famous zoo with Norway's biggest amusement park (10 km toward Oslo on the main road), a daily bus to Bergen, and lots of big boats going to England and Denmark. It's the closest thing to a beach resort in Norway. The Posebyen neighborhood, around the bustling pedestrian market street, is the shopping/eating/browsing/people-watching town center. Stroll along the Strand Promenaden (marina) to the Christiansholm Fortress.

The TI is at Dronningensgate 2 (Monday–Saturday 8:00–19:30, Sunday 12:00–19:30; off-season Monday–Friday 8:00–16:00 only, tel. 38 12 13 14). The bank at the Color Line terminal opens for each arrival and departure (even the midnight ones) and is reasonable. The cinema complex is within 2 blocks of the Color Line docks and the TI (50 kr, seven screens, showing movies in English, check schedules at TI or cinema).

Sleeping and Eating in Kristiansand

Your best modern, comfy, and cozy bet is **Hotel Sjøgløtt**. Friendly Helene Ranestad gives this small hotel lots of class (S-390 kr, Sb-490 kr, D-530 kr, Db-590 kr with breakfast, CC:VM, near the harbor on a quiet street at Østre Strandgt 25, tel. & fax 38 02 21 20). **Villa Frosbusdal B&B**, once a shipbuilder's mansion, has friendly hosts and modern bathrooms (Frosbusdalen 2, tel. 38 07 05 15). Otherwise, Kristiansand hotels are expensive and nondescript. Consider the newly renovated but still traditional **Bondeheimen** (Sb-490 kr, Db-680 kr with breakfast, CC:VMA, tel. 38 02 44 40, fax 38 02 73 21). The **Rainbow Hotel Norge** is more modern and expensive but reduces its rates to 750 kr for a double on Friday, Saturday, and Sunday and from mid-June through mid-August (regular rates: Db-870 kr, Dronningensgate 5, tel. 38 02 00 00, fax 38 02 35 30).

Villa Frobusdal Hotel, outside the city center, is a 1917 villa and classy B&B run by the friendly Herigstads (Sb-525 kr, Db-690 kr, includes breakfast, Frobusdalen 2, access from E-18 going east, tel. 38 07 05 15, fax 38 07 01 15). The **hostel** is cheap, but not central (tel. 38 02 83 10).

In the town center you'll find plenty of *kafeterias*, a **Peppe's Pizza** (open until 23:00, salad bar, on Gyldenløvesgate), and budget ethnic restaurants. For the best dinner in town, splurge at **Bak Gården** (dinner 250 kr, Tollbodgaten 5, hiding in the center, tel. 38 02 79 55).

Transportation Connections—Kristiansand

By boat to Hirtshals, Denmark: The Color Line ferry sails from Kristiansand in Norway to Hirtshals in Denmark (usually daily departures at about 8:00, 13:30, 14:30, 21:00, and 00:30, mid-June to late August; 8:15 and 19:15 the rest of the year). Fast boats take 2.5 hours, regular boats take four hours, and the overnight ride is slower, to arrive at 6:30. Passengers pay 100 kr to 360 kr (July and weekends are most expensive). A car costs 200 kr to 500 kr. The "car package" lets five in a car travel for 1,390 kr (summer Monday–Thursday). There are decent smørgåsbords, music, duty-free shopping, a desk to process your Norwegian duty-free tax rebates, and a bank for small changes (no fee).

When you can commit yourself to a firm date, call Color Line to make a reservation. They accept telephone reservations payable when you get to the dock. Color Line's information and reservation line is open daily 8:00 to 23:00, tel. 38 07 88 00, in Kristiansand. Or you can use their office in Oslo (tel. 22 94 44 70), Bergen (tel. 55 54 86 00), or New York (c/o Bergen Line, tel. 212/319-1300, fax 212/319-1390). Ask about specials. Round-trip fares can be lower than one-way fares.

Take the night boat to save the cost of a hotel. Enjoy an evening in Kristiansand, then sleep (or vomit) as you sail to Denmark. Beds are reasonable (reclining seats euphemistically called "sleeperettes" are 40 kr; simple couchettes are 60 kr; a bed in a four-berth room is 110 kr; and a private double with shower ranges 130–260 kr per person). You owe yourself the comfort of a private room if you're efficient enough to spend this night traveling. I slept so well that I missed the Denmark landing and ended up crossing three times! After chewing me out, the captain said it happens a lot. Set your alarm or spend an extra day at sea.

Route Tips for Drivers

Bergen to Kristiansand (ten hours): Your first key connection is the Kvanndal–Utne ferry (a two-hour drive from Bergen, departures hourly from 6:00 to 23:00, tel. 55 23 87 80 to confirm times, reservations not possible or even necessary if you get there 20 minutes early, breakfast in cafeteria). If you make the 8:00, your day will be more relaxed. Driving comfortably, with no mistakes or traffic, it's two hours from your Bergen hotel to the ferry dock. Leaving Bergen is a bit confusing. Pretend you're going to Oslo on the road to Voss (signs for Nestune, Landas, Nattland, R-7). About a half-hour out of town, leave the Voss road, after a long tunnel on Road 7, for Norheimsund. This road, as treacherous for the famed beauty of the Hardanger Fjord it hugs as for its skinniness, is faster and safer if you beat the traffic (which you will with this plan).

The ferry drops you in Utne, where a lovely road takes you to Odda and up into the scenic mountains. From Haukeligrend, turn south and wind up to Sessvatn at 3,000 feet. Enter Setesdal Valley. Follow the Otra River downhill for 140 miles south to the major port town of Kristiansand. Skip the secondary routes. As you enter Kristiansand, follow signs for Denmark.

SWEDEN

STOCKHOLM

If I had to call one European city home, it would be Stockholm. Surrounded by water and woods, bubbling with energy and history, Sweden's stunning capital is green, clean, and underrated.

Crawl through Europe's best-preserved old warship and relax on a canal-boat tour. Browse the cobbles and antique shops of the lantern-lit Old Town and take a spin through Skansen, Europe's first and best open-air folk museum. Marvel at Stockholm's glittering city hall, modern department stores, and art museums.

While progressive and sleek, Stockholm respects its heritage. In summer, mounted bands parade daily through the heart of town to the royal palace, announcing the changing of the guard, and turning the most dignified tourist into a scampering kid. The Gamla Stan (Old Town) celebrates the Midsummer festivities (late June) with the vigor of a rural village, forgetting that it's part of a gleaming 20th-century metropolis.

Stockholm is Europe's "Culture Capital" in 1998. The year will be filled with special events with this theme: "Culture holds a society together." All the details can be found at www.kulture98.stockholm.se or on the city's Web site: www.stoinfo.se.

Planning Your Time

On a two- to three-week trip through Scandinavia, Stockholm is worth two days. Efficient train travelers sleep in and out for two days in the city with only one night in a hotel. (Copenhagen and Oslo trains arrive at about 8:00 and depart

at about 23:00.) To be even more ec
you could use the luxury Stockholm-
hotel for two nights (spending a day
two days in Stockholm without a hot
night train to Stockholm, day in Stoc
Helsinki, day in Helsinki; night boat
Stockholm; night train to Oslo). That
gives you three interesting and inexpe......ve days of travel fun.

Spend two days in Stockholm this way:

Day 1: Arrive by train (or the night before by car), do station chores (reserve next ride, change money, pick up map, *Stockholm This Week*, and a Stockholm Card at the Hotellcentralen TI), check into hotel. At 10:00 catch one-hour bus tour from Opera; 11:00 tour *Vasa* warship and have a picnic; 13:00 tour Nordic Museum; 15:00 Skansen (ask for an open-air folk museum tour); 19:00 folk dancing, possible smørgåsbord, and popular dancing, or wander Gamla Stan.

Day 2: Do the 10:00 city hall tour and climb the city hall tower for a fine view; 12:00 catch the changing of the guard at the palace, tour royal palace and armory, explore Gamla Stan, or picnic on one-hour city boat tour; 16:00 browse the modern city center around Kungsträdgården, Sergels Torg, Hötorget market and indoor food hall, and Drottninggatan area.

Orientation (tel. code: 08)

Greater Stockholm's 1.8 million residents live on 14 islands that are woven together by 50 bridges. Visitors need only concern themselves with five islands: **Norrmalm** is downtown, with most of the hotels, shopping areas, and the train station. **Gamla Stan** is the old city of winding lantern-lit streets, antique shops, and classy, glassy cafés clustered around the royal palace. **Södermalm**, aptly called Stockholm's Brooklyn, is residential and untouristy. **Skeppsholmen** is the small, very central traffic-free park island with the Museum of Modern Art and two fine youth hostels. **Djurgården**, literally "deer garden" and now officially a national city park, is Stockholm's wonderful green playground with many of the city's top sights (bike rentals just over the bridge as you enter the island).

Tourist Information

Hotellcentralen is primarily a room-finding service (in the central train station), but its friendly staff adequately handles all

Greater Stockholm

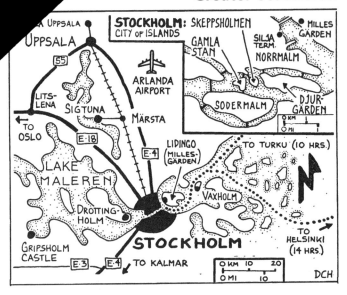

your sightseeing and transportation questions. This is the place for anyone arriving by train to arrange accommodations, buy the Tourist Card or Stockholm Card (see below), and pick up a city map, *Stockholm This Week* (which lists opening hours and directions to all the sights, special events, and all the tedious details: lost and found, embassies, post offices, etc.), and brochures on whatever else you need (city walks, parking, jazz boats, excursions, bus routes, shopping, and so on). While *This Week* has a decent map of the sightseeing zone, the 15-kr map covers more area and bus routes. It's worth the extra money if you'll be using the buses (daily June–August 7:00–21:00; May and September 8:00–19:00; off-season 9:00–18:00; tel. 08/789-2425, fax 08/791-8666, e-mail: hotels@stoinfo.se).

Sverige Huset (Sweden House), Stockholm's official tourist information office (a short walk from the station on Kungsträdgården), is very good but usually more crowded than Hotellcentralen. They've got pamphlets on everything; an "excursion shop" for transportation, day-trip, and bus-tour information, and tickets; and an English library and reading room upstairs with racks of 5-kr information on various aspects of Swedish culture and one state's attempt at cradle-to-grave happiness (July–September Monday–Friday 9:00–18:00, Saturday–Sunday 9:00–17:00; off-season weekdays 9:00–18:00, weekends 9:00–15:00; Hamngatan 27, tel. 08/789-2490 for info, 08/789-2415 for tickets; T-bana: Kungsträdgården).

The **City Hall TI** is smaller but with all the information and a bit less chaos (daily 9:00–17:00, May–October only, at the Stadshuset or City Hall, tel. 08/5082-9000).

Arrival in Stockholm

By Train: Stockholm's central train station is a wonderland of services, shops, and people going places. The Hotellcentralen TI is as good as the city TI nearby. If you're sailing to Finland, check out the Viking Line office. The FOREX long-hours exchange counter changes traveler's checks for only a 15-kr fee (two offices, upstairs and downstairs, in the station).

By Plane: Stockholm's Arlanda Airport is 45 kilometers north of town. Shuttle buses run between the airport and the City Terminal next to the station (6/hour, tel. 08/600-1000). Airport information tel. 08/797-6000 (SAS tel. 08/910-150, British Air tel. 08/679-7800).

Helpful Hints

The Kulturhus on Sergels Torg has a cyber café (Monday–Saturday 11:00–18:00, 20 kr for 30 minutes with assistance, 30 kr same with coffee and a roll). There are three kinds of public phones: coin-op, credit card, and phone card. For operator assistance, call 0018. Numbers starting with 020 are toll-free. For medical help, call 08/644-9200. There's a 24-hour pharmacy near the central station at Klarabergsgatan 64 (tel. 08/454-8100). To get a taxi within three minutes, call Taxi Stockholm (tel. 08/150-000) or Taxi Kurir (tel. 08/300-000).

Getting Around Stockholm

By Bus and Subway: Stockholm complements her many sightseeing charms with great information services, a fine bus and subway system, and special passes that take the bite out of the city's cost (or at least limit it to one vicious budgetary gash).

Buses and the subway work on the same tickets. Ignore the zones since everything I mention (except Drottningholm and Carl Millesgården) are in Zone One. Each 14-kr ticket is valid for one hour (ten-packs cost 95 kr). The subway, called T-bana or Tunnelbana, gets you where you want to go very quickly. Ride it just for the futuristic drama of being a human mole and to check out the modern public art (for instance, in the Kungsträdgården station, transit info tel. 08/600-1000). The **Tourist Card**, which gives you free use of all public transport and the harbor ferry (24 hours/60 kr, 72 hours/120 kr, sold at TIs and newsstands), is not necessary if you're getting the Stockholm Card (see below). The 72-hour pass includes admission to Skansen, Gröna Lund, and the Kaknäs Tower.

It seems too good to be true, but each year I pinch myself and the **Stockholm Card** is still there. This 24-hour, 185-kr pass (sold at TIs and ship terminals) gives you free run of all public transit, free entry to virtually every sight (70 places), free parking, a handy sightseeing handbook, and the substantial pleasure of doing everything without considering the cost (many of Stockholm's sights are worth the time but not the steep individual ticket costs). This pays for itself if you do Skansen, the *Vasa*, and the Royal Palace and Treasury tour. If you enter Skansen on your 24th hour (and head right for the 50-kr aquarium), you get a few extra hours. (Parents get an added bonus: two children under 18 go along for free with each adult pass.) The same pass comes in 48-hour (350-kr) and 72-hour (470-kr) versions.

By Harbor Shuttle Ferry: Throughout the summer, ferries connect Stockholm's two most interesting sightseeing districts. They sail from Nybroplan and Slussen to Djurgården, landing next to the *Vasa* and Skansen (15 kr, not covered by Stockholm Card, every 20 min).

Sights—Downtown Stockholm

▲**Kungsträdgården**—The King's Garden Square is the downtown people-watching center. Watch the life-sized game of chess and enjoy the free concerts at the bandstand. Surrounded by the Sweden House, the NK department store, the harborfront, and tour boats, it's the place to feel Stockholm's pulse (with discretion).

▲▲**Sergels Torg**—The heart of modern Stockholm, between Kungsträdgården and the station, is worth a wander. Enjoy the colorful, bustling underground mall and dip into the Gallerien mall. Visit the Kulturhuset, a center for reading, relaxing, and socializing designed for normal people (but welcoming tourists), with music, exhibits, hands-on fun, and an insight into contemporary Sweden (free, Tuesday–Sunday

Stockholm Center

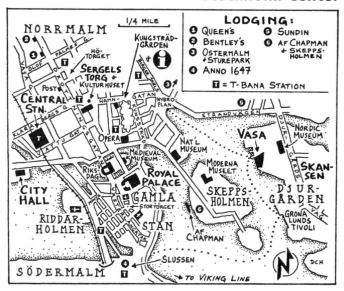

NORRMALM

1/4 MILE

KUNGSTRÄD-
GÅRDEN

HÖ-
TORGET

PALME G.

OLOF

SERGELS
TORG +
KULTURHUSET

POST

CENTRAL
STN.

KLARA
BERGS G.

HAMN-
GATAN

GATAN

NYBRO-
PLAN.

STRANDVÄGEN

NORDIC
MUSEUM

LODGING:
❶ QUEEN'S   ❺ SUNDIN
❷ BENTLEY'S   ❻ AF CHAPMAN
❸ OSTERMALM   + SKEPPS-
   + STUREPARK   HOLMEN
❹ ANNO 1647

🚇 = T-BANA STATION

VATTU GAT.

OPERA

MEDIEVAL
MUSEUM

RIKS-
DAG

NAT'L
MUSEUM

VASA

MODERNA
MUSEET

SKAN-
SEN

ROYAL
PALACE

CITY
HALL

GAMLA

RIDDAR-
HOLMEN

STORTORGET

STAN

SKEPPS-
HOLMEN

DJUR-
GÅRDEN

GRÖNA
LUNDS
TIVOLI

AF
CHAPMAN

SLUSSEN

SÖDERMALM

TO VIKING LINE

DCH

11:00–17:00, often later, tel. 08/700-0100). From Sergels Torg, walk up the Drottninggatan pedestrian mall to Hötorget (see Eating, below).

▲▲**City Hall**—The Stadshuset is an impressive mix of 8 million bricks, 19 million chips of gilt mosaic, and lots of Stockholm pride. One of Europe's most impressive public buildings (b. 1923) and site of the annual Nobel Prize banquet, it's particularly enjoyable and worthwhile for its entertaining tours (30 kr, daily June–August at 10:00, 11:00, 12:00, and 14:00; off-season at 10:00 and 12:00; just behind the station, bus #48 or #62, tel. 08/5082-9059). Climb the 350-foot tower (an elevator takes you halfway) for the best possible city view (15 kr, daily 10:00–16:30, May–September only). The City Hall also has a TI and a good cafeteria with complete lunches for 60 kr (11:00–14:00, Monday–Friday).

▲**Orientation Views**—Try to get a bird's-eye perspective on this wonderful urban mix of water, parks, concrete, and people from the City Hall tower (see above), the Kaknäs Tower (at 500 feet, the tallest building in Scandinavia, 20 kr, daily May–August 9:00–22:00, daily September–April

10:00–21:00, bus #69 from Nybroplan or Sergels Torg, tel. 08/789-2435), the observatory in Skansen, or the Katarina elevator (5 kr, daily 7:30–21:00, circa 1930s, ride 40 meters to the top, near Slussen subway stop, then walk behind Katarinavagen for grand views, a classy residential neighborhood, and the lively Mosebacke evening scene—strolling, dancing, and beer gardens).

▲Quickie Orientation Bus Tour—Several different city-bus tours leave from the Royal Opera House: 50 minutes for 85 kr with a Swedish/English guide (mid-June through mid-August at 10:30, 11:30, 12:30, 13:30, 14:30) or 90 minutes for 130 kr (mid-April–October at 10:00, 12:00, 14:00, 17:00, tel. 08/411-7023). They also organize 75-minute Old Town walks (75 kr, daily in summer at 11:30 and 14:30). For a free self-guided tour, follow the Gamla Stan walk laid out below.

▲City Boat Tour—For a good floating look at Stockholm, and a pleasant break, consider a sightseeing cruise. Tour boats leave regularly from in front of the Grand Hotel (tel. 08/240-470). The "Historical Canals of Stockholm" tour offers the best informative introduction (80 kr, one hour, departing on the half-hour 10:30–16:30 from mid-June–mid-August). The "Under the Bridges" tour goes through two locks and under 15 bridges (live guide, 130 kr, 2 hours, hourly departures mid-April–mid-October). The "Royal Canal" tour is a scenic joyride through lots of greenery (80 kr, one-hour tape-recorded spiel, departs at half-past each hour from mid-May–August).

▲National Museum—Though mediocre by European standards, this museum is small, central, uncrowded, and very user-friendly. The highlights of the collection are several Rembrandts, Rubens, a fine group of Impressionists, and works by the popular and good-to-get-to-know local artists Carl Larsson and Anders Zorn (60 kr, Tuesday–Sunday 11:00–17:00, Tuesday and Thursday until 20:00, closed Monday, tel. 08/666-4250). A worthwhile audiotape (20 kr) guides you through a 50-minute tour of the collection's highlights.

Museum of Modern Art—Newly reopened after a major renovation, this bright and cheery gallery is as far out as can be, with Picasso, Braque, and lots of goofy Dada art (such as the *Urinal* and the *Goat with Tire*). It's in a pleasant park on Skeppsholmen (60 kr, Tuesday–Thursday 11:00–22:00, Friday–Sunday 11:00–18:00, closed Monday, tel. 08/666-4363).

Sights—Stockholm's Gamla Stan

▲▲**Gamla Stan self-guided walk**—Stockholm's old island
core is charming, fit for a film, and full of antique shops,
street lanterns, painted ceilings, and surprises. While many
will happily just wander around, take this guided walk first:

Slottsbacken: Start at the base of the palace (bottom of
Slottsbacken) where a statue of King Gustav III gazes at the
palace, formerly the site of Stockholm's first castle. Walk up
the broad cobbled boulevard. Behind the obelisk stands the
Storkyrkan, Stockholm's cathedral (and most interesting
church, which we'll visit later in the walk). Opposite the
palace (orange building on left) is the Finnish church (Finska
Kyrkan), which originated as the royal tennis hall. Walk
behind the church into the shady churchyard where you'll
find the 3-inch-tall "iron boy," the tiniest statue in Stockholm (often with a little gift). Continue through the yard
onto Tradgardsgatan, which leads (turn right) to the old
stock exchange.

Stortorget: Left of the stock exchange is the oldest square
in town, Stortorget. The town well is now dry but this is still a
popular meeting point. Scan the fine old facades. This square
has a notorious history. It was the site of Stockholm's blood-
bath of 1520—during a royal power-grab, most of the town's
aristocracy was beheaded. Rivers of blood were said to have
run through the streets. Later, this was the location of the
town's pillory. At the far end of the square (under the finest
gables) turn right and follow Trangsund toward the cathedral.

Cathedral: Just before the church you'll see my favorite
phone booth (Rikstelefon) and the gate to the churchyard
being guarded by statues of Caution and Hope. Enter the
cathedral (10 kr, daily 9:00–18:00, until 16:00 off-season, pick
up the free English flier describing interior). The fascinating
interior is paved with centuries-old tombstones; more than
2,000 people are buried under the church. In front on the left
is an impressive sculpture of *Saint George and the Dragon* made
of oak, gilded metal, and elk horn (1489). Near the exit is a
painting with the oldest existing depiction of Stockholm (from
1535, showing a walled city filling only today's Gamla Stan).

Prastgatan: Exiting through the churchyard, continue
down Trangsund. At the next corner go downhill on
Storkyrkobrinken and take the first left—where the priests
used to—on Prastgatan. Enjoy a quiet wander down this

peaceful lane. After 2 blocks (at Kakbrinken) you'll see a cannon on the corner guarding a prehistoric rune stone. (In case you can't read ancient Nordic script, it says: "Torsten and Trogun erected this stone in memory of their son.") Continue farther down Prastgatan until you see the German-strength brick steeple of the *Tyska Kyrkan* (German church). This is a reminder of the days when German merchants worked here. Wander through its churchyard and out the back onto Svartmangatan. Follow it downhill to its end at a couple of benches and an iron railing overlooking Østerlånggatan.

   Østerlånggatan: From this perch, survey the street to the left and right. Notice how it curves. This marks the old shoreline. In medieval times piers stretched out like many fingers into the harbor. Gradually, as land was reclaimed and developed, these piers were extended and what were originally piers became lanes leading to piers farther away. Walk left along Østerlånggatan. At the cobbled Y in the road head uphill (up Kopmanbrinken) past a copy of *George and the Dragon*. (Or, for a quick finish, Østerlånggatan takes you back to your starting point at the palace.)

   Shopping, Jazz, and Food: From Kopmantorget (the statue), Kopmangatan leads past fine antique shops (some with their medieval painted ceilings still visible) back to Stortorget. Crossing the square, follow the crowds downhill 2 blocks to Stora Nygatan. This is Gamla Stan's main commercial drag, a festival with all the distractions which keep most visitors from seeing the historic charms of the old town—which you just did. Now you can shop and eat.

   ▲▲**Military Parade and Changing of the Guard**—Starting at the Army Museum (daily at 12:00), the parade marches over either Norrbro Bridge or Strombron Bridge and up to the palace courtyard where the band plays and the guard changes (every other day the band is mounted . . . on horses). These days, the royal family lives out of town at Drottningholm, but the guards are for real. If the guard by the cannon in the semicircular courtyard looks a little lax, try wandering discreetly behind him.

   ▲▲**Royal Palace**—The palace is a complex of sights. Drop by the info booth in the semicircular courtyard (at the top where the guard changes) for an explanatory brochure with a map marking the different entrances. In a nutshell: The apartments of state are lavish, as worthwhile as any; the treasury is the best in Northern Europe; the chapel is no big deal; Gustav III's museum of antiquities—skip it; and the Royal Armoury is awesome—plan to spend some time. An 80-kr combo ticket covers the apartments, treasury, and antiquities (more info below).

▲▲**Apartments of State**—The stately palace exterior encloses 608 rooms (one more than Britain's Buckingham Palace) of glittering Baroque and rococo decor. Clearly the palace of Scandinavia's superpower, it's richly decorated (18th century) and steeped in royal history. The guided tour is heavy and tedious; the place is more interesting on your own—pick up English descriptions where available and don't miss the Bernadotte rooms (45 kr, daily June–August 10:00–16:00; off-season Tuesday–Sunday 12:00–15:00, closed Monday; free English-language tours at 12:00 and 13:15).

▲▲**Royal Treasury**—You'll find great crowns, scepters, jeweled robes, and plenty of glitter that's gold. Nothing is explained, so get the 2-kr description at the entry (40 kr, same hours as above, no samples, often tours at 11:00 and 14:15, tel. 08/402-6000).

Gustav III's Museum of Antiquities—In the 1700s, Gustav III traveled through Italy and brought home an impressive gallery of classical Roman statues. This was a huge deal if you'd never been out of Sweden. It's worth a look only if you've never been to the rest of Europe. Nothing is explained in English (40 kr, same hours).

▲▲▲**Royal Armoury (Livrust Kammaren)**—This, the oldest museum in Sweden, has the most interesting and best displayed collection of medieval royal armor I've seen anywhere in Europe. The incredible, original 17th-century gear includes royal baby wear, outfits kings wore when they were killed in battle or assassinated, and five centuries of royal Swedish armor—all wonderfully described in English. An added bonus is a basement lined with royal coaches, including coronation coaches, all beautifully preserved and richly decorated (40 kr, daily 11:00–16:00, closed winter Mondays, tours daily in summer at 13:00, entry at the bottom of Slottsbacken at the base of the palace, tel. 08/666-4475).

Riksdaghuset—You can tour Sweden's parliament buildings if you'd like a firsthand look at its government (free hourly tours in English from June through August, usually Monday–Friday at 11:00, 12:30, and 14:00, enter at Riksgatan 3a, but call 08/786-4000 to confirm times).

Museum of Medieval Stockholm (Medeltidsmuseet)—
While grade-schoolish, this gives you a good look at medieval
Stockholm (30 kr, daily July–August 11:00–16:00, Tuesday,
Wednesday, Thursday until 18:00; Monday–Saturday
September–June 11:00–16:00, closed Monday; free 30-minute
English tours at 14:00 daily in summer enlivens the exhibits;
enter from the park in front of the Parliament, tel. 08/700-
0593). The Stromparterren park, with its Carl Milles statue
of the *Sun Singer* greeting the day, is a pleasant place for a
sightseeing break (but an expensive place for a potty break—
use the free WC in the museum).

Riddarholm Church—This final resting place for about 600
years of Sweden's royalty is pretty lifeless (20 kr, daily
June–August 11:00–16:00, less in May and September, closed
in winter, tel. 08/402-6000). In a futile attempt to make this
more interesting, they'll loan you the church guidebooklet.
The cathedral next to the palace (see Gamla Stan walk, above)
is far more interesting.

Sights—Stockholm's Djurgården ⁵/₂₆/₉₉

▲▲▲**Skansen**—Europe's original and best open-air folk
museum, Skansen is a huge park gathering more than 150
historic buildings (homes, churches, shops, and schoolhouses)
transplanted from all corners of Sweden. Tourists can explore
this Swedish-culture-on-a-lazy-Susan, seeing folk crafts in
action and wonderfully furnished old interiors (lively only in
the summer). In the town quarter (top of the escalator),
craftspeople such as potters are busy doing their traditional
thing in a re-created Old World Stockholm. Don't miss the
glassblowers if you'll be missing Sweden's Glass Country to
the south.

Spreading out from there, the sprawling park is designed
to show northern Swedish culture and architecture in the
northern part of the park (top of park map) and southern Sweden in the south (bottom of map). Excellent, free one-hour
guided walks (from Bollnästorget info stand at top of escalator)
paint a fine picture of old Swedish lifestyles (usually daily at
14:00 and 16:00 June–August). There's fiddling nightly (except
Sunday) at 18:15, folk dancing demonstrations daily in summer
at 19:00, Sunday at 14:30 and 16:00, and public dancing to live
bands weeknights (20:30–23:30, call for evening theme—jazz,
folk, rock, or disco, nightly except Sunday). Admission to the

aquarium is the only thing not covered on your entry ticket (45 kr, 10:00–20:00, shorter hours off-season).

Kids love Skansen, especially its zoo (ride a life-size wooden Dala-horse and stare down a hedgehog) and Lill' Skansen (Punch 'n' Judy, mini-train, and pony ride fun daily from 11:00 till at least 16:00). There are lots of special events and several restaurants. The main restaurant serves a grand smørgåsbord (200 kr) and the Ekorren café offers the least expensive self-service lunches with a view. Tre Byttor (next to Ekorren) serves 18th-century-style food in a candlelit setting. Another cozy inn, the old-time Stora Gungan Krog, at the top of the escalator, has better food (60-kr indoor or outdoor lunches with a salad and cracker bar).

Skansen is great for people-watching and picnicking, with open and covered benches all over (especially at Torslunden and Bollnästorget, where peacenik local toddlers don't bump on the bumper cars). Get the map or the 30-kr museum guidebook that has the same map, and check the live crafts schedule at the information stand at Bollnästorget to confirm your Skansen plans.

Use the west entrance (Hazeliusporten) if you're heading to or from the Nordic Museum. (55-kr entry, 30-kr in winter; daily May–August 9:00–22:00, buildings 11:00–17:00; winter 9:00–17:00, some buildings 11:00–15:00; take bus #47 or #44 from the station; call 08/5789-0005 for a recording of the day's tour, music, and dance schedule, or 08/442-8000.) You can miss Gröna Lund, the second-rate amusement park across the street.

▲▲▲*Vasa*—Stockholm turned a titanic flop into one of Europe's great sightseeing attractions. This glamorous but unseaworthy warship—top-heavy with a tacked-on extra cannon deck—sank 20 minutes into her 1628 maiden voyage when a breeze caught the sails and blew her over in the Stockholm harbor. After 333 years she rose again from the deep (with the help of marine archeologists) and today is the best-preserved ship anywhere, housed in a state-of-the-art museum. The masts on the roof are placed to show their actual height.

Catch the 25-minute English-subtitled movie (at the top of each hour, dubbed versions often play at 11:30 and 13:30), and for more information, take the free 25-minute English tours (at the bottom of each hour from 10:30, every other hour off-season) to best enjoy and understand the ship. Learn about ship's rules (bread can't be older than eight years), why it sank (heavy bread?), how it's preserved, and so on. Private tours are easy to freeload on, but the displays are so well described that a tour is hardly necessary. (50 kr, daily mid-June–mid-August 9:30–19:00; off-season 10:00–17:00, winter on Wednesday until 20:00, tel. 08/666-4800.) Take bus #47 to the big brick Nordic Museum or catch the boat from Nybroplan or Slussen, or walk from Skansen.

▲▲**Nordic Museum**—This museum, built to look like a Danish palace, offers a look at how Sweden lived over the last 500 years. Highlights include the Food and Drink section, with its stunning china and crystal table settings; the Nordic folk art (second and third floors); the huge statue of Gustav Vasa, father of modern Sweden, by Carl Milles (top of second flight of stairs); and the Sami (Lapp) exhibit in the basement (Tuesday–Sunday 11:00–17:00, summer Tuesdays and Thursdays until 21:00, closed Monday, tel. 08/666-4600). Worth your time if you have the Stockholm Card, but it's overpriced at 60-kr admission. The 30-kr guidebook isn't necessary, but pick up the English brochure at the entrance.

▲**Thielska Galleriet**—If you liked the Larsson and Zorn art in the National Gallery and/or if you're a Munch fan, this charming mansion on the water at the far end of the Djurgården park is worth the trip (40 kr, Monday–Saturday 12:00–16:00, Sunday 13:00–16:00; bus #69 from the central station, tel. 08/662-5884).

Sights—Outer Stockholm

▲▲**Carl Millesgården**—The home and garden housing a museum and the major work of Sweden's greatest sculptor is dramatically situated on a cliff overlooking Stockholm. Milles' entertaining, unique, and provocative art was influenced by Rodin. There's a classy café and a great picnic spot (50 kr, daily May–September 10:00–17:00; off-season Tuesday–Sunday 12:00–16:00, closed Monday; tel. 08/446-7590.) Catch the T-bana to Ropsten, then take any bus (except #203 and #213) to the first stop (Torsvik). It's a five-minute walk from there (follow the signs).

▲▲**Drottningholm**—The queen's 17th-century summer castle and present royal residence has been called, not surprisingly, Sweden's Versailles. The adjacent, uncannily well-preserved Baroque theater is the real highlight, especially with its 40-kr guided tours (English theater tours normally depart 12:30, 13:30, 14:30, 15:30, and 16:30 May–September).

Get there by a relaxing but overpriced boat ride (70 kr round-trip, two hours) or take the subway to Brommaplan and bus #301 or #323 to Drottningholm. (40-kr entry, palace open daily May–August 11:00–16:30; September weekdays 13:00–15:30, weekends 12:00–15:30; tel. 08/402-6280 for palace tours in English, scheduled often at 11:00.)

The 18th-century Drottningholm court theater performs perfectly authentic operas (about 30 performances each summer). Tickets to these very popular and unique shows go on sale each March. Prices for this time-tunnel musical and theatrical experience are 100 kr to 470 kr. For information, write to Drottningholm's Theater Museum, Box 27050, 10251 Stockholm, or phone 08/660-8225, fax 08/665-1473.

▲▲**Archipelago**—The world's most scenic islands (24,000 of them!) surround Stockholm. Europeans who spend entire vacations in and around Stockholm rave about them. If you cruise to Finland, you'll get a good dose of this island beauty. Otherwise, consider the pleasant hour-long cruise (90 kr each way) from Nybroplan downtown to the quiet town of Vaxholm. The tourist office has a free archipelago guide booklet.

Sauna

Sometime while you're in Sweden or Finland, you'll have to treat yourself to Scandinavia's answer to support hose and a face-lift. (A sauna is actually more Finnish than Swedish.) Simmer down with the local students, retired folks, and busy executives. Try to cook as calmly as the Swedes. Just before bursting, go into the shower room. There's no luke-cold, and the trickle-down theory doesn't apply—only one button, bringing a Niagara of liquid ice. Suddenly your shower stall becomes a Cape Canaveral launch pad, as your body scatters to every corner of the universe. A moment later you're back together. Rejoin the Swedes in the cooker, this time with their relaxed confidence; you now know that exhilaration is just around the corner. Only very rarely will you feel so good.

Any tourist office can point you toward the nearest birch twigs. Good opportunities include a Stockholm–Helsinki cruise, any major hotel you stay in, some hostels, or cheapest, a public swimming pool. In Stockholm, consider the Eriksdalsbadet (Hammarby Slussvag 8, near Skanstull T-bana, tel. 08/643-0673). Use of its 50-meter indoor/outdoor pool and first-rate sauna costs 35 kr.

For a classier experience, the newly refurbished Central-badet lets you enjoy an extensive gym, "bubblepool," sauna, steam room, and an elegant Art Nouveau pool from 1904 (79 kr, long hours, last entry 20:30, closed Sunday, Drottningsgatan 88, five minutes up from Sergels Torg, tel. 24 24 03). Bring your towel into the sauna; the steam room is mixed, the sauna is not. Massage and solarium cost extra, and the pool is more for floating than for jumping and splashing. The leafy courtyard is an appropriately relaxing place to enjoy their restaurant (reasonable and healthy light meals).

Shopping

Modern design, glass, clogs, and wooden goods are popular targets for shoppers. Browsing is a free, delightful way to enjoy Sweden's brisk pulse. Cop a feel at the Nordiska Kompaniet (NK, also meaning "no kroner left") just across from the Sweden House or close by in the Gallerian mall. The nearby Åhlens is less expensive. Swedish stores are open 9:30 to 18:00, until 14:00 on Saturday, and closed Sunday. Some of the bigger stores (like Åhlens and NK) are open later on Saturday and on Sunday afternoon. Take a short walk to Norrmalms Torg to the new bank branch of Scandia Insurance for its ATMs, clean design, Internet access, and free coffee, tea, or chocolate.

For a smørgåsbord of Scanjunk, visit the Loppmarknaden (northern Europe's biggest flea market) at the planned suburb of Skärholmen (free on weekdays, 10 kr on weekends, Monday–Friday 11:00–18:00, Saturday 9:00–15:00, Sunday 10:00–15:00, busiest on weekends, T-bana: Skärholmen, tel. 08/710-0060).

Sleeping in Stockholm
(7 kr = about $1, tel. code: 08)
Sleep Code: **S** = Single, **D** = Double/Twin, **T** = Triple, **Q** = Quad, **b** = bathroom, **CC** = Credit Card (**V**isa, **M**asterCard, **A**mex). "Summer rates" mean mid-June to mid-August, and Friday and Saturday (sometimes Sunday) the rest of the year. Prices include breakfast unless otherwise noted.

Stockholm has plenty of money-saving deals for the savvy visitor. Its hostels are among Europe's best ($15 a bed), and plenty of people offer private accommodations ($50 doubles). Peak season for Stockholm's expensive hotels is business time—workdays outside of summer. Rates drop by 30 to 50 percent in the summer or on weekends, and if business is slow, occasionally any night—ask. To sort through all of this, the city has helpful, English-speaking room-finding services with handy locations and long hours (see Hotellcentralen and Sweden House, above).

The **Stockholm Package** offers business-class doubles with buffet breakfasts from 790 kr, includes two free Stockholm Cards, and lets two children up to 18 years old sleep for free. This is limited from mid-June to mid-August, and Friday and Saturday throughout the year. Assuming you'll be getting two Stockholm Cards anyway (370 kr), this gives you a $200 hotel room for about $50. This is for real (summertime is that dead for business hotels). The procedure (through either tourist office) is easy: a 100-kr advance booking fee (you can arrange by fax, pay when you arrive) or a 40-kr in-person booking fee if you just drop in. Arriving without reservations in July is never a problem. It gets tight during the Water Festival (ten days in early August) and during a convention stretch for a few days in late June.

My listings are a good value only outside of Stockholm Package time, or if the 790 kr for a double and two cards is out of your range and you're hosteling. Every place listed here has staff who speak English and will explain their special deals to you on the phone. If money is limited, ask if they have cheaper rooms. It's not often that a hotel will push their odd misfit room that's 100 kr below all the others. And at any time of year, prices can be soft.

About the only Laundromat in central Stockholm is Tvättomaten, at Våstmannagatan 61 on Odenplan, bus route #53 from Upplandsgaten to Central Station (60 kr, 80 kr full-serve, weekdays 8:30–18:30, Saturday 9:30–15:00, closed Sunday, across from Gustav Vasa church, helpful manager, tel. 08/346-480).

Sleeping in Hotels

Queen's Hotel is cheery, clean, and just a ten-minute walk from the station, located in a great pedestrian area across the street from the Centralbadet (city baths, listed on all maps). With a fine TV and piano lounge, coffee in the evenings, and a staff that enjoys helping its guests, this is probably the best cheap hotel in town (summer and Friday-Saturday rates: S-450 kr, Ss-480 kr, Sb-595 kr, D-550 kr, Ds-580 kr, Db-695–895 kr, winter rates: D-550–680 kr, Ds-580–780 kr, Db-1,050–1,150 kr, CC:VMA, Drottninggatan 71A, tel. 08/249-460, fax 08/217-620, e-mail: queenshotel@queenshotel.se, run by the Bergman family). Their simple rooms have no sinks. If you're arriving early from the train or boat, you're welcome to leave your bags and grab a 45-kr breakfast.

Bentley's Hotel is an interesting option with old English flair and renovated rooms (summer rates include winter Sundays: very small Db-490 kr, Db-690 kr, suite Db-750–850 kr, winter Db-1,090 kr, CC:VMA, a block up the street from Queen's at Drottninggatan 77, 11160 Stockholm, tel. 08/141-395, fax 08/212-492). Klas and Agi Kallstrom attempt to mix elegance, comfort, and simplicity into an affordable package. Each room is tastefully decorated with antique furniture but has a modern full bathroom.

The proud little **Stureparkens Gästvåning** is a carefully run, traditional-feeling place with lots of class and ten thoughtfully appointed rooms. It's a better value during the high season (July rates: S-400 kr, D-600 kr, Db-700 kr; high season: S-460 kr, D-660 kr, Db-760 kr, two-night minimum, elevator, CC:VM, near T-bana: Stadion, across from Stureparken at Sturegatan 58, tel. 08/662-7230, fax 08/661-5713).

Hotel Gustav Vasa has classy Old World rooms in a listed building with a family-run feel on a convenient square a 15-minute walk from the center (Sb-550 kr, D-550 kr, Db-650 kr, rates 100–150 kr higher outside of summer and weekends, they have some cheaper very small doubles, family deals, CC:VMA, elevator, subway to Odenplan, exit Våstmannagatan, to Våstmannagatan 61, tel. 08/343-801, fax 08/307-372).

Drottning Victorias Orlogshem, formerly a hotel for Navy personnel, now accepts the public, offering functional quiet rooms with hardwood floors and naval decor in a great neighborhood just a block off the central harbor behind the National Museum (35 rooms, Sb-450 kr, Db-650 kr, Tb-750 kr, Qb-1,000 kr, family deals, same prices all year, breakfast-35 kr, no double beds—only twins, Teatergatan 3, 11148 Stockholm, tel. 08/611-0113, fax 08/611-3150).

Prize Hotel is unique—a super-modern, happy place with tight 'n' tidy rooms 2 blocks from the station in Stockholm's World Trade Center. Designed for business travelers, it has mostly singles (with wall-beds which fold down to make doubles) and major summer and weekend discounts (not worth the high-season price, low prices Friday, Saturday, and June 8 through August 10: Sb-550 kr, Db-650 kr, they have a few real doubles for the same price as their wall-bed doubles—worth asking for, low rates offered during slow winter times—ask, breakfast-55 kr, CC:VMA, Kungsbron 1, tel. 08/566-2200, fax 08/5662-2444, e-mail: prize.sth@prize.se, www.prize.se).

City Hotel is also unique. Filling the top floors of a down-sized department store and a leader in environmental friendliness, this modern place offers hardwood floors and all the comforts in a "one-star delux" package (200 rooms, discount rates for Friday, Saturday, and June 20–August 15: Sb-550 kr, Db-790 kr, Qb-990 kr, some Db with no windows but good ventilation-690 kr, all D are twins shoved together, high season Db-1,100 kr, breakfast included, CC:VMA, free loaner bikes, overlooking Hotorget market at Kungsgatan 47, tel. 08/723-7220, fax 08/723-7299).

Sleeping in Rooms in Private Homes

Stockholm's centrally located private rooms are nearly as expensive as discounted hotels—a deal only in the high season. More reasonable rooms are a few T-bana stops just minutes from the center. Stockholm's tourist offices refer those in search of a room in a private house to **Hotelljänst** (near station, Vasagatan 15, tel. 08/104-467, fax 08/213-716). They can set you up for about 430 kr per double without breakfast for a minimum two-night stay. Go direct—you'll save your host the listing service's fee. Be sure to get the front door security code when you call, as there's no intercom connection with front doors.

Else Mari Sundin is an effervescent retired actress who rents her homey apartment, beautifully located just 2 blocks from the bridge to Djurgården (D-600 kr for up to four people, bus #47 or #69 to Torstenssonsgatan 7, go through courtyard to "garden house" and up to second floor, tel. 08/665-3348, 0884 door code). Since she lives out of town, this can be complicated. But once you're set up, it's great.

Mrs. Lichtsteiner offers rooms with kitchenettes and has a family room with a loft (Sb-300 kr, Db-400 kr without breakfast, a block from T-bana: Rådhuset, exit T-bana direction Polishuset, at Bergsgatan 45, once inside go through door on left and up elevator to second floor, tel. 08/746-9166, call ahead to get the security code, e-mail: lichtsteiner@monitor-akuten.se).

Sleeping in Hostels

Stockholm has Europe's best selection of big-city hostels offering good beds in simple but interesting places for 100 kr. If your budget is tight, these are right. Each has a helpful English-speaking staff, pleasant family rooms, good facilities, and good leads on budget survival in Stockholm. All will hold rooms for a phone call. Hosteling is cheap only if you're a member (guest membership: 35 kr a night necessary only in IYHF places); bring your own sheet (paper sheets rent for 30 kr), and picnic for breakfast (breakfasts cost 40 kr). Several of the hostels are often booked up well in advance but hold a few beds for those who are left in the lurch.

Af Chapman (IYHF), Europe's most famous youth hostel, is a permanently moored cutter ship. Just a five-minute walk from downtown, this floating hostel has 140 beds—two to eight per stateroom. A popular but compassionate place, it's often booked far in advance, but saves some beds each morning for unreserved arrivals (given out at 7:00) and gives away unclaimed rooms each evening after 18:00. If you call at breakfast time and show up before 12:00, you may land a bed, even in summer (110 kr per bed, D-240 kr, open April–mid-December, sleeping bags allowed, has a lounge and cafeteria that welcomes non-hostelers, reception open 24 hours, rooms locked up 11:00–15:00, STF Vandrarhem Af Chapman, Skeppsholmen, 11149 Stockholm, tel. 08/679-5015 for advance booking or 08/679-5016).

Skeppsholmen Hostel (IYHF), just ashore from the Af Chapman, is open all year. It has better facilities and smaller rooms (120 kr per bed in doubles, triples, and quads, only 90 kr in dorms, nonmembers pay 40 kr extra, tel. 08/679-5016), but it isn't as romantic as its seagoing sister.

Zinken Hostel (IYHF) is a big, basic hostel in a busy suburb, with 120-kr dorm beds (40 kr extra for sheets and nonmembers), plenty of 355-kr doubles without sheets, a Laundromat, and the best hostel kitchen facilities in town (STF Vandrarhem Zinken, open 24 hours all year, Zinkens Väg 20, T-bana: Zinkensdamm, tel. 08/616-8100 or 08/616-8188 in evenings). This is a great no-nonsense, user-friendly value.

Vandrarhemmet Brygghuset, in a former brewery near Odenplan, is small (57 beds in 12 spacious rooms), bright, clean, and quiet, with a Laundromat and a kitchen. Since this is a private hostel, its two- to six-bed rooms are open to all for 125 kr per bed (no sleeping bags allowed, sheets rent for 35 kr). Sheetless doubles are 310 kr. (Open June–mid-September 7:00–12:00, 15:00–23:00, 02:00 curfew, good lockers, Norrtullsgatan 12 N, tel. 08/312-424.)

Café Bed and Breakfast is Stockholm's newest cozy hostel, with only 30 beds (130 kr per bed in eight- to 12-bed rooms, breakfast-30 kr, sheets-30 kr, near Radmansgatan T-bana stop, just off Sveavägen at Rehnsgatan 21, tel. & fax 08/152-838). Bjorn and Daniela also offer three 335-kr doubles and a free sauna.

Stockholm has 12 **campgrounds** (located south of town) that are a wonderful solution to your parking and budget problems. The TI's "Camping Stockholm" brochure has specifics.

Eating in Stockholm

Stockholm's elegant department stores (notably NK and Åhlens, near Sergels Torg) have cafeterias for the kroner-pinching local shopper. Look for the 50-kr "rodent of the day" (*dagens rett*) specials. Most museums have handy cafés. The café at the **Af Chapman hostel** (open to the public in summer daily 11:30–18:00) serves a good salad/roll/coffee lunch in an unbeatable deck-of-a-ship atmosphere (if the weather's good).

The Old Town (Gamla Stan) has lots of restaurants. Try the wonderfully atmospheric **Kristina Restaurang** (Västerlånggatan 68, Gamla Stan, tel. 08/200-529). In this 1632 building, under a leather ceiling steeped in a turn-of-the-century interior, you'll find good dinners from 145 kr, including a salad and cracker bar and a cheaper "summer" menu. They serve a great 55-kr lunch (from 11:00 to 15:00) that includes an entrée, salad bar, bread, and a drink. The place is best Wednesday through Saturday 20:00 to 23:00, when live jazz accompanies your meal (silent in July and August). You can enjoy the music over just a beer or coffee, too. **Hermans** has good vegetarian food and daily specials (Stora Nygatan 11, also in Gamla Stan).

Café Michaelangelo, + Pagnim

Picnics

With higher taxes almost every year, Sweden's restaurant industry is suffering. You'll notice many fine places almost empty. Swedes joke that the "local" cuisine is now Chinese,

Italian, and hamburgers. Here more than anywhere, budget travelers should picnic.

Stockholm's major department stores and the many small corner groceries are fine places to assemble a picnic. **Åhlens** department store has a great food section (open until 21:00, near Sergels Torg). The late-hours supermarket downstairs in the central train station is picnic-friendly, with fresh, ready-made sandwiches (weekdays 7:00–23:00, weekends 9:00–23:00).

The market at **Hötorget** is a fun place to picnic shop, especially in the indoor, exotic ethnic Hötorgshallen (fun café and restaurant in fish section). The outdoor market closes at 18:00, and many merchants put their unsold produce on the push list (earlier closing and more desperate merchants on Saturday).

For a classy vegetarian buffet lunch (70 kr, Monday–Friday until 17:00), often with a piano serenade, or dinner (85 kr, evenings and weekends), eat at **Örtagården** (literally, "the herb garden," Nybrogatan 31, tel. 08/662-1728), above the colorful old Östermalms food market at Östermalmstorg.

Transportation Connections—Stockholm

By train to: Uppsala (30/day, 45 min), **Kalmar** (12/day, 5 hrs, including evening service 18:18–23:06), **Copenhagen** (6/day, 8 hrs, night service 22:30–7:00), **Oslo** (3/day, 7 hrs, night service 23:40–7:30). For train information, call 020/757-575 (toll-free in Sweden) for domestic trains, 08/227-940 for international trains.

By boat to: Helsinki (daily/nightly boats, 14 hrs; see Helsinki chapter), **Turku** (daily/nightly boats, 10 hrs).

Estline runs a regular ferry from Stockholm to **Tallinn, Estonia** (every other night at 17:30, arriving at 9:00 the next morning, 445 kr each way, 590 kr round-trip with breakfasts and a bed in a quad, cheaper off-season). It offers a 36-hour tour (no visa necessary, round-trip, simple two-bed cabins, two breakfasts, two dinners) for 1,030 kr per person (tel. 08/667-0001).

Parking in Stockholm: Only a Swedish meatball would drive his car in Stockholm. Park it and use the public transit. But parking is confusing, a major hassle, and expensive. Unguarded lots generally aren't safe. Take everything into your hotel or hostel, or pay for a garage. The tourist office has a "Parking in Stockholm" brochure. Those hosteling on Skeppsholmen feel privileged with their 25-kr-a-day island parking passes. Those with the Stockholm Card can park free in a big central garage or at any meter for the duration of the ticket. Ask for your parking card and specifics when you get your Stockholm Card. There's a safe and reasonable (10 kr per day) lot at Ropsten—the last subway station (near the Silja Line terminal). Those sailing to Finland can solve all parking worries by long-term parking on arrival in Stockholm at either terminal's safe and reasonable parking lot (60 kr per day).

NEAR STOCKHOLM: UPPSALA AND SIGTUNA

Uppsala

Uppsala is a compact city with a cathedral and university that win "Sweden's oldest/largest/tallest" awards. Allow the better part of a day, including the train from Stockholm.

The sights of historic Uppsala, along with its 30,000 university students, cluster around the university and cathedral. Just over the river is the bustling shopping zone.

Tourist Information: The Uppsala TI has a branch near the cathedral (Monday–Friday 10:00–18:00, Saturday 10:00–15:00, Sunday 12:00–16:00; closed Sunday off-season) and one in the castle (daily in summer, tel. 018/274-800). Pick up their free, entertaining, and helpful *Uppsala Guide*.

Sights—Uppsala

▲▲**Uppsala Cathedral**—One of Scandinavia's largest and most historic cathedrals, it has a breathtaking interior, the tomb of King Gustavus Vasa, and twin 400-foot spires. Ask about a guided tour. Otherwise, push the English button and listen to the tape-recorded introduction in the narthex opposite the TI table (daily 8:00–18:00).

University—Scandinavia's first university was founded here in 1477. Linnaeus and Celsius are two famous grads. Several of the old buildings are open. A historic (but not much to see) silver-bound Gothic Bible is on display with other rare medieval books in the Carolina Rediviva (library). The anatomy theater in the Gustavianum is thought-provoking. Its only show was a human dissection.

Gamla Uppsala—Old Uppsala is rooted deeply in history but now almost entirely lost in the sod of centuries. Look at the postcards of Gamla Uppsala's 15 grassy burial mounds from downtown. That's all you'll see if you go out there. Easy by car, not worth the headache by bus (#2, #5, #20, #24, or #54).

Other Uppsala Sights—Uppland Museum is on the river by the waterfall (20 kr, daily 12:00–17:00). Near the **Carl Linnaeus Garden and Museum,** the 16th-century **castle** on the hill has slice-of-castle-life exhibits.

Eating in Uppsala

Browse through the lively **Saluhallen,** the riverside indoor market near the cathedral. The university district abounds with inexpensive eateries. Try **Kung Kral** for great food; ask about a five-shot sampler of schnapps (St. Persgata 4, tel. 018/12 50 90).

Sigtuna

Between Stockholm and Uppsala you'll pass Sigtuna. Possibly Sweden's cutest town, Sigtuna is basically fluff. You'll see a medieval lane lined with colorful wooden tourist shops, a pleasant TI, a café, a romantic park, a lakeside promenade, an old church, and some rune stones. The TI organizes walking tours in English (40 kr, 3/day except Monday, call 08/5925-0020 for info). If it's sunny, Sigtuna is worth a browse and an ice-cream cone, but little more. Sigtuna is 60 minutes from Stockholm (2 trains/hr to Marsdal, then catch bus #570 or #575).

Route Tips for Drivers

Stockholm to Oslo: From downtown, follow Sveavägen West to Nortull/Gottberg/E-3/E-4 South. Take the second E-18 (immediately after the first). From Uppsala to Oslo, it's about 325 miles—that's seven hours of mostly freeway. Leaving Uppsala, follow signs for Route 55 and Nörrköping. When you hit E-18, just follow the Oslo signs. You'll pass *loppmarkets* (flea markets), Ester's Café (before Arjang), and hostel signs (90-kr dorm beds.)

Arjang, just before the Norwegian border, is worth a stop if you don't make it to Oslo. The Arjang TI (9:00–20:00, less on weekends and off-season, tel. 0573/14136) books rooms (D-240 kr plus a 50-kr fee). **Hotel Karl XII** is cheap (D-300 kr, Sveavägen 22, near marketplace, tel. 0573/10156, fax 0573/711-426).

At the border, change money at the little TI kiosk (left side, under flags, daily summer 10:00–19:00, fair rates, standard 20-kr-per-traveler's-check fee). If you change a traveler's check, convert your extra Swedish paper and coins for no extra fee. Pick up the Oslo map and *What's On*.

The freeway zips you into downtown Oslo. Follow "E-18" signs to Sentrum, then Sentral Stasjon (train station) and Paleet P (a central parking garage). If you're going directly to a room on the west end, keep left, following signs to Oslo V, veering right toward the palace immediately after passing the harborfront and twin brick towers of the city hall. If your hotel is near the station, don't take the Sentrum O exit; instead, follow the sign for Paleet P. (At the Paleet P parking garage, turn right on Fred Olsens Gate, 1.5 blocks for the Sjømannshjem.)

SOUTH SWEDEN: VÄXJÖ AND KALMAR

Outside of Stockholm, the most interesting region in Sweden is Småland. This Swedish province is famous for its forests, lakes, great glass, and the many immigrants it sent to the U.S.A. More Americans came from this area than any other part of Scandinavia, and the immigration center in Växjö tells the story well. Between Växjö and Kalmar is Glass Country, a 70-mile stretch of forest sparkling with glassworks. Of the prestigious glassworks that welcome curious visitors, Kosta's best. Historic Kalmar has a rare Old World ambience and the most magnificent medieval castle in Scandinavia. From Kalmar, you can cross Europe's longest bridge to hike through the Stonehenge-type mysteries of the strange island of Öland.

Planning Your Time

By train, on a three-week Scandinavian trip, I'd skip this area in favor of the slick night train from Copenhagen to Stockholm (and side trips to Helsinki and Estonia). If you're driving, the sights described below make that same trip an interesting way to spend a couple of days. While I'm not so hot on the Swedish countryside (okay, blame my Norwegian heritage), you can't see only Stockholm and say you've seen Sweden. Växjö and Kalmar give you the best possible dose of small-town and countryside Sweden. (I find Lund and Malmö, both popular side trips from Copenhagen, really dull. And I'm not old or sedate enough to find a sleepy boat trip along the

South Sweden: Växjö and Kalmar

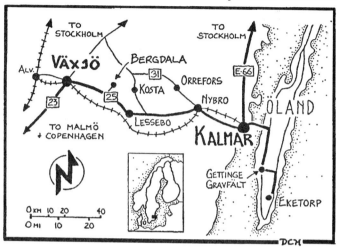

much-loved Göta Canal appealing.) Drivers spend three days getting from Copenhagen to Stockholm this way:

Day 1: Leave Copenhagen after breakfast, tour the Frederiksborg Castle, picnic under the Kronborg Castle; take the 14:00 ferry to Sweden, then drive northeast; 18:00 set up in Växjö.

Day 2: Tour Växjö's House of Emigrants, drive into Glass Country, tour the Kosta glassworks (or the smaller, more traditional Bergdala works); 14:30 set up in Kalmar in time to tour the castle and its provincial museum; evening in Kalmar.

Day 3: 8:00 begin five-hour drive north along the coast to Stockholm; 10:30 break in Västervik; 12:00 stop in Söderköping for a picnic lunch and a walk along the Göta Canal; 13:30 continue drive north; 16:00 arrive in Stockholm and possibly catch the night boat to Helsinki.

Thinking ahead to your Helsinki cruise: boat tickets may be cheaper (off-weekend) and your drive to Oslo more reasonable (earlier start) if you do the Helsinki excursion immediately after Kalmar, before seeing Stockholm.

VÄXJÖ

A pleasant but rather dull town of 70,000, Växjö (vek-fwah, the Swedish "xj" is like our "k") is in the center of Småland.

A stroll through downtown Växjö is perhaps the purest
Swedish experience you can have.

The town is compact, with the train station, town square,
two important museums, and the tourist office all within 2
blocks of each other. Växjö has an easy-to-enjoy pedestrian
center, and the nearby lake is encircled by a pleasant 3-mile
path. Train travelers not interested in glass can make this a
convenient three-hour stopover en route to Kalmar. A farmers' market bustles on the main square on Wednesday and
Saturday mornings.

Tourist Information: The busy TI is off the main
square (mid-June–August Monday–Friday 9:30–18:00, Saturday 10:00–14:00, Sunday 11:00–15:00; September–mid-June
Monday–Friday 9:00–16:30; from the station, walk straight
up Kungsgatan 3 blocks to #11, tel. 0470/41410).

Sights—Växjö

▲▲**House of Emigrants**—This tidy brick box is a user-
friendly archive filled with letters home to the old country,
ships' registers, and Minnesotans pondering their roots. A
large part of the 1,300,000 Swedes who moved to the U.S.A.
came from this neck of the Swedish woods. If you have
Swedish roots, this place is really exciting. Even if you don't,
this small exhibit is more interesting than you might expect. In
1900, Chicago was the second-largest Swedish town. Back
then, one in six Swedes lived in the U.S.A. The "Dream of
America" exhibit tells the story of the 1850s–1920s "American
Fever" in beautiful English (30 kr, June–August Monday–
Friday 9:00–18:00, Saturday 11:00–16:00, closed Sunday,
shorter hours off-season, tel. 0470/20120.) The emigration festival, three days around the second Sunday in August, is a real
hoot, as thousands of Minnesotans storm Växjö.

Upstairs is an excellent library and research center. You're
welcome to take a peek. Interview an American Swede at work.
Root-seekers (10,000 a year from the U.S.A.) are welcome,
encouraged to write well in advance (Box 201, S-35104, Växjö,
for research form and information), and advised to bring whatever information they have—such as ship names and birthdates. (Research center open Monday–Friday 9:00–16:00, 50 kr
per half-day.)

The Liv Ullman movie about the emigration, *The Immigrants*, and its sequel, *The New Land*, are great pre-trip viewing.

▲**Småland and Swedish Glass Museum**—Unfortunately, a recent renovation cost this museum its charm and its English descriptions. It offers a good look at local forestry, a prehistoric exhibit, a wonderful traditional costume display (top floor), and a look at the local glass industry but is meaningless unless you speak Swedish (30 kr, Monday–Friday 11:00–18:00, weekends 11:00–16:00, next to the House of Emigrants).

Domkyrka—Växjö's fine church (dedicated to the 11th-century English missionary, Saint Sigfrid) features some fine sacred art—in glass, of course. The thoughtfully written 10-kr brochure describes it well. The church offers free summer concerts many Thursday evenings at 20:00.

Linneparken—This lovely park, behind the cathedral, is dedicated to the great Swedish botanist Carl von Linne (a.k.a. Carolus Linnaeus). It has an arboretum, lots of well-categorized perennials, and a big children's playground.

Swimming—From the House of Emigrants you can see the town's super-modern lakeside swimming hall (Simhall) a five-minute walk away (25 kr including the sauna, plus a little more if you want to tan or use the exercise room, towels 5 kr, call for open swim hours, tel. 41204).

Sleeping in Växjö
(7 kr = about $1, tel. code: 0470)
Sleep Code: **S** = Single, **D** = Double/Twin, **T** = Triple, **Q** = Quad, **b** = bathroom, **CC** = Credit Card (Visa, MasterCard, Amex). Rates include breakfast.

Sleeping in Hotels and Motels
Hotel Esplanad is your best central hotel value. This quiet, comfortable old hotel, run by Birgit, is just 3 blocks from the town center (summer rates are mid-June–mid-August, Friday, Saturday, and Sunday nights: S-265 kr, Sb-420 kr, D-350 kr, Db-440 kr; high-season rates: D-520 kr, Db-690 kr, CC:VM, N. Esplanaden #21A, 35231 Växjö, tel. 0470/22580, fax 0470/26226). From the station, walk 5 blocks up Kungsgatan and turn left on N. Esplanaden; it's 2 blocks to the hotel. From the freeway, follow "Centrum" signs into town. At the Royal Corner Hotel, turn left; 200 yards later, at the first light, turn right onto N. Esplanaden. The yellow hotel is on the right.

Best Western Hotel Statt, in the town center, is more traditional and borderline-luxurious (small Sb-665, Db-1,125 kr; summer and weekend rates—which can stretch during slow times: small Sb-400 kr, Db-750 kr, CC:VMA, a block in front of the station at 6 Kungsgatan, tel. 0470/13400, fax 0470/44837, Web site: www.hotelstatt.se).

Hotell Teaterparken, in the Konserthus complex, has sleekly designed rooms that are a good value when discounted (in summer and on winter weekends: Sb-500 kr, Db-690 kr, CC:VMA, V. Esplanaden 10-12, tel. 0470/39900, fax 0470/47577).

Sleeping in Rooms in Private Homes

For a 50-kr fee, the tourist office can find private rooms at 140 kr per person, 125 kr if you have sheets. Breakfast is usually 35 kr extra. To save money and be assured of a good value, go or call direct to the following places.

Eva and Håkan Edfeldt are a professional couple with a teenage son who live in a woodsy 80-year-old house in a folksy old neighborhood (140 kr per person, one double and one triple share a bathroom on the top floor up some steep stairs, 30-kr breakfast baskets in the room, kitchenette, Telestadsgatan 6, 35235 Växjö, tel. 0470/19242, or during the day at their workplace, tel. 0470/88279). The whole family speaks great English. Their home is an eight-minute walk from the station: take the bridge over the tracks, jog right and follow Värendsgatan to the lake, at Skånegatan turn right— Skånegatan ends at the Edfeldts' driveway.

The **Emigrant's Cabin** is remotely situated deep in a forest near a lake, 200 meters from a tiny road, and 25 miles from Växjö. This hundred-year-old rustic cabin is furnished oldtime, with no modern conveniences. Consider a peaceful escape/adventure here (book in advance, 500 kr per night for two to four people, minimum two nights, includes a rowboat, emergency cell phone, "guided visit" to a grocery store, and round-trip drive from Växjö by the owners, the Edfeldts—see previous listing). While I haven't done this, after hearing this charming couple describe the experience, it's high on my list.

Siv Kidvik, a more comfortable, newer home run by an older couple, is fine for families with a car and has a great garden and four rooms (May–August only, D-150 kr, children half-price, breakfast-35 kr, kitchenette, Kastanjevägen 70, tel.

0470/17053, speak slowly and clearly). Drive north from the center on Linnegatan, which becomes Sandsbrovägen. At the end of the cemetery before the Shell Tankomat station, go right on Lillestadsvägen, take the first left onto Gamla Norrvägen, then the first left onto Kastanjevägen.

Sleeping in the Hostel
Växjö has a fine **hostel** on a lake 2 miles out of town (open 8:00–10:00, 17:00–20:00, 100-kr beds in two- to four-bed rooms, breakfast-40 kr, nonmembers pay 35 kr extra; STF Vandrarhem Evedal—IYHF, 35590 Växjö, tel. 0470/63070, telephone reservations required in summer). Take bus #1C from the TI to the last stop (summer only, last ride 16:15, first ride 9:15, so hitch a ride into Växjö with a fellow hosteler).

Eating in Växjö
Växjö after hours has precious little charm. You might consider dining out. These splurges come recommended by locals: **Lager Lunden** (150-kr meals, in front of the Statt Hotel), **Nygatan 26** (Swedish nouveau cuisine, 200-kr meals, at Nygatan 26), **PM** (100- to 200-kr meals, modern European cuisine in a bistro ambience popular with discerning local yuppies, across from the theater at V. Esplanaden 9, tel. 0470/45445), **Spisen** (60-kr lunch specials, 100- to 200-kr dinners, traditional Swedish, a bit smoky, across from the station, tel. 0470/12300), and **Café Momento** in the Småland museum (Swedish-French).

Transportation Connections—Växjö
By train to: Copenhagen (6/day, 5 hrs, change in Alvesta), **Kalmar** (11/day, 1.5 hrs). While there are **buses** from Växjö to Kosta and **bus tours** of the Glass Country from Växjö, the glassworks aren't worth the time and trouble unless you have a car. Instead, take a careful look at the glass exhibit in the Växjö museum and train straight to Kalmar.

Sights—Between Växjö and Kalmar
Lessebo Paper Mill—The town of Lessebo has a 300-year-old paper mill that's kept working for visitors to see. If you've never seen handmade paper produced, this mill is worth a visit. Get the English brochure. (Monday–Friday 7:00–17:00, tours in English at 9:30, 10:30, 13:00, and 14:15 in summer; the mill makes paper 7:00–11:15, 12:30–15:00; otherwise it's open but

dead, tel. 0478/10600.) By car, Lessebo is an easy stop between
Växjö and Kosta. Just after the Kosta turnoff, you'll see a
black-and-white "Handpapersbruk" sign.

▲▲The Kingdom of Crystal—This is Sweden's Glass Country. Frankly, these glassworks cause so much excitement
because of the relative rarity of anything else thrilling in Sweden, outside of greater Stockholm. Pick up the Glasriket
"Kingdom of Crystal" brochure in Växjö or Kalmar. The following three glassworks give tours and welcome visitors.
Bergdala is cutest; Kosta treats its tourists best; Orrefors is the
most famous. The fourth glassworks makes art.

Bergdala has a glassworks that offers a fine close-up look
at actual craftsmen blowing and working the red-hot glass, a
good shop (with Bergdala's tempting blue-ringed cereal
bowls), and a fine picnic area with covered tables in case it's
wet (Monday–Friday 9:00–14:30, Saturday 10:00–15:00, Sunday 12:00–15:00, no action 12:00–12:30; 30 minutes east of
Växjö, exit Road 25 at "Bergdala" sign, drive 3 miles north;
tel. 0478/31650).

Kosta is your best major glassworks stop. This town
boasts the oldest of the *glasbruks*, dating back to 1742. Today
the glassworks is a thriving tourist and shopping center (open
year-round Monday–Friday 9:00–18:00, Saturday 9:00–16:00,
Sunday 11:00–16:00; actual glassblowing is seen only on workdays but not from 10:00–11:00, tel. 0478/50705, book tours at
tel. 0478/34529). On arrival, report to the information desk to
get your English tour. Tours start in the historic and glass display rooms, then go to the actual blowing room, where guides
are constantly narrating the ongoing work.

Making great strides toward getting the lead out, Kosta's
crystal is already 80 percent lead-free. Visitors show the most
enthusiasm in the shopping hall, where crystal "seconds" and
discontinued models are sold at very good prices. This is duty-
free shopping, and they'll happily mail your purchases home.
Kosta's best picnic tables (rainproof) are at the Gamla Kosta
museum. Kosta is a well-signposted 15-minute drive from
Lessebo. In town, follow signs for "Glasbruk."

Orrefors has the most famous of the several renowned
glassworks in Glass Country, but its glassworks are quite a tourist
racket and offer mediocre 30-minute tours (hourly, tel. 0481/
34000 to confirm tour times). Most visitors just observe the work
from platforms. There's glassblowing action from 8:00 to 15:00

except for the 10:30 to 11:30 lunch-break. Like Kosta, their shop sells nearly perfect crystal seconds at deep discounts (June–mid-July Monday–Friday 9:00–18:00, Saturday 9:00–16:00, Sunday 11:00–16:00; off-season closes an hour earlier). Don't miss the dazzling "museum" (open same hours as shop).

Transjö Glashytta offers a much different experience. Set up in an old converted farm, a ten-minute drive south of Kosta, this tiny glassworks does expensive but fine art pieces (tel. 0478/50700 for hours and specifics).

KALMAR

Kalmar feels formerly strategic and important. In its day, the town was called "the gateway to Sweden"—back when the Sweden/Denmark border was just a few miles to the south. Today it's just a sleepy has-been, and gateway only to the holiday island of Öland. Kalmar's salty old center, fine castle, and busy waterfront give it a wistful sailor's charm. The town is wonderfully walkable or bike-able.

History students remember Kalmar as the place where the treaty establishing the Kalmar Union was signed. This 1397 "three crowns" treaty united Norway, Sweden, and Denmark and created a huge kingdom—impressive for its day, as most of Europe was fragmented and bickering. But the union, which was dominated by Denmark, lasted only a little more than a hundred years. When Gustav Vasa came to power in 1523, it was dissolved.

Tourist Information: The TI is central and helpful (mid-June to mid-August Monday–Friday 9:00–21:00, Saturday 9:00–17:00, Sunday 12:00–18:00; closing at 17:00 other months and closed on winter weekends, from station walk 2 blocks down Sodra Langgatan and turn right on Larmgatan to #6, tel. 0480/15350). Get the handy town map, city guidebooklet, and confirm your sightseeing plans.

Bike Rental: Kalmar, with its cheery lanes, surrounding parks, and brisk harborfront, makes for happy biking. Team Sportia, a big sport shop near the station, rents fine bikes for 40 kr a day (weekdays 10:00–18:00, Saturday 10:00–15:00, closed Sunday, leaving station, turn left on Stationsgatan and walk 300 meters to the roundabout, tel. 0480/21244). The Frimurare Hotellet rents bikes to its guests for the same price. The TI has a "Vasa Stigen" flier outlining a pleasant bike/hike past the castle and around the Stenso Peninsula.

Kalmar

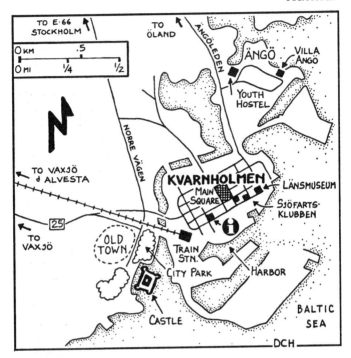

Arrival in Kalmar: Arriving by train couldn't be easier. At the station (lockers available), get a reservation for your departure. The TI and town are dead ahead, bikes are to your left, and the castle is behind you.

Sights—Kalmar

▲▲**Kalmar Castle**—This moated castle is one of Europe's great medieval experiences. The stark exterior, cuddled by a lush park, houses a fine Renaissance palace interior, which is the work of King Gustavus Vasa and his sons. You'll walk up steps made of Catholic grave stones into faded but still grand halls alive with Swedish history. The elaborately furnished rooms are entertainingly explained in English (50 kr, mid-June to mid-August Monday–Saturday 10:00–18:00, Sunday 12:00–18:00; shoulder season 12:00–18:00; November–March much shorter hours, tel. 0480/56351). English tours are worthwhile for the goofy medieval antics of Sweden's kings (free, 45 minutes, daily in summer at 11:30 and 14:30). Check out the eerie exhibit on the women's prison; find the book with English descriptions.

▲**Krusenstiernska Garden**—This early 19th-century middle-class home is lovingly cluttered with old family photos, toys, and Gustavian-style furniture. A helpful English leaflet gives a room-by-room inventory. The garden, with its breezy café selling traditional homemade cakes, is also a treat (15 kr, Monday–Friday 10:00–17:00, weekends 13:00–16:00, closed off-season, 200 yards in front of the castle at St. Dammgatan 11, tel. 0480/411-552). Between this house, the castle, and the station is Kalmar's **Gamla Stan** (old town), a toy village of well-painted wooden homes, tidy yards, and perfect fences.

▲**Kalmar Town**—The old town of Kalmar is more interesting than its grid plan. Stroll the Storgatan spine to the main square, Stortorget, where you'll find the biggest Baroque church in Sweden. The quieter lanes and Lilla Torget have fine old wooden homes. The ramparts survive and mark the old harbor line. The 20th-century extension is filled with parked cars and a modern shopping center.

▲▲**Kalmar County (Lans) Museum**—The second floor of this museum displays the impressive salvaged wreck of the royal ship *Kronan*, which sank nearby in 1676. Lots of interesting soggy bits and rusted pieces giving a here's-the-buried-treasure thrill are well-described in English. (For maximum info, borrow the *Kronan* English booklet). While the actual ship has yet to be recovered, this museum gives a much more intimate look at life at sea than Stockholm's grander *Vasa* exhibit. See the excellent 12-minute film (to avoid a delay, request an English showing as you enter). The third floor is worth a quick look for its Jenny Nystrom exhibit (a turn-of-the-century Kalmar artist who gained fame for her cute Christmas decorations featuring gidgets, elves, and pixies), a little old-time Kalmar city life exhibit, and a cozy cafeteria (daily 11:30–13:30, 40-kr salad buffet). From the harborfront museum's door you can see the distant half of the long bridge leading to the island of Öland (40 kr, daily mid-June–mid-August 10:00–18:00, off-season closes at 16:00, tel. 0480/56300).

Maritime History Museum (Sjöfartsmuseum)—This humble little three-room exhibit behind the Lans Museum is a jumble of model boats, charts, and paraphernalia interesting only to sailors who speak Swedish.

▲Island of Öland—Europe's longest bridge (free, 4 miles) connects Öland with Kalmar and the mainland. The island, 90 miles long and only 8 miles wide, is a pleasant local resort known for its birds, windmills, flowers, beaches, and prehistoric sights. Public transportation is miserable, and the island is worthwhile only if you have a car and three extra hours. A 60-mile circle south of the bridge will give you a good dose of the island's windy rural charm.

Gettlinge Gravfalt (just off the road about 10 miles up from the south tip) is a wonderfully situated, boat-shaped, Iron Age grave site littered with monoliths and overseen by a couple of creaky old windmills. It offers a commanding view of the windy and mostly treeless island.

Farther south is the **Eketorp Prehistoric Fort**, a very reconstructed fifth-century stone fort that, as Iron Age forts go, is fairly interesting. Several evocative huts and buildings are filled with what someone imagines may have been the style back then, and the huge rock fort is surrounded by strange, runty, pig-like creatures that were common 1,500 years ago. A sign reads: "For your convenience and pleasure, don't leave your children alone with the animals." (45 kr, daily May–August 9:00–18:00, free English tours usually at 13:00 in summer, tel. 0485/62023.)

Sleeping in Kalmar
(7 kr = about $1, tel. code: 0480)
The tourist office can nearly always find you a room in a private home (230 kr per double, 40 kr per person for sheets, and a 50-kr fee per booking, no breakfast). They can also get you special last-minute discounts on fancy hotels. The first three places are great but cheap or open only during summer.

Frimurare Hotellet fills a grand old building overlooking a fine square. While quite large, it has soul and feels family-run. Rich public areas, broad hardwood floors, chandeliers, and pilasters give it a neoclassical elegance (regular Db rate: 890 kr, mid-June–mid-August and Friday/Saturday/Sunday all-year rates: Sb-460 kr, Db-645 kr with breakfast, CC:VMA, five rooms—while no more expensive—are saved for honeymooners and tourists like you who ask for them, free sauna, bikes rented for 40 kr/day, yellow building 50 meters in front of the train station at Larmtorget 2, 39232 Kalmar, tel. 0480/15230, fax 0480/85887).

The **Sjöfartsklubben (Seaman's Club)** opens its ship-shape little dorm to tourists June through mid-August. This historic home, built as a girls' school in 1820, now houses student sailors during the school year (13 rooms, S-175 kr, D-230 kr, T-300 kr, Q-360 kr, sheets-40 kr, breakfast-30 kr, kitchen privileges, lively common room, Olandsgatan 45, reception open same hours as TI, tel. 0480/10810). With harbor views and a lazy garden protected by a salty picket fence, this has by far the best cheap beds in Kalmar.

Söderportsgården is a university dorm that opens mid-June to mid-August for tourists (35 simple yet classy rooms, two to a "flat" sharing a bathroom and kitchen, S-350 kr, D-450 kr, includes sheets and breakfast, Slottsvägen 1, tel. 0480/12501). It's beautifully located next to a park, directly in front of the castle.

A 15-minute walk from the center, you'll find a fine **IYHF hostel** and hotel annex. The hostel has two- or seven-bed rooms, laundry, TV, and sauna (40 kr/hour per couple, 120 kr per bed, sheets-45 kr, nonmembers pay 40 kr extra, breakfast-45 kr, closed 10:00–16:30, reservations recommended). The hotel annex, **Kalmar Lagprishotell Svanen**, offers more comfort and privacy (S-305 kr, Sb-385 kr, D-420 kr, Db-490 kr, includes sheets and breakfast, CC:VMA, STF Vandrarhem, Rappegatan 1, 39230 Kalmar, tel. 0480/25560, fax 0480/88293). You'll see a blue-and-white hotel sign and hostel symbol at the edge of town on Angoleden Street, less than a mile from the train station.

In the same residential neighborhood, a few blocks farther out, consider **Hotel Villa Angö**, a big old house with a peaceful garden on the water and homey ground-floor rooms (S-195 kr, D-300 kr, Db-350–500 kr with breakfast in summer, basement sauna, a 15-minute walk out of town, Bagensgatan 20, tel. 0480/85415). The management lets the place virtually run itself, leaving the door open and the room key waiting for you in the door.

Best Western Stadts Hotel is a 1,100-kr place with an affordable summer price (summer rate: Sb-495 kr, Db-670 kr, includes breakfast, CC:VMA, central at Stortorget 14, tel. 0480/15180, fax 0480/15847, e-mail: reservation@calmarstadshotell.se).

Eating in Kalmar

In the old center: I'd stroll the two busy cross streets, Storgatan and Kaggensgatan, to survey the many competitive

places—both ethnic and Swedish. **Bistro Matisse** is popular
for French cuisine (1 Kaggensgatan). At the intersection of
those two streets, upstairs in the Kvasten department store, the
4 Kok cafeteria serves a hearty *dagens rett* special (50 kr,
11:00–14:00).

On the modern harborfront: Consider **Calmar
Hamnkrog** for classy harbor-view dining (200-kr dinners,
daily 13:00–23:00, Skeppsbrogatan 30, call 0480/411-020 to
reserve seats by a window). For a meal for half the price from
the same kitchen, with less ambience but the same harbor
views, consider **Dåcket** (100-kr dinners, daily from 17:00,
closed Sunday, outside or inside seating).

Near the castle: There are cafeterias in the castle and
directly in front of the castle at Söderportsgärden. For classier
dining (or just a coffee break) in the city park with a view of
the castle, consider the venerable **Byttan Restaurant** (55-kr
lunch special 11:00–14:00, more expensive dinners; you'll pass
it as you walk to the castle).

Transportation Connections—Kalmar

By train to: Växjö (10/day, 1.5 hrs, reservation not required),
Stockholm (10/day, 6 hrs, normally a transfer in Alvesta,
reservation required; night train possible but with a change,
nightly except Saturday), **Copenhagen** (6 hrs, one change,
reservation required).

Route Tips for Drivers

Copenhagen to Sweden: See "Route Tips for Drivers" at the
end of Copenhagen chapter.

Helsingborg to Växjö to Kalmar: In Helsingborg, follow
signs for E-4 and Stockholm. The road's good, traffic's light,
and towns are clearly signposted. At Ljungby, Road 25 takes
you to Växjö. Entering Växjö, skip the first Växjö exit and follow the freeway into "Centrum," where it ends.

The 70-mile drive from Växjö to Kalmar is a joy—light
traffic with endless forest and lake scenery punctuated by
numerous glassworks. The TI's free "Kingdom of Crystal" map
lists them all and is your best navigational tool. Leave Växjö on
Road 25 to Kalmar. The driving time between Växjö and Kosta
is 45 minutes; between Kosta and Kalmar, 45 minutes.

Kalmar to Stockholm: Leaving Kalmar, follow E-22
"Lindsdal" and "Nörrköping" signs. The Kalmar–Stockholm

drive is 240 miles and takes 5.5 hours. Sweden did a cheap widening job, paving the shoulders of the old two-lane road to get 3.8 lanes. Still, traffic is polite and sparse. There's little to see, so stock the pantry, set the compass on north, and home in on Stockholm.

Make two pleasant stops along the way. Ninety miles north is Vastervik, with a pleasant 18th-century core of wooden houses (3 miles off the highway, "Centrum" signs lead you to the harbor). Park at the little salty, six-days-a-week-and-great-smoked-fish market on the waterfront next to the seven-days-a-week, picnic-perfect Exet supermarket and a public WC.

Söderköping is just right for a lunch on the Göta Canal stop. Stay on E-22 past the town center, turn right at the TI/Kanalbåtarna/Slussen/Kanal P signs. Park by the canal, 1 block toward the hill from the town square and TI.

Sweden's famous Göta Canal is 110 miles of canals cutting Sweden in half, with 58 locks (*slussen*) working up to a summit of 300 feet. It was built 150 years ago, with more than 7 million 12-hour man-days (60,000 men working about 22 years) at a low ebb in the country's self-esteem—to show her industrial oats. Today it's a lazy three- or four-day tour. Take just a peek at the Göta Canal over lunch, in the medieval town of Söderköping.

The TI on Söderköping's Rådhustorget (a square about a block off the canal) has good town maps, canal information, and Stockholm maps. From there go to the canal. The Toalett sign points to the Kanulbatiquen, a yachters' laundry (40 kr, wash and dry, open daily), shower, shop, and WC, with idyllic canalside picnic tables just over the lock. From the lock, stairs lead up to the Utsiktsplats pavilion (a nice view but not quite worth the hike).

Leaving Söderköping, E-22 takes you to Nörrköping. Follow "E-4" signs through Nörrköping, then past a handy over-the-freeway rest stop into Stockholm. The Centrum is clearly marked. (Viking's ferry terminal for Helsinki is in Södermalm, while Silja's terminal is northeast of town in Ropsten.)

FINLAND

HELSINKI

Finland is the odd duck in this book, and, as such, it deserves special comment. First, a brief history lesson. As far as the sightseer is concerned, Finland's history breaks into three parts:

Swedish—Finland was dominated by Sweden before the 1809 Russian takeover. Because of city fires, very little remains of this era.

Russian—Between 1809 and 1917, under Russian control, most of Helsinki's great buildings were built.

Independent—From 1918 on, Finland's bold, trendsetting modern design and architecture blossomed.

After World War II, Finland teetered between independence and the U.S.S.R., treading very lightly on matters concerning her fragile autonomy and relations with her giant neighbor to the east. The collapse of the U.S.S.R. has done to Finland what a good long sauna might do to you.

When the menace of Moscow vanished, so did about 20 percent of Finland's trade. Along with the loss of a major trading partner, unemployment and a high cost of living have been Finland's main problems. The average income is roughly $30,000—with about 35 percent going to taxes. About 70 percent of the people rent apartments that can be had in Helsinki for about $800 a month including heat.

Money
There are about 5 Finnish markka (mk) in a U.S. dollar. One markka is about 20 cents.

Weather in Finland

They say the people of Finland spend nine months in winter and the other three months waiting for summer. The weather dictates a brief (June–August) tourist season. February in Finland is not my idea of a good time. During particularly cold winters, Helsinki's bus #19 used to extend its route over the frozen bay to a suburban island. When summer arrives, the entire population jumps in with street singing and beach-blanket vigor.

Finnish

Finnish is a difficult-to-learn Finno-Ugric language originating east of Russia's Ural Mountains and related in Europe only to Estonian (closely) and Hungarian (distantly). Finland is officially bilingual; 6 percent of the country's population speaks Swedish as a first language. You'll notice that Helsinki is called Helsingfors in Swedish. Many street signs list places in both Finnish and Swedish. Nearly every educated young person will speak effortless English and the language barrier is very small.

The only essential word needed for a quick visit is, "*Kiitos*" (key-toes)—that's "thank you," and locals love to hear it. "*Kippis*" ("Keep peace") is what you say before you down a shot of Finnish vodka or cloudberry liqueur.

And now, on to Helsinki—via a cruise ship.

SAILING FROM STOCKHOLM TO HELSINKI

The next best thing to being in Helsinki is getting there. Europe's most enjoyable cruise starts with lovely archipelago scenery, a setting sun, and a royal smørgåsbord dinner. Dance 'til you drop and sauna 'til you drip. Budget travel rarely feels this hedonistic. Fourteen hours after you depart, it's "Hello, Helsinki."

Planning Your Time

When planning your cruise, consider how much time you'd like to spend in Helsinki (one day is normally enough) and the day you'd like to depart (Friday and Saturday are more crowded and expensive). Also consider the schedule ripples caused by the ship. Assuming you sleep into and out of Stockholm by train and take two night boats, you'll have two days in Stockholm with no nights. Stockholm is worth two days on a three-week Scandinavian trip, but four in-transit nights in a row is pretty intense. Doable, but intense.

Sailing from Stockholm to Helsinki

The Cruise Lines: Viking and Silja

Two fine and fiercely competitive lines, Viking and Silja, connect the capitals of Sweden and Finland daily and nightly. Each line offers state-of-the-art ships with luxurious smørgåsbord meals, reasonable cabins, plenty of entertainment (discos, saunas, gambling), and enough duty-free shopping to sink a ship.

The Pepsi and Coke of the Scandinavian cruise industry vie to outdo each other with bigger and fancier boats. The ships are big—at 56,000 tons, nearly 200 yards long, and with 2,700 beds, they're the largest (and some of the cheapest) luxury hotels in Scandinavia. Many other shipping lines buy their boats used from Viking and Silja.

Which line is best? You could count showers and compare smørgåsbords, but each line goes overboard to win the loyalty of the 9 million duty-free-crazy Swedes and Finns who make the trip each year. Viking, with an older, less luxurious fleet, is cheaper by about 100 kr per round-trip. Silja requires passengers to rent a bed (about 195 kr each way high season for a bed in a four-bed cabin, double that in a double), and Viking lets stowaways (or those who find the boat booked up) sleep for free on chairs, sofas, and under the stars or stairs. Eurailers get free deck passage on Viking and discounts from Silja.

Cruise Schedules

Both lines sail daily from Stockholm and Helsinki, usually leaving at 18:00 and arriving the next morning between 8:00 and 9:00. There are morning departures, too, but overnight crossings are more fun and efficient. Both lines also sail daily between Stockholm and Turku, Finland.

Scenery: The first three hours are filled with island scenery. The first hour after departure is least interesting. The third hour features the most exotic island scenery—tiny islets with cute red huts and very happy people. I'd have dinner at the first sitting (immediately upon departure) and get out on the deck for the sunset. Stockholm departures pass their counterparts coming in from Finland about an hour into the cruise.

Time Change: Finland is one hour ahead of Sweden. Sailing from Stockholm to Helsinki, operate on Swedish time until you go to bed, then reset your watch. Morning schedules are Finnish time (and vice versa when you return).

Cost

Fares vary with the season and are inconsistent. Fridays throughout the year and mid-June to mid-August are most expensive (and crowded). Even in high season, a round-trip with the cheapest bed (in a below-sea-level, under-car-deck quad) is remarkably cheap: about $110 (800 kr on Viking, 900–1,000 kr on Silja). Fares are as low as 560 kr (round-trip with a bed) in low season. Each ship offers a whale of a smørgåsbord.

Beds cost the same throughout the year, starting at around 120 kr (on Viking, under the car deck, quads) and going up with the elevator. Viking also lets vagabonds sail without a bed (600-kr round-trip, deck class, peak season, add 100 kr per bed in a quad each way or 200 kr per bed in a double each way).

The fares are so cheap because the boats operate tax-free and the hordes of locals who sail to shop and drink duty- and tax-free spend a fortune on board. It's a very large operation—mostly for locals. The boats are filled with about 60 percent Finns, 35 percent Swedes, and 5 percent cruisers from other countries. Last year, the average passenger spent nearly as much on booze and duty-free items as for the boat fare—about

600 kr. (Note: As European unification continues, the lure of duty-free shopping will diminish.)

Sleeping Free

Most new boats lack cheap "slum" beds, but some older boats may have a few free dorm beds for vagabonds. To get one (on Viking only), get to the boat as soon as it opens (usually 16:00) and head straight for the bottom of the boat. There may be eight to ten bunks with no closing doors. Those camping out can lock up their bags from port to port in the luggage checkroom.

Reservations

Reserve your spot in advance from Copenhagen, Stockholm, or the U.S.A. Call and compare deals (Silja 800/323-7436; Viking 800/688-3876). You'll save money by booking in Scandinavia, but if you want a bed and are traveling in summer or on a Friday, make a reservation as soon as you can commit. Pick up your reserved ticket at the terminal an hour before sailing. (Viking Line tel. 08/452-4000 in Stockholm, 33 32 60 36 in Copenhagen; Silja Line tel. 08/222-140 in Stockholm, 33 14 40 80 in Copenhagen.) You can also get a ticket through any travel agent in Scandinavia (same price plus a 30-kr-or-so booking fee).

Terminals

Locations: In Stockholm, the Viking terminal is more central. Take the bus (20 kr) from Central Station's gate #24 or take bus #53 to "London Viaducten." The ship is parked just past the Gamla Stan. For Silja, take the bus (20 kr) from Central Station's gate #35. In Helsinki, both lines are perfectly central, each on opposite sides of the harbor, a ten-minute walk from the market, Senate Square, and shopping district. (If staying at Helsinki's Eurohostel, Viking is more convenient.)

Terminal Buildings: These are well organized with cafés, lockers, tourist information desks, lounges, and phones. Remember, 2,000 passengers come and go with each boat. Customs is a snap. Boats open two hours before departure.

Parking: Both lines offer safe and handy 70 kr/day parking in Stockholm. Viking's ticket machine takes 5- and 10-kr coins (come with 110 kr for 46 hours or credit cards). For

Silja it's wise to reserve a parking spot (tel. 08/662-0046).
Keep inserting money until you see the date and time of your
return on the meter, then hit the red button and leave the
ticket on your dashboard. Park your car here on arrival in
Stockholm, and leave it while you sightsee Stockholm, take
the cruise, and tour Helsinki.

Services On Board

Meals: The cruise is famous for its smørgåsbords, and under-
standably so. Board the ship hungry. Dinner is self-serve in two
sittings, one immediately upon departure, the other two hours
later. The scenery is worth being on deck for, but if you call in
advance, you can reserve a window seat. If you board without a
reservation, go to the headwaiter and make one. Breakfast buffets
are 50 kr; dinner buffets, 150 kr (buy with your ticket and save
10 percent). Pick up the "How to Eat a Smørgåsbord" brochure.
The key is to take small portions and pace yourself. Drinks or
free water can be ordered from waiters (free beer and wine on
Viking). There are also reasonable or classy restaurants for
lighter eaters or those on a budget.

Sauna: Each ship has a sauna. This costs about 60 kr extra.
Reserve a time upon boarding. Saunas on Silja are half-price or
even free in the morning (for those with a cabin towel).

Banking: The change desk on board has bad rates but no
fee, which means it's actually a better deal than a Helsinki bank
for those changing less than $100. There are about 5 Finnish
markka (mk) in a U.S. dollar. Helsinki banks charge 15 mk to
exchange cash and 20 mk for traveler's checks, while the
change desk in the boat changes cash for no fee and charges 30
mk for checks. FOREX (with offices at N. Esplanaden 27 in
Helsinki and in Stockholm's train station) gives the best rates
for small exchanges. For a quick visit to Helsinki, just change
some of your Swedish kroner. While city sightseeing tours can
be paid for in kroner, you'll need local currency for public
transport, shops, and museums.

Day Privileges: If you're spending two nights in a row on
the Stockholm–Helsinki boat, you have access to your stateroom all day long. If you like, you can sleep in and linger over
breakfast long after the boat has docked. But there's really way
too much to do in Helsinki to take advantage of these privileges (unless you take the round-trip passage twice, on four
successive nights—a reasonable option given the high cost of

hotels and meals on shore and the frustration of trying to see Helsinki in a day).

Options

Staying Overnight in Helsinki: If you're staying in Helsinki, your boat line can get you a $100 double in a $200 hotel when you book your tickets, but you can find a cheaper room by telephoning my budget listings (see below).

Open Jaws: Consider an "open jaws" plan, sailing from Stockholm into Helsinki and returning to Stockholm from Turku. The cheaper round-trip boat fare saves enough to pay for the two-hour train ride from Helsinki to Turku. Turku boats may have free airplane seats or couchettes in the bilge, but the boats are usually smaller and lack cruise-ship excitement. Passengers are rushed on and off, since the boat stays only one hour in the port.

HELSINKI

Helsinki feels close to Russia. It is. Much of it reminds me of St. Petersburg. It's no wonder Hollywood chose to film *Dr. Zhivago*, *Reds*, and *Gorky Park* here. (They filmed the Moscow Railway Station scenes in *Dr. Zhivago* in the low red-brick building near the Viking Terminal.) There is a huge and impressive Russian Orthodox church overlooking the harbor, a large Russian community, and several fine Russian restaurants.

In the early 1800s, the Russians took Finland from Sweden, and moved the capital eastward from Turku, making Helsinki the capital of their "autonomous duchy." I asked a woman in the TI if a particular café was made for Russian officers. In a rare spasm of candor (this was during the Cold War), she said, "All of 19th-century Helsinki was made for Russian officers."

Today Helsinki is gray and green. A little windy and cold, it looks like it's stuck somewhere in the north near the Russian border. But it makes the best of its difficult situation and will leave you impressed and glad to have dropped in. Start with the two-hour "Hello, Helsinki" bus tour that meets the boat at the dock. Enjoy Helsinki's ruddy harborfront market, count goosebumps in her churches, and dive into Finnish culture in the open-air folk museum.

Europe's most neoclassical city has many architectural overleafs, and it tends to turn guests into fans of architecture. Its buildings, designs, fashions, and people fit sensitively into their surroundings. An architect might say, "Dissimilar elements are fused into a complex but comfortable whole." It's an intimate and human place.

Planning Your Time

On a three-week trip through Scandinavia, Helsinki is worth the time between two successive nights on the cruise ship—about nine hours. Take the orientation bus tour upon arrival, mingle through the market, buy and eat a picnic, and drop by the TI. People-watch and browse through downtown to the National Museum (closed until October 1, 1999). For the afternoon, choose between the Open-Air Folk Museum or a harbor boat tour. Enjoy a cup of coffee in the Café Kappeli before boarding time. Sail away while sampling another smørgåsbord dinner.

Orientation (Helsinki's tel. code: 09; from outside Finland: 358-9)

Helsinki is a colorful shopping town of 500,000 people. The compact city center is great for roaming and brisk walking.

Tourist Information: Helsinki has TIs at the boat terminals, inside the train station, and on Market Square (Market Square office open Monday–Friday 9:00–19:00, weekends 9:00–15:00, shorter hours off-season, tel. 09/169-3757 or 09/174-088, fax 09/169-3839, web site: www.hel.fi). The TIs are uniformly friendly, helpful, well stocked in brochures, and blond(e). Pick up the city map; the "Route Map" (public transit); "Helsinki on Foot" (six well-described walking tours with maps); the monthly *Helsinki This Week* magazine (lists sights, hours, and events); and *City* magazine (good opinionated restaurant listings, geared for the younger crowd). Ask for the brochure on the scenic #3T tourist tram and go over your sightseeing plans. **Tour Expert,** a travel agency at the TI, is efficient and helpful for hotels and excursions, especially to the Baltics (same hours as TI, tel. 09/622-6990, fax 09/6226-9914).

Money Exchange: FOREX exchange desks are all over town (daily 8:00–21:00).

Telephoning: Helsinki's area code is 09 and Finland's country code is 358. When calling Helsinki from outside Finland, add the country code and drop the 0. Dial the international access code of the country you're calling from (usually 00 in Europe), then dial 358-9-local number.

Ferries: If you're returning to Stockholm, the boat

Helsinki Center

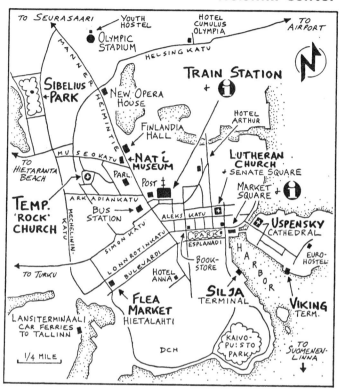

departs Helsinki at Finnish time. Remember, Finland is one hour ahead of Sweden. Ferry info: Silja Line, tel. 9800-74552.

Museum Pass: The **Helsinki Card** is worth considering (24 hours/105 mk, includes free entrance to sights, use of buses and trams, and a 70-mk bus tour; 48 hours for 135 mk; buy at TI).

Getting Around Helsinki

By Bus and Tram: With the public transit route map and a little mental elbow grease, the buses and trams are easy, giving you the city by the tail. Tickets (7 mk per ride, 9 mk for an hour of travel) are purchased from the driver.

The Tourist Ticket (25 mk for 24 hours of unlimited travel) pays if you take three or more rides. The Helsinki Card

(105 mk) gives you free entry to city sights and use of all buses and trams for 24 hours.

The tourist tram, #3T, makes the rounds of most of the town's major sights, letting you stop and go for 9 mk an hour. The TI has a helpful explanatory brochure (not available on the bus). Bus #24 goes farther afield but is similar to the tourist tram #3T (with great guide brochure, also from TI). Each of these give you a great, cheap, go-any-time, once-over-lightly, do-it-yourself tour. In summer the red "Pub Tram" makes a 40-minute circle through the city while its passengers get looped on the (one) beer that comes with the 30-mk ticket (hourly from 11:00–15:00 and 17:00–22:00, from Mikaelsgata in front of Fennia building across from the train station).

By Bike: Citysafari rents bikes at the old market hall (near the Silja Terminal, 50 mk for two hours, 20 mk per hour thereafter, tel. 0400-50-3939). Greenbike also rents bikes (at Mannerheimintie 13, across from the Parliament House).

Do-It-Yourself "Welcome to Helsinki" Walk

Start at the harbor. The colorful **produce market** on Market Square thrives from 7:00 to 14:00 and 15:30 to 20:00 (closed Saturday afternoon and sometimes on Sunday). The head of the harbor, facing the cruise ships, is Helsinki's center. The fountain features the symbol of Helsinki, the Daughter of the Baltic. The pale blue building facing the market is the City Hall. Beyond that is the Presidential Palace. Don't miss the busy, two-tone, red-brick, indoor market hall adjacent. Across the street you'll see the **Tourist Office**. The round door next to the TI leads into the delightful **Jugendsalen**. Designed, apparently, by a guy named Art Deco, this free and pleasant information center for locals offers interesting historical exhibits and a public WC (Monday–Friday 9:00–16:00, Pohjoisesplanadi 19).

One block inland behind the tourist office are the fine neoclassical **Senate Square** and **Lutheran Cathedral**. You'll pass the Schroder Sport Shop on Unioninkatu, with a great selection of popular Finnish-made Rapula fishing lures—ideal for the fisherfolk on your gift list.

Across the street from the TI, in the park facing the square, is my favorite café in northern Europe, **Café Kappeli**. When you've got some time, dip into this turn-of-the-century gazebo-like oasis of coffee, pastry, and relaxation. Built in the

19th century, it was a popular hangout for local intellectuals and artists. Today the café offers the romantic tourist waiting for his ship a great 10-mk-cup-of-coffee memory (unguarded WC just inside the door).

Behind the café runs the entertaining park, sandwiched between the north and south **Esplanadi**—Helsinki's top shopping boulevard. Walk it. The north (tourist office) side is interesting for window-shopping, people-watching, and sun-worshiping. You'll pass several stores specializing in Finnish design. The huge Academic Bookstore, designed by Alvar Aalto (nearby at 1 Keskuskatu), has a great map and travel guide section and café. Finally you'll come to the prestigious Stockman's department store—Finland's Harrods. This biggest, best, and oldest store in town has fine displays of local design. Just beyond is the main intersection in town, Esplanadi and Mannerheimintie. Nearby you'll see the famous ***Three Blacksmiths*** statue. (Locals say, "If a virgin walks by, they'll strike the anvil." It doesn't work. I tried.)

A block to the right, through a busy shopping center, is the harsh (but serene) architecture of the central **train station,** designed by Eliel Saarinen in 1916. The four people on the facade symbolize the peasant farmers with lamps coming into the Finnish capital. Wander around inside. Continuing past the Posti and the statue, return to Mannerheimintie, which leads to the large white **Finlandia Hall,** another Aalto masterpiece. While it's not normally open, there are often two tours a day in the summer (ask at the TI). Across the street is the excellent little Finnish **National Museum** (looks like a church, designed by Finland's first three great architects, closed until October 1, 1999), and a few blocks behind that is the sit-down-and-wipe-a-tear beautiful rock church, **Temppeliaukio.** Sit. Enjoy the music. It's a wonderful place to end this Welcome to Helsinki walk.

From nearby Arkadiankatu Street, bus #24 will take you to the **Sibelius Monument** in a lovely park. The same ticket is good on a later #24. Ride to the end of the line—the bridge to Seurasaari island and Finland's open-air folk museum. From here, bus #24 returns to the Esplanadi.

Sights—Helsinki
▲▲▲**Orientation Bus Tour**—A fast, very good two-hour introductory tour leaves daily from both terminals immediately after the ships dock (unless there are two arrivals, in which case

some travelers will have an hour to walk down and see the market in action). The rapid-fire two- or three-language tour costs 80 mk (120 Swedish kroner) and gives a good historic overview—a look at all the important buildings from the newly remodeled Olympic Stadium to embassy row, with too-fast ten-minute stops at the Lutheran Cathedral, the Sibelius monument, and the Church in the Rock (Temppeliaukio). You'll learn strange facts, such as how they took down the highest steeple in town during World War II so the Soviet bombers flying in from Estonia couldn't see their target.

If you're on a tight budget and don't mind missing the more distant sights, you can do the core of this tour on your own, as explained in my city walk (above). But I thoroughly enjoyed listening to the guide. He sounded like an audio shredder that was occasionally turned off so English could come out.

For more time in the Church of the Rock, leave the tour there and consider walking 3 blocks to the National Museum (closed until October 1, 1999) and Finlandia Hall.

A shorter, cheaper bus tour is nearly as good (70 mk and included on the Helsinki Card, daily in summer at 11:30 and 13:30 from the train station or near the TI at 10:30 or 12:30, no stop at the Lutheran Cathedral), but I like the "pick you up at the boat and drop you at your hotel or back on Market Square" efficiency of the 9:30 tour. Buy your ticket on board or at the tourist desk in the terminal (availability is no problem).

▲▲**Lutheran Cathedral**—With its prominent green dome overlooking the city and harbor, this church is Carl Ludwig Engel's masterpiece. Open the pew gate and sit to savor neoclassical nirvana. Finished in 1852, the interior is pure architectural truth (Monday–Saturday 9:00–18:00, Sunday 12:00–16:00; off-season 10:00–16:00).

Senate Square—From the top of the steps of the Lutheran Cathedral, study Europe's finest neoclassical square. The Senate building is on your left. The small blue stone building with the slanted mansard roof in the far left corner is from 1757, one of just two pre–Russian-conquest buildings remaining in Helsinki. On the right is the university building. Czar Alexander II, a friend of Finland's, is honored by the statue in the square. The huge staircase leading up to the cathedral is a popular meeting and tanning point in Helsinki. Cafe Engel is a popular hangout on the square opposite the church.

▲▲**Uspensky Russian Orthodox Cathedral**—Hovering above Market Square and facing the Lutheran Cathedral as Russian culture faces Europe's, is a fine icon experience and western Europe's largest Russian Orthodox church (built 1868, daily 9:30–16:00 except Tuesday 9:30–18:00 and Sunday 12:00–15:00).

▲▲▲**Temppeliaukio Church**—Another great piece of church architecture, this was blasted out of solid rock and capped with a copper-and-skylight dome. It's normally filled with live or recorded music and awestruck visitors. I almost cried. Another form of simple truth, it's impossible to describe. Grab a pew. Gawk upward at a 14-mile-long coil of copper ribbon. Look at the bull's-eye and ponder God. Forget your camera. Just sit in the middle, ignore the crowds, and be thankful for peace—under your feet is an air-raid shelter that can accommodate 6,000 people (Monday–Friday 10:00–20:00, Saturday 10:00–16:00, Sunday 12:00–13:45 and 15:15–17:45). To experience the church in action, attend the Lutheran English service (Sunday at 14:00, tel. 09/494-698) or one of the many concerts. You can buy individual slides or the picture book.

▲**Sibelius Monument**—Six hundred stainless-steel pipes shimmer over a rock in a park to honor Finland's greatest composer. Notice the face of Sibelius (which the artist was forced to add to silence the critics of this abstract work). Bus #24 stops here (or catch a quick glimpse on the left from the bus) on its way to the open-air folk museum. The #3T tram, which runs more frequently, stops a few blocks away. By the way, music lovers enjoy the English-language tours of the slick new Finnish National Opera (closed in June and July).

▲**Seurasaari Open-Air Folk Museum**—Inspired by Stockholm's Skansen, also on a lovely island on the edge of town, this is a collection of 100 historic buildings from every corner of Finland. It's wonderfully furnished and gives rushed visitors an opportunity to sample the far reaches of Finland without leaving the capital city. Buy the 10-mk guidebook. (The park is free, 20 mk to enter the buildings, daily June–August 11:00–17:00; late May and early September weekdays 9:00–15:00, weekends 11:00–17:00.) Off-season it's quiet. Just you, log cabins, and birch trees—almost not worth a look. In winter, the park is open but the buildings are closed. Ride bus #24 to the end and walk across the quaint footbridge. Call the museum or ask at the TI about free English tours (daily except

Wednesday at 11:30 and 15:30) and evening folk-dance schedules (usually Tuesday, Thursday, and Sunday at 19:00, tel.
09/484-712).

For a 10-mk bottomless cup of coffee in a cozy-like-some-
one's-home setting, stop by the café near the Seurasaari
Bridge, up the road at Tamminiementie 1 (June–August
11:00–23:00). Great bagels—and Chopin, too.

▲▲National Museum—It is closed until October 1, 1999. Its
pleasant, easy-to-handle collection (covering Finland's story
from A to Z with good English descriptions) is in a grand building designed by three of Finland's greatest early architects.
While the neoclassical furniture, portraits of Russia's last czars
around an impressive throne, and the folk costumes are interesting, the highlight is the Finno-Ugric exhibit downstairs, with a
20-page English guide to help explain the Finns, Estonians,
Lapps, Hungarians, and their more obscure Finno-Ugric cousins
(tel. 09/40501). The museum café has light meals and Finnish
treats such as lingonberry juice and reindeer quiche.

Finlandia Hall—Alvar Aalto's most famous building in his
native Finland means little to the non-architect without a tour
(20 mk, summer only, tel. 09/40241 for hours).

▲Harbor tours—Several boat companies line Market
Square, offering 90-minute, 60-mk cruises around the waterfront nearly every hour 10:00 to 18:00. The narration is
slow-moving—often tape-recorded and in as many as four
languages. But if the weather's good and you're looking for
something one step above a snooze in the park, it's a nice
break. If you like fish with your harbor views, IHA-Lines
offers a fish-buffet boat tour (70 mk, 90 minutes, 10:30,
12:15, 14:30, from the Market Square).

▲Flea Market—If you brake for garage sales, the Hietalahti
Market, Finland's biggest flea market, is worth the 15-minute
walk from the harbor (Monday–Saturday 8:00–14:00, summer
evenings Monday–Friday 15:30–21:00 and some summer Sundays 10:00–16:00).

Suomenlinna—This "fortified island," a popular park with
several museums, will be particularly busy in 1998 as it celebrates its 250th birthday (20-minute ferry or water-bus ride,
18–25 mk round-trip, on the half-hour from Market Square,
museums open 10:00–17:00 in summer).

Sauna—Finland's vaporized fountain of youth is the sauna.
Public saunas are a dying breed these days, since saunas are

standard equipment in nearly every Finnish apartment and home. Your boat or hotel has a sauna. Your hostel probably even has one. Saunas are generally not mixed—they usually come in pairs. You go in with a towel not to cover your body but to sit on. For hygienic reasons, it's bad form to sit directly on the wooden benches. For a real experience, ask about the Finnish Sauna Society (70 mk, bus #20 for 20 minutes in a park on the waterfront, men-only most nights, Thursday is women's night, tel. 09/678-677). For a cheap and easy public sauna, go to the Olympic swimming pool at the Olympic Stadium (12 mk, pool and sauna open Monday–Saturday 7:00–20:00, Sunday 9:00–20:00).

Concerts—Concerts in churches are heavenly. Ask at the TI and keep a lookout for posters. The Kallio Church has a magnificent new organ.

Nightlife—Remember that Finland was the first country to give women the vote. The sexes are equal in the bars and on the dance floor. Finns are easily approachable, and tourists are not a headache to the locals (as they are in places like Paris and Munich). While it's easy to make friends, anything alcoholic is very expensive. For the latest on hot nightspots, read the English insert of the *City* magazine that lists the "best" of everything in Helsinki. For very cheap fun, Suomenlinna and Hietaranta beach is where the local kids hang out (and even skinny-dip) at 22:00 or 23:00. This city is one of Europe's safest after dark.

Sleeping in Helsinki
(5 mk = about $1, tel. code from outside Finland: 358-9)
Sleep Code: **S** = Single, **D** = Double/Twin, **T** = Triple, **Q** = Quad, **b** = bathroom, **CC** = Credit Card (Visa, MasterCard, Amex).

Standard budget hotel doubles start at $100. But there are many special deals, and dorm and hostel alternatives. You have four basic budget options: cheap hostels, student dorms turned "summer hotels," plain and basic low-class hotels, or expensive business-class hotels at special summer or weekend clearance sale rates.

Summer (mid-June–mid-August) is "off-season" in Helsinki, as are Friday, Saturday, and Sunday nights the rest of the year. You can arrive in the morning and expect to find a budget room. Two room-finding services can get you a double room in a three-star hotel with breakfast for 500 mk. This can be done by fax in advance or upon arrival. **Tour Expert** is in the harborside tourist office (see TI above, tel. 09/622-6990, fax 09/6226-9914). In the train station is the **Hotellikeskus** room-finding service (June–August Monday–Saturday 9:00–19:00, Sunday 10:00–18:00; off-season 10:00–17:00 Monday–Friday only; facing the tracks, it's on the left side, a pleasant 20-minute walk from your boat, or tram #3B from Silja, bus #13 from Viking, arrival only). Each charges 15 mk for the service. They know what wild bargains are available. Consider a luxury-hotel clearance deal, which may cost $20 more than the cheapies.

Sleeping in Classy "Real" Hotels

Hotel Anna, plush and very central, is one of the best values in town (Sb-350 mk-summer, 470 mk-winter, Db 470 mk-summer, 600 mk-winter, includes breakfast, CC:VMA, near Mannerheimintie and Esplanadi, a 15-minute walk from the boat, 1 Annankatu, tel. 09/616-621, fax 09/602-664).

    Hotel Arthur, a five-minute walk from the train station and Senate Square, has spacious rooms (Sb-330–395 mk, Db-400–495 mk, CC:VMA, Vuorikatu 19, 00100 Helsinki, tel. 09/173-441, fax 09/626-880).

    Hotel Skatta was originally for sailors. Now it's a stark but comfortable place just a block from the Viking Terminal on the harbor, offering very cheap rooms in a quiet locale (23 rooms, Sb-250 mk, Db-300 mk, breakfast extra, CC:VMA, elevator, kitchenettes in each room, call long in advance to reserve, Linnankatu 3, 00160 Helsinki, tel. 09/659-233, fax 09/631-352).

    Hotel Cumulus Olympia is often about the least expensive hotel in town (Db-380 mk-summer, 580 mk-winter, includes breakfast, CC:VMA, not so central but on the #3B or #1 tram line at the Sport Hall stop, 2 Lantinen Brahenkatu, tel. 09/69151, fax 09/691-5219).

Sleeping in Hostels

Eurohostel is a wonderful modern hostel located a block from the Viking Terminal or a ten-minute walk from Market Square renting 250 beds (S-185 mk, D-240 mk, T-360 mk, including sheets, private lockable closets, and morning sauna; less 15 mk per person with hostel cards, breakfast-28 kr, doubles can be shared with a stranger of the same sex for 115 mk per bed, CC:VMA, handy tram stop around the corner, Linnankatu 9,

00160 Helsinki, tel. 09/622-0470, fax 09/655-044, Web site: www.eurohostel.fi). It's packed with facilities including a TV room, laundry room, a members' kitchen with a refrigerator that lets you lock up your caviar and beer, a cheap cafeteria, and plenty of good budget information on travel to Russia or the Baltics including an overnight visa service for Russia and hostel booking service.

Kallio Retkeilymaja is cozy, cheery, central, well run, and very cheap (only 35 beds; 70 mk for dorm bed for boys, or a bed in five-bed rooms for girls, lockers, kitchen facilities, closed 10:00–15:00, open July–August, Porthaniankatu 2, tel. 09/7099-2590). From Market Square, take the metro or tram #3T, #1, or #2 to Hakaniemi Square Market.

Olympic Stadium Hostel (Stadionin Retkeilymaja, IYHF) is big, crowded, impersonal, and a last resort. (55 mk per bed in eight- to 12-bed rooms, D-160 mk, sheets-15 mk, nonmembers pay 15 mk extra, open all year, dorm closed daily 10:00–16:00 off-season, tel. 09/496-071.) Take tram #7A to the Olympic Stadium.

Eating in Helsinki

The best food values are, of course, the department store cafeterias and a picnic assembled from the colorful stalls on the harbor and nearby bakery. Take advantage of the red-brick indoor market on the edge of the square. At the harbor you'll also find several local "tent" cafes and fast-food stalls and delicious fresh fish (cooked if you like), explosive little red berries, and sweet carrots. While the open-air market is the most fun, produce is cheaper in large grocery stores.

At the Eurohostel, **Café Pinja** serves decent cheap meals (the fish is better than the pepper steak). In the train station, the **Eliel Self-Service** restaurant offers reasonable midday specials in a splendid architectural setting.

In Helsinki, Russian food is an interesting option. Most popular, with meals around 100 mk, are the **Troikka** (good Russian food in a tsarific setting, Caloniukesenkatu 3, tel. 09/445-229 for reservations) and **Kasakka** (old Russian style, Meritullinkatu 13, tel. 09/135-6288). Seafood is another local specialty. Many restaurants serve daily lunch specials for around 30 mk to 40 mk.

Holvari serves tasty Finnish lunches in an art-filled setting (Yrjonkatu 15, tel. 09/642-394). **Könstan Mölja** features an all-you-can-eat lunch for 45 mk on weekdays. This family-run restaurant, decorated with old photos and farming tools, serves Finnish cooking and hearty home-baked Karelian bread (Hietalahdenkatu 14, just a couple of blocks from the flea market at the end of Bulevardi).

The Lutheran Cathedral and Academic Bookstore have handy **cafés**. For a dinner with folk music, ask the TI about the show at **Seurasaari Open-Air Folk Museum.**

Transportation Connections—Helsinki

For train info, call 09/707-5700.

By boat to Stockholm: The Silja and Viking lines sail between Helsinki and Stockholm daily and nightly. (See the beginning of this chapter for details.)

By boat to Tallinn, Estonia: Several boats sail daily between Helsinki's West Terminal and Tallinn. One-way fares for ferries cost 110 mk (50-mile 4-hr trip). The hydrofoil takes 100 minutes and 270 mk (round-trip with 10 hours in Tallinn—tickets from Tour Expert). Tallink has the most frequent departures (tel. 358/9/228-2177 in Helsinki). Eurohostel has more information (358/9/622-0470).

NEAR HELSINKI: TURKU, NAANTALI, AND PORVOO

Turku is a pale shadow of Helsinki, and Naantali is cute, commercial, and offers little (if you've seen or will see Sigtuna, near Stockholm). Porvoo may be for you.

Turku, the historic, old capital of Finland, is a two-hour train ride from Helsinki (10/day, 90 mk, free with Eurail or save 50 percent by getting train connection with an "open jaws" boat ticket). Turku has a handicraft museum in a cluster of wooden houses (the only part of town to survive a devastating fire in the early 1800s), an old cathedral, and a market square. Viking and Silja boats sail from Turku to Stockholm at 21:30, or 20:00 off-season (the cheap fare saves enough to pay for the train from Helsinki to Turku).

Naantali, a well-preserved medieval town with a quaint harbor, is an easy bus ride from Turku (4/hr, 20 min, 16 mk).

Porvoo, the second-oldest town in Finland, has wooden architecture that dates from the Swedish colonial period. This coastal town can be reached from Helsinki by boat from Market Square or by train (4/hr, 60 min, 74 mk round-trip).

APPENDIX

Let's Talk Telephones

In Europe, card-operated public phones are s
coin-operated phones. Each country sells telephone cards good
for use within its borders. In Scandinavia, get a phone card at a
post office, newsstand, or tobacco shop. To make a call, pick
up the receiver, insert your card in the slot in the phone, dial
your number, make your call, then retrieve your card. The
price of your call is automatically deducted from your card as
you use it. If you have a phone-card phobia, you'll usually find
easy-to-use "talk now–pay later" metered phones in post
offices. Avoid using hotel-room phones, which are major rip-
offs for anything other than local and calling-card calls (see
below). Incidentally, using directory assistance in Scandinavia
costs about the same as telephone sex. Really.

Calling-Card Operators

Calling home from Europe is easy from any type of phone if
you have a calling card. From a private phone, just dial the toll-
free number to reach the operator. If you're using a public
phone, first insert a coin or a Scandinavian phone card. Then
dial the operator, who will ask you for your calling-card number
and place your call. You'll save money on calls of three minutes
or more. When you finish, your coin should be returned (or if
using a card, no money should have been deducted). Your bill
awaits you at home (one more reason to prolong your vacation).
For more information, see the Introduction chapter, Telephones and Mail.

USA Direct Services

Country	AT&T	MCI	Sprint
Denmark	800 100 10	800 100 22	800 108 77
Finland	9800 100 10	9800 102 80	9800 102 84
Norway	800 190 11	800 199 12	800 198 77
Sweden	020 795 611	020 795 922	020 799 011

Dialing Direct

Calling Between Countries: First dial the international access
code, then the country code, followed by the area code (if it
starts with zero, drop the zero), then the local number.

Calling Long Distance Within a Country: First dial the area code (including its zero), then the local number.

Some of Europe's Exceptions: A few countries lack area codes, such as Denmark, Norway, and France; you still use the same sequence and codes to dial, just skip the area code. In Spain, area codes start with nine instead of zero (just drop or add the nine as you would a zero when calling in other countries).

International Access Codes

When dialing direct, first dial the international access code of the country you're calling from.

Austria:	00	France:	00	Norway:	00
Belgium:	00	Germany:	00	Portugal:	00
Britain:	00	Ireland:	00	Russia:	810
Czech Rep.:	00	Italy:	00	Spain:	07
Denmark:	00	Latvia:	00	Sweden:	009
Estonia:	800	Lithuania:	810	Switzerland:	00
Finland:	990	Netherlands:	00	U.S.A./Canada:	011

Country Codes

After you've dialed the international access code, then dial the code of the country you're calling.

Austria:	43	France:	33	Norway:	47
Belgium:	32	Germany:	49	Portugal:	351
Britain:	44	Ireland:	353	Russia:	7
Czech Rep.:	42	Italy:	39	Spain:	34
Denmark:	45	Latvia:	371	Sweden:	46
Estonia:	372	Lithuania:	370	Switzerland:	41
Finland:	358	Netherlands:	31	U.S.A./Canada:	1

Public Transportation

You can tour Scandinavia efficiently and enjoyably by train and bus. You even have a few options that drivers don't. If you sleep on the very comfortable Nordic trains, destinations not worth driving to on a short trip become feasible. Add your own Scandinavian highlights. Consider a swing through Finland's eastern lakes district or the scenic ride to Trondheim. I'd go overnight whenever possible on any ride six or more hours long.

The Norway chapter is heavy on fjord scenery (my kind of problem). Fjord country buses, boats, and trains connect, but not without one- to three-hour layovers. "Norway in a Nutshell" is an exception. The Flåm–Bergen boat is a great fjord finale.

Train, Bus, and Boat Connections

Pick up exact schedules as you travel, available free at any tourist office. Some lines make fewer runs or even close in the off-season.

Departures Copenhagen to:	Daily	Hours
Amsterdam	2	11
Berlin via Gedser	2	9
Frankfurt/Rhine castles	4	10
Helsingør (ferry to Sweden)	40	.5
Hillerød (Frederiksborg)	40	.5
Louisiana (Helsingør train to Humlebæk)	40	.5
Odense	16	.5
Oslo	4	10
Roskilde	16	.5
Stockholm	6–8	8
Växjö via Alvesta	6	5
Stockholm to:		
Helsinki	2	14
Helsinki to Turku	7	2.5
Kalmar	6	8
		(1-night train)
Oslo	3	7
Turku	2	10
Uppsala	30	1
Växjö to glassworks	TI tour or side trip by bus	
Växjö to Kalmar	9	1.5
Oslo to:		
Åndalsnes	3	6.5
Bergen	4	7–8
Lillehammer	12	2.5
Trondheim	3	7–8

Scandinavia: Main Train Lines

Departures	Daily	Hours
Norway's Mountain and Fjord Country		
Lillehammer to Åndalsnes	4	4
Åndalsnes over Trollstigvege	early	4
to Geiranger Fjord	each morning	
Åndalsnes to Ålesund		
by bus (with each arriving train)	2	.5
Lillehammer to Lom (change at Otta)	3	4

Departures	Daily	Hours
Lom to Sogndal	2	
(bus departures 8:50 and 15:50, summer only)		

Bergen to:		
Ålesund	1	10
Kristiansand	1 (bus)	12
Stavanger	3 (boat)	4

South Norway
Setesdal Valley, Hovden to:

Kristiansand	2	5

Kristiansand to:		
Hirtshals, Denmark (by ferry)	4	4
Oslo	6	4–5

Denmark		
Ærø to Copenhagen	5	5
Århus to Odense	16	2
Halsskov–Knudshoved	26	1
Hirtshals to Århus	16	2.5
Odense to Svendborg	16	1
Svendborg to Ærø (by ferry)	5	1

Numbers and Stumblers

- Europeans write a few numbers differently than we do:
  1 = 1, 4 = 4, 7 = 7. Learn the difference or miss your train.
- In Europe, dates appear as day/month/year, so Christmas is 25/12/99.
- Commas are decimal points and decimals commas. A dollar and a half is 1,50 and there are 5.280 feet in a mile.
- When pointing, use your whole hand, palm downward.
- When counting with fingers, start with your thumb. If you hold up your first finger to request one item, you'll get two.
- What we Americans call the second floor of a building is the first floor in Europe.
- Europeans keep the left "lane" open for passing on escalators and moving sidewalks. Keep to the right.

Metric Conversion (approximate)

1 inch = 25 millimeters   32 degrees F = 0 degrees C

1 foot = 0.3 meter   82 degrees F = about 28 degrees C
1 yard = 0.9 meter   1 ounce = 28 grams
1 mile = 1.6 kilometers   1 kilogram = 2.2 pounds
1 centimeter = 0.4 inch   1 quart = 0.95 liter
1 meter = 39.4 inches   1 square yard = 0.8 square meter
1 kilometer = .62 mile   1 acre = 0.4 hectare

Climate

First line, average daily low temperature; second line, average daily high; third line, days of no rain

	J	F	M	A	M	J	J	A	S	O	N	D
Copenhagen,	29	28	31	37	44	51	55	54	49	42	35	32
DENMARK	36	36	41	50	61	67	72	69	63	53	43	38
	22	21	23	21	23	22	22	19	22	22	20	20
Helsinki,	17	15	22	31	41	49	58	55	46	37	30	22
FINLAND	27	26	32	43	55	63	71	66	57	45	37	31
	20	20	23	22	23	21	23	19	19	19	19	20
Oslo,	20	20	25	34	43	51	56	53	45	37	29	24
NORWAY	30	32	40	50	62	69	73	69	60	49	37	31
	23	21	24	23	24	22	21	20	22	21	21	21
Stockholm,	23	22	26	32	41	49	55	53	46	39	31	26
SWEDEN	31	31	37	45	57	65	70	66	58	48	38	33
	23	21	24	24	23	23	22	21	22	22	21	22

Faxing Your Hotel Reservation

Most hotel managers know basic "hotel English." Faxing is the preferred method for reserving a room. It's more accurate and cheaper than telephoning and much faster than writing a letter. Use this handy form for your fax. Photocopy and fax away.

One-Page Fax

To: _____ @ _____
                hotel   *fax*

From: _____ @ _____
              name   *fax*

Today's date: ___ / ____ / ___
            day *month* *year*

Dear Hotel _____,

Please make this reservation for me:

Name: _____

Total # of people: _____ # of rooms: _____ # of nights: _____

Arriving: ___ / ____ / ___ My time of arrival (24-hr clock): _____
        day *month* *year* (I will telephone if I will be late)

Departing: ___ / ____ / ___
         day *month* *year*

Room(s): Single___ Double___ Twin___ Triple___ Quad___

With: Toilet___ Shower___ Bath___ Sink only___

Special needs: View___ Quiet___ Cheapest Room___

Credit card: Visa___ MasterCard___ American Express___

Card #: _____

Expiration date:_____

Name on card: _____

You may charge me for the first night as a deposit. Please fax or mail me confirmation of my reservation, along with the type of room reserved, the price, and whether the price includes breakfast. Thank you.

_____
Signature

_____
Name

_____
Address

_____
City   *State*   *Zip Code*   *Country*

Road Scholar Feedback for
SCANDINAVIA

We're all in the same travelers' school of hard knocks. Your feedback helps us improve this guidebook for future travelers. Please fill this out (attach more info or any tips/favorite discoveries if you like) and send it to us. As thanks for your help, we'll send you our quarterly travel newsletter free for one year. Thanks! Rick

I traveled mainly by: ___ Car   ___ Train/bus tickets
___ Railpass   Other (please list _____)

Number of people traveling together:
___ Solo   ___ 2   ___ 3   ___ 4   ___ Over 4   ___ Tour

Ages of traveler/s (including children):

_____

I visited _____ **countries in** _____ **weeks.**

I traveled in: ___ Spring ___ Summer ___ Fall ___ Winter

My daily budget per person (excluding transportation):
___ Under $40   ___ $40–$60   ___ $60–$80   ___ $80–$120
___ over $120   ___ Don't know

Average cost of hotel rooms: Single room $_____
Double room $_____   Other (type _____) $_____

Favorite tip from this book:

_____

Biggest waste of time or money caused by this book:

_____

Other Rick Steves books used for this trip:

_____

Hotel listings from this book should be geared toward places that are:
___ Cheaper   ___ More expensive   ___ About the same

Of the recommended accommodations/restaurants used, which was:

Best _____

    Why? _____

Worst _____

    Why? _____

I reserved rooms:

____ from USA   ____ in advance as I traveled

____ same day by phone   ____ just showed up

Getting rooms in recommended hotels was:

____ easy   ____ mixed   ____ frustrating

Of the sights/experiences/destinations recommended by this book, which was:

Most overrated _____

    Why? _____

Most underrated _____

    Why? _____

Best ways to improve this book:

_____

I'd like a free newsletter subscription:

___ Yes   ___ No   ___ Already on list

_____
Name

_____
Address

_____
City, State, Zip

_____
E-mail Address

Please send to:
ETBD • Box 2009, Edmonds, WA 98020

INDEX

Rick Steves' Phrase Books

Unlike other phrase books and dictionaries on the market, my well-tested phrases and key words cover every situation a traveler is likely to encounter. With these books you'll laugh with your cabby, disarm street thieves with insults, and charm new European friends.

Each book in the series is 4" x 6", with maps.

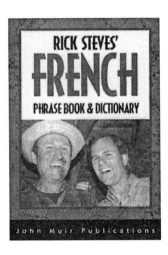

RICK STEVES' FRENCH PHRASE BOOK & DICTIONARY
U.S. $5.95/Canada $8.50

RICK STEVES' GERMAN PHRASE BOOK & DICTIONARY
U.S. $5.95/Canada $8.50

RICK STEVES' ITALIAN PHRASE BOOK & DICTIONARY
U.S. $5.95/Canada $8.50

RICK STEVES' SPANISH & PORTUGUESE PHRASE BOOK
& DICTIONARY
U.S. $7.95/Canada $11.25

RICK STEVES' FRENCH, ITALIAN & GERMAN PHRASE
BOOK & DICTIONARY
U.S. $7.95/Canada $11.25

Books from John Muir Publications

Rick Steves' Books

Asia Through the Back Door, $17.95
Europe 101: History and Art for the Traveler, $17.95
Mona Winks: Self-Guided Tours of Europe's Top Museums, $18.95
Rick Steves' Europe Through the Back Door, $19.95
Rick Steves' Best of Europe, $18.95
Rick Steves' France, Belgium & the Netherlands, $16.95
Rick Steves' Germany, Austria & Switzerland, $15.95
Rick Steves' Great Britain & Ireland, $16.95
Rick Steves' Italy, $14.95
Rick Steves' Russia & the Baltics, $9.95
Rick Steves' Scandinavia, $13.95
Rick Steves' Spain & Portugal, $14.95
Rick Steves' French Phrase Book, $5.95
Rick Steves' German Phrase Book, $5.95
Rick Steves' Italian Phrase Book, $5.95
Rick Steves' Spanish & Portuguese Phrase Book, $7.95
Rick Steves' French/Italian/German Phrase Book, $7.95

City•Smart™ Guidebooks

Albuquerque, $12.95 (avail. 4/98)
Anchorage, $12.95
Austin, $12.95
Calgary, $12.95
Cincinnati, $12.95 (avail. 5/98)
Cleveland, $14.95
Denver, $14.95
Indianapolis, $12.95
Kansas City, $12.95
Memphis, $12.95
Milwaukee, $12.95
Minneapolis/St. Paul, $14.95
Nashville, $14.95
Portland, $14.95
Richmond, $12.95
San Antonio, $12.95
St. Louis, $12.95 (avail. 5/98)
Tampa/St. Petersburg, $14.95

Travel✦Smart™ Guidebooks

Alaska, $14.95
American Southwest, $14.95
Carolinas, $14.95
Colorado, $14.95
Deep South, $17.95
Eastern Canada, $15.95
Florida Gulf Coast, $14.95
Hawaii, $14.95
Kentucky/Tennessee, $14.95
Michigan, $14.95
Minnesota/Wisconsin, $14.95
Montana, Wyoming, & Idaho, $16.95
New England, $14.95
New York State, $15.95
Northern California, $15.95
Ohio, $14.95 (avail. 5/98)
Pacific Northwest, $14.95
Southern California, $14.95
South Florida and the Keys, $14.95
Texas, $14.95
Western Canada, $16.95

Adventures in Nature Series

Alaska, $18.95
Belize, $18.95
Guatemala, $18.95
Honduras, $17.95

Kidding Around™ Travel Titles

$7.95 each
Kidding Around Atlanta
Kidding Around Austin
Kidding Around Boston
Kidding Around Chicago
Kidding Around Cleveland
Kids Go! Denver
Kidding Around Indianapolis
Kidding Around Kansas City
Kidding Around Miami
Kidding Around Milwaukee
Kidding Around Minneapolis/St. Paul
Kidding Around Nashville
Kidding Around Portland
Kidding Around San Francisco
Kids Go! Seattle
Kidding Around Washington, D.C.

Ordering Information

Please check your local bookstore for our books, or call **1-800-888-7504** to order direct and to receive a complete catalog. A shipping charge will be added to your order total.

Send all inquiries to:
**John Muir Publications
P.O. Box 613
Santa Fe, NM 87504**